God Speaks to Us, Too

God Speaks to Us, Too

Southern Baptist Women on Church, Home, and Society

Susan M. Shaw

THE UNIVERSITY PRESS OF KENTUCKY

Scholarly publisher for the Commonwealth,
serving Bellarmine University, Berea College, Centre
College of Kentucky, Eastern Kentucky University,
The Filson Historical Society, Georgetown College,
Kentucky Historical Society, Kentucky State University,
Morehead State University, Murray State University,
Northern Kentucky University, Transylvania University,
University of Kentucky, University of Louisville,
and Western Kentucky University.
All rights reserved.

Editorial and Sales Offices: The University Press of Kentucky
663 South Limestone Street, Lexington, Kentucky 40508-4008
www.kentuckypress.com

12 11 10 09 08   5 4 3 2 1

Library of Congress Cataloging-in-Publication Data

Shaw, Susan M. (Susan Maxine), 1960–
  God speaks to us, too : Southern Baptist women on church, home, and
society / Susan M. Shaw.
     p. cm.
  Includes bibliographical references and index.
  ISBN 978-0-8131-2476-6 (hardcover : alk. paper)
  1. Baptist women. 2. Baptists—Doctrines. I. Title.
  BV4415.S48 2008
  286'.132082—dc22

                              2007048492

This book is printed on acid-free recycled paper meeting
the requirements of the American National Standard
for Permanence in Paper for Printed Library Materials.

∞ ✪

Manufactured in the United States of America.

 Member of the Association of
American University Presses

For Mom and the Clique
(JoAnn Shaw, Lidia Abrams, Doris Bailey, Alicia Bennett,
Kayne Carter, Shelby Christie, Judy Masters, Nancy Moore)
and for Tisa Lewis and Paula Sheridan, Queen Regent in Service

In memory of Melodie Yocum (1953–2007)

Contents

Preface

A FEW YEARS AGO, my dear friend Paula Sheridan saw a play about Southern Baptist boys growing up in Texas. After telling me about the play, Paula said to me, "Susu, somebody needs to tell our story"—"our" meaning the girls, the women. Southern Baptist women are an interesting lot. They're diverse, but they share certain common experiences that have marked their identity in significant ways. In particular, these living generations of Southern Baptist women reflect the cultural conditions and changes of a unique period in history during which Southern Baptists were involved in unprecedented controversy, particularly with regard to the roles of women. For one group of Southern Baptist women, of which Paula and I are a part, the social changes of the 1960s and 1970s created a brief period of freedom for women in ministry that had not been seen before among Southern Baptists and did not last long. Propelled by biblical literalism, inerrancy, and a conservative social agenda, fundamentalists within the denomination achieved a power shift, disenfranchising moderate Southern Baptists over a fifteen-year period. The issues of women in ministry and women's roles in the family were primary in the fundamentalists' agenda; therefore, the generations of women who participated in my interviews have a particularly heightened awareness of gender.

Having grown up Southern Baptist, attended a Southern Baptist seminary, and taught at Southern Baptist institutions, I was keenly aware of the importance of gender both in the denomination and in women's individual lives as members of Southern Baptist congregations. I was also well aware of all the contradictions folded into these lives. So, inspired by Paula's lament, I decided to tell our story—or at least my version of it.

The changes in the Southern Baptist Convention caused me a lot of personal pain. I had attended the Southern Baptist Theological Seminary during a time of openness for women, only to find the Convention changing into a place that was no longer hospitable to my theology or my gender. The years I spent teaching for Southern Baptists were difficult ones, and after I left the denomination, I carried a lot of bitterness for quite a while. Fortunately, time and distance, a teaching position in a state university in the Northwest, and a loving church home in the United Church of Christ have allowed me to work through my strong emotional responses and find value in those precious things that were part of my upbringing and remain part of my identity. Actor and playwright Leslie Jordan, a former Southern Baptist, told Paula how he accomplishes this: "When I go back home, when I go to my church, I put the ugly things under my chair. And I take the precious things back to California with me."

In Rebecca Wells's *The Divine Secrets of the Ya-Ya Sisterhood,* the main character has a lot of issues with her mother. At last, in learning how to deal with her mother, she comes to this conclusion: "Be as tender as you can bear to be." That is what I'm doing with this book: being as tender as I can bear to be. Much in Southern Baptist history is to be celebrated; much is also to be denounced. As I tell the stories of many Southern Baptist women, myself included, I hope to be tender—critical and analytical, but also tender. This doesn't mean that I've ignored difficult issues, but whenever I've offered a critique, I've tried to be kind. After all, as one of my participants put it, "These are my people."

I am a feminist, one who believes in and works toward social, political, economic, and religious equality between women and men and who recognizes the significant ways that differences such as race or ethnicity, age, and social class affect individuals' experiences of gender. As a feminist, I bring certain perspectives to this book. My participants may or may not agree with them, but I have worked especially hard to represent their views accurately. A great deal of the book is phenomenological—it attempts to understand the meanings my participants have constructed of their lives. It is also autobiographical and historical. I make no claim that this book is objective or represents all Southern Baptist women. At most, it is a glimpse into the diverse lives of these women, situated within the context of the complex history of Southern Baptists as I understand it. At best, I hope this book will foster conversations, bring back good memories, and challenge closely held assumptions.

The assistance I received in researching and writing this book was overwhelming in its generosity. I met Kryn Freehling-Burton in the late 1980s when she was my student at California Baptist College, and we even acted together in a student-directed one-act play at the college. Many years later, after I'd moved to Oregon, Kryn started reading feminist theology on her own. She reconnected with me and ended up taking some of Oregon State University's online women studies courses. Over the next year, she often lamented how much she'd like to be in graduate school. At last I said to her, "Would you come to OSU if we gave you a teaching assistant position?" She turned me down. She couldn't ask her family—a husband and four children—to move. A few weeks later she called me back. Her husband, Eric, had said to her, "We have to do this. You can't spend the rest of your life wondering, 'What if?'" With her background in Southern Baptist life, Kryn was the ideal research assistant for this project. She conducted some of the interviews, tracked down innumerable books and articles, and helped code and organize the data. Without her, this book would have been another year in the making. I wish OSU had a PhD program in women studies just so we could keep her around for another four years. My other graduate research assistants—Mehra Shirazi, Marcia Chambers, and Heather Ebba Maib—were also invaluable. They created Excel files, tracked down obscure references, and managed the numerous minutiae of research.

My transcriptionist, Janet Lockhart, is another former student who became a friend; we have coauthored several teaching guides and book chapters. She performed the most tedious part of the work, and I will be forever grateful that I didn't have to transcribe all those hours of recordings. Janet was also the perfect foil for this material. With no background in Baptist life, she helped me realize just how much coded language we Baptists use and how important it was to explain it clearly.

Many of my colleagues at OSU helped me think through the book's methodology and analysis and give shape to my four thick notebooks of data. Over the past three years, Janet Lee, Becky Warner, Sally Gallagher, and Nancy Rosenberger listened to my ideas, helped me dissect my data, offered theoretical perspectives, and provided general encouragement when I felt overwhelmed. I especially appreciate the willingness of Tisa Lewis, my best friend of twenty-five years, to help me refine my ideas and support me as I struggled to make sense of so much data from so many diverse participants.

Kathy Sylvest and Bill Sumners at the Southern Baptist Historical Library and Archives, Amy Cook and Diane Baker at the Woman's Missionary Union Library and Archives, Pat Brown at Lifeway, Pam Durso at the Baptist Historical Society, and Ellen Brown at Baylor University helped me find obscure references, old Sunday school literature, Lottie Moon photographs, and a host of other necessary resources. Carolyn Goodman Plampin helped me make connections with a number of the women in ministry who participated in the interviews. Funding for the project was provided by the Louisville Institute, the Southern Baptist Historical Library and Archives, and Oregon State University's Valley Library. OSU's Center for the Humanities also provided me with a fellowship during the 2004–2005 academic year to work on the book.

Along my journey, a lot of strangers opened their homes and church fellowship halls to me; they organized focus groups or made other arrangements to facilitate my research. Special thanks go to Jennifer Adamson, Sheryl Churchill, Candi Finch, Tammy Hayes, Becky Kennedy, Joan Lewis, Karen Massey, Becky Metheny, Dorothy Kelley Patterson, Julie Pennington-Russell, Shirley Powell, Lilla Schmeltekopf, and Jorene Swift. My colleagues Stephanie Sanford and Ken Williamson loaned me their coastal home in Yachats, allowing me to get away and focus on my writing without interruption. My friend and former colleague Janet Melnyck provided me with a place to stay whenever I was in Atlanta, and Paula Sheridan took me in whenever I was in Southern California; she later read the manuscript and gave me feedback. Carrie Baker, the director of women's studies at Berry College, invited me to share some of my early findings at my college alma mater.

My participants generously took the time to share their stories with me. In particular, I want to thank the Clique—my mother, JoAnn Shaw, and her friends Lidia Abrams, Doris Bailey, Alicia Bennett, Kayne Carter, Shelby Christie, Judy Masters, and Nancy Moore—who provided so much of the inspiration for this book. They were some of my earliest connections with Southern Baptist women, and they have supported and cared for me, in some cases, for more than forty-five years.

I also want to thank all the women who participated in my interviews. They honored me with their stories, welcomed me into their homes, and reminded me of all the things that are so wonderful about Southern Baptist women.

Finally, I want to thank my editor at the University Press of Kentucky, Joyce Harrison, who encouraged me along the way and helped this project become a reality. I also thank Bill Leonard and Susan Willhauck, who provided helpful reviews of the manuscript.

Introduction

Raised Right—The Making of Southern Baptist Identity

Living for Jesus a life that is true,
Striving to please him in all that I do,
Yielding allegiance glad-hearted and free,
This is the pathway of blessing for me.
—Thomas O. Chisholm, "Living for Jesus"

Mama said, "I just don't believe a woman should be the pastor of a church." We were sitting in the living room of the house in which I'd grown up. Mom was kicked back in her overstuffed recliner, and I was on the sofa. The lavalier microphone cords linked us to each other and to my digital recorder.

"Why not?" I asked, walking the fine line between researcher and goading prodigal daughter.

"Because women are more emotional creatures, and we're supposed to be protected. And God put that man here to protect us. We're the weaker sex; I believe that. Not weaker in the mind. But we're supposed to . . . we have a road."

I asked the women who participated in my interviews to allow me to use their real names and thus preserve their words and experiences as a piece of Baptist history. All but three of the names used in this book are real; the three people who chose to use pseudonyms were concerned about possible conflicts of interest with their work. Because these women honored me with their time, their trust, their words, and their real names, I felt compelled to mention each participant's name at least once in the book. To help readers keep everyone straight, I provide on page 269 a "cast of characters"—because, indeed, these women are characters—that lists each participant's name and some brief identifying information.

Then, in the next breath, she said, "Without women in the church, there'd be no church either, because women do most of the work in the church."

"So why wouldn't it make sense to . . . ?"

She cut me off. "And I believe a woman can be a preacher too. But I believe being a pastor is more than just getting up there like an evangelist and preaching the Word."

"What else do you see as the role of the pastor?"

"The pastor is supposed to feed the flock; that's number one. But he also is supposed to minister to that flock, by showing love and compassion and visiting them, and getting to know them like his family."

"You don't think women are better . . . ?"

She interrupted me again. "Yeah, women can be a complement; and that's what a wife is, a helpmeet to the man."

"I'm trying to figure out what specifically for you excludes women from the pastorate, because everything you're describing women do well."

"Probably administration," she answered, then added without taking a breath, "I know women are good at administration. One of my gifts was administration. When I did that treasurer's job I knew that without a doubt."

She paused, realizing what she was saying. "I guess maybe it was the way I was brought up, but I just . . . men, the world respects men more in a leadership capacity. It's just like what I was talking about, in church if a man gets up and says something, they all listen; if a woman gets up, she's running her mouth."

I asked her whether she thought things might change as more women moved into leadership positions in society.

"If I were younger, I might believe that. I can see women in leadership positions in the church, maybe *under* a pastor, as assistant or something like that, but not the head of the church. To me, the pastor is the head of the church under Christ, and even though God is no respecter of persons. . . ." The irony of what she was saying struck her. "I guess it's just because of the way I was raised, and my age, and everything, that I just don't believe a woman should be the pastor of a church," she concluded.

"But you believe in local church autonomy?" I asked.

"Right. I believe in the autonomy of the local church. If you have a church that votes a woman as the pastor or co-pastor, that church has the right to do that."

In many ways, my mother is a typical Southern Baptist woman. She's conservative, Bible believing, missions minded, and civically engaged, and she's full of contradictions. She has spent her entire life in the Deep South, where she married young, had children, and made a home in which my sister and I were raised to be good Southern Baptist girls. She tells me that my father is the head of the house, although I can't imagine his daring to make a family decision without her input. She herself did not go to college or have a career, but she made sure that my sister and I both got an excellent higher education and would always be able to be self-sufficient. She teaches Sunday school at her church, serves on church committees, and helps provide for needy people in her community. She reads her Bible daily and has definite ideas about what's right and wrong. She also feels perfectly free to challenge her pastor or anyone else in authority about the Bible, theology, or the church budget. I asked her, "I take it you think it's okay to disagree with the pastor?"

"Oh, yes," she answered, "He knows it too. . . . And he knows that if he preaches something, and my little light goes off that that's not the way I see it, that I'll ask him about it."

Although she taught me to be respectful of others, she also told me that I had to think for myself, and she certainly models that. Yet we've ended up thinking pretty differently about a lot of things—something fairly characteristic of Baptists. Put two Baptists in a room together, the saying goes, and you'll get three opinions. Or, as one of my participants put it, "If you've met one Baptist, you've met one Baptist."

Baptist is by far the predominant religion in the South: Baptists account for 44.9 percent of all religious adherents in Kentucky, 42.4 percent in Alabama, 40.9 percent in Mississippi, 40.8 percent in Tennessee, 35.5 percent in Georgia, 34.9 percent in South Carolina, and 33.8 percent in North Carolina.[1] Baptists had their beginnings in seventeenth-century England when two distinct groups emerged at almost the same time with very different ideas about free will and predestination. And Baptists have been fighting ever since.[2] Controversy has always attended Baptists because they believe that each individual has equal and direct access to God and therefore possesses the ability to determine what is true and right for herself or himself. They've disagreed—and sometimes parted ways—over missions, their origins, the Bible, hymn singing, and women, among other things. But disagreement hasn't always been a bad thing, because it has kept Baptist faith alive, vibrant, and relevant as its adherents have engaged in debates over the important issues of the day, including (from the seventeenth century on) the status, rights, and roles of women. And for Baptist women, these debates have played a pivotal role in how they've constructed their own identities, as well as fostered a great deal of diversity among Baptist women themselves. Though they've had their differences, Baptists have also typically agreed on a number of important points that distinguished them from the other Reformation offspring. From the beginning, one belief in particular characterized Baptists: freedom.

Most Americans probably would not think of Baptists as radicals, but in the seventeenth century, Baptists were on the cutting edge of radical changes in Protestant faith and practice. They were called a "base sect," a "scab of error," a "seduced and . . . schismatical rabble of deluded children, servants, and people," "a profane and sacrilegious sect," an "impure and carnal sect," and "anarchists."[3] Surprisingly, the belief that raised such an outcry from the conservative establishment, the belief that threatened both church and crown, was freedom. Baptists demanded complete liberty of conscience. They believed that one could enter Christianity only through a conscious, voluntary choice, free of coercion. In practice, this meant that infant baptism had to be replaced by believer's baptism, and the requisite for church membership became one's own free decision to join rather than induction into membership through baptism as an infant. More than theological heretics, Baptists were considered political traitors. Baptists called for the separation of church and state, and they disobeyed the laws of the state when those laws conflicted with their beliefs. For their convictions, Baptists were persecuted, whipped, and imprisoned—both in England and in America.

Today, people hardly think of Baptists as dissenters and nonconformists who started out demanding freedom of conscience for all people. In particular, Southern Baptists tout themselves as conservatives, and in recent years they have made far-reaching changes to redefine the Southern Baptist Convention (SBC). They have embraced Republican politics[4] and have become vocal proponents of pastoral authority and women's subordination. When fundamentalists took control of the Convention in the early 1990s, many moderate Southern Baptists left the denomination to form alternative organizations that highlighted historic Baptist characteristics such as soul freedom and the separation of church and state. Nonetheless, although the public face of Southern Baptists may seem entirely fundamentalist, the ideals of soul freedom still have great sway in Southern Baptist churches. This is especially significant for women, whose roles and identities have been central in the changing rhetoric of the Convention since 1979 and the beginning of what is known as "the Controversy" among Southern Baptists.

Being Baptist

The central theme of this book is soul competency—the notion of a free soul that stands alone before God and is therefore competent and responsible for its own decisions without the need for any other mediator—and how this Baptist distinctiveness shapes (consciously and unconsciously) the identities of Southern Baptist women. These women are more complex, more thoughtful, kinder, and usually more rebellious than outside observers might think. This book reveals that complexity and suggests that even in the midst of patriarchy (in which they are often willing participants), Southern Baptist women create ways to claim their own identity and to act independently because they are, in their own eyes, competent before God.

I asked each participant what being Baptist means to her. There was a surprising consistency in their answers. Many mentioned issues such as Baptists' high view of scripture or their emphasis on missions. Some named specific elements, such as the Cooperative Program, which is the financial support mechanism for the denomination's work. Others noted theological propositions, such as eternal security, which may or may not be a belief shared by other Baptists. By far, however, most of their answers had to do with soul competency. Raquel Ellis, a twenty-nine-year-old graduate student in Illinois, answered the question this way: "[Being Baptist] means that we can approach God directly (no middleman) and have a personal relationship with him, that Christians should be baptized to publicly profess their acceptance of Christ, and that the Bible is God-breathed." Joanne Parker, editor of the Woman's Missionary Union's *Missions Mosaic* magazine, grew up Catholic and became Southern Baptist as an adult. When I asked her what being Baptist means to her, she immediately responded, "Being Baptist means that I have the freedom to go directly to God in prayer; I have the freedom to open my Bible and study it without someone else telling me, 'This is what you need to learn.'" Judy Masters, a lifelong friend of my mother's, told me, "I think [being Baptist has] given me the independence to believe as I feel like the Bible teaches me to believe. It gives me the independence to study [God's] Word and not have to trust what somebody else tells me. It gives me a firm conviction that directs which paths I choose." For each participant, in some way, the idea that God speaks directly to her and that she has the ability to discern God's direction in her own life is paramount to her experience of being Baptist. In many ways, this belief in their soul competency lies at the heart of their identities.

Because they believe in their own competence in matters of religion, Southern Baptist women tend to exhibit a strong sense of agency and autonomy—they are able to act and to govern themselves.[5] Although outsiders tend to see Southern Baptist women as dominated by men because of the patriarchal context of Southern Baptist life, the reality is that agency always occurs within a social context that defines the parameters of the choices available to people.[6] Within the parameters of Southern Baptist life, women are able to utilize creative strategies that expand those boundaries while remaining fully involved in their relationships and their communities. Thus, although the public face of Southern Baptists is unapologetically patriarchal (and many Southern Baptist women themselves espouse notions of subordination and submissiveness), the reality is that within their contexts, Southern Baptist women develop a variety of strategies to adapt to and challenge the constraints they face in church, at home, and in society, and these strategies are closely interwoven with these women's understanding of themselves as Southern Baptists.

Southern Baptist Identity

That I would grow up Southern Baptist seems inevitable. I was born in Georgia, the heart of the Bible Belt and a stronghold for Southern Baptists. In fact, my little county of 69,000 inhabitants had sixty Southern Baptist churches in 1960 when I made my appearance at McCall Hospital in Rome, Georgia, just three days after my mother's twenty-first birthday. The first place my parents ever took me to was a Southern Baptist church. My father grew up Southern Baptist, and when I recently asked his mother about her own churchgoing experiences, my now ninety-eight-year-old grandmother told me, "I'm a Baptist, teeth and toe." My mother's family was not particularly religious, so she attended a Christian church on her own while she was growing up. When she married my father in 1957, four months before her eighteenth birthday (he was twenty-three), she started going to a Southern Baptist church with him. And my path was set.

Southern Baptists came into being in 1845 in response to northern Baptists' increasing opposition to slavery.[7] Until this point, Baptists in the North and South had cooperated to support missionaries, and the mission societies had a policy of neutrality with regard to slavery. As northern Baptists became more and more abolitionist, however, Baptists in the South, on the whole, became more entrenched in their defense of slavery. Tensions reached a breaking point in 1844, when Baptists in Georgia nominated a slave owner for appointment as a home missionary, constituting a test case of the Home Mission Society's neutrality. The society refused to act on the test case. Then Alabama Baptists questioned whether slaveholders could be appointed as foreign missionaries. The neutrality stance was cited in response, but the following sentence was added: "one thing is certain; we can never be a party to any arrangement which would imply approbation of slavery."[8] Some Baptists in the South called for a cautious response, but delegates from various southern Baptist bodies gathered in Augusta, Georgia, on May 8, 1845, and formed the Southern Baptist Convention with 4,126 churches and 351,951 members.[9]

For the next 100 years, Southern Baptists continued as one of many strong Christian denominations in the South. But with its successful "Million More in '54" campaign, the Convention experienced unprecedented growth. Coupled with southern economic expansion, this campaign catapulted Southern Baptists to the forefront of Christianity in the South. Soon, Southern Baptists became the largest Protestant denomination in the United States. One of the keys to the denomination's success was its ability to create a common identity for Southern Baptist church members. To be Southern Baptist was not simply to hold membership in a Southern Baptist church. Rather, it was to construct a sense of self shaped by Southern Baptist theology, polity, educational programs, and church practices.

As early as 1963, Southern Baptist religious educator Findley Edge critiqued the institutionalization of Southern Baptists and the resulting concern for numbers and programs over authentic faith.[10] He warned that numerical success could not be equated with faithful Christian living and pointed out that Southern Baptists' emphasis on growth and efficiency had led to unregenerate church membership—that is, those who had had conversion experiences but who had not gone on to lead authentic Christian lives. For Edge, the division of salvation from discipleship was problematic at best and heretical at worst. He worried that the denomination's packaging of curricular materials and programs rooted in secular educational and management scholarship rather than theology would lead to programmed rather than experiential faith. Yet for most leaders in the denomination, unprecedented growth equated with God's blessing, so they did not heed Edge's warning. They continued to develop materials that turned Christian education into a series of step-by-step guidelines instead of a dynamic experience of the divine. Though theologically problematic, these materials worked—if the goal was to create a simple and singular identity for Southern Baptists.

So, I was born not so much into a church or a denomination as into an identity. And for me, that identity was gendered and racialized in the sociohistorical context of the 1960s and 1970s South. Developmental theorist James Fowler contends that the process of meaning-making is central to faith.[11] As I thought about my own life and the lives of other Southern Baptist women, I became interested in this process of meaning-making. I wanted to understand how Southern Baptist women make meaning of their lives, how they construct gendered identities that are complex and often contradictory, and how they understand themselves as Southern Baptist women.

So I decided to ask them. Funded by the Louisville Institute, I spent a year and a half talking to 159 current and former Southern Baptist women. Support from the Southern Baptist Historical Library and Archives and Oregon State University's Valley Library allowed me to comb Southern Baptist archives to find out what women of the past had to say for themselves—and what others had to say about them. Oregon State University's Center for the Humanities provided me with a fellowship that gave me the time and space to travel and write.

Gathering the Stories

I set out to talk to the broadest spectrum of Southern Baptist women possible, because I wanted to reflect their great diversity. I talked to fundamentalist, conservative, moderate, and liberal women; to laywomen and women in ministry; to white, black, Asian American, and Latina women; to young and old women; to southern, midwestern, and western women. Many of the women in my study are now former Southern Baptists. They are among the thousands of people who left the denomination after the fifteen-year struggle between moderates and fundamentalists resulted in the latter making radical changes in the denomination's public stance on issues related to women. Yet their identities were forged in Southern Baptist churches, and most of them continue to identify with some Baptist group.

Diana Garland once led the social work program at the Southern Baptist Theological Seminary, but she was a casualty of the Controversy and left to join the faculty of another Baptist institution—Baylor University. Paula Sheridan, a professor of social work at Whittier College in California, asked Diana, "Why are you doing this at Baylor when you could do it anywhere?" Diana answered, "Because these are my people."

"I understand that," I said, when Paula told me of their conversation.

"And I will say to people who make fun of Southern Baptists," Paula continued, "'These are my people.' This is a part of my family, and if I separated myself from that I would be fragmenting myself."

Many consider themselves Baptists in exile. That metaphor seems to predominate among those who either were forced out of Southern Baptist life or left of their own free will. In fact, a volume of essays written by a number of moderate leaders during the Controversy is entitled *Exiled*.[12] Speaking of the people who left, Paula said, "We're all in exile." She believes that the trick is learning how to love what has both birthed and harmed us.

Nan Cook, a member of First Baptist Church in Batesburg, South Carolina, has remained a Southern Baptist. She explained, "A preacher told me one time if you were ever raised a Baptist, you were always a Baptist!" Interestingly, the women who stayed and the women who left have many more similarities than differences. Those who left provide a much more vocal alternative narrative to the Convention's official stance on women, but even the women who stayed present a more subtle and nuanced picture of simultaneous complicity and resistance than most outside observers would predict. For simplicity's sake, I refer to all these women as Southern Baptists, noting their affiliation with other groups or denominations when it is relevant.

Perhaps the most poignant moment of my research came when I sat down to lunch with Dorothy and Paige Patterson. Paige is now president of Southwestern Baptist Theological Seminary, and Dorothy teaches there. Paige was one of the leaders of the conservatives during the Controversy, and Dorothy was an outspoken advocate of the changes in the Convention. In every way we were (and are) on opposite sides of most issues, yet I found myself in their home, eating lunch, and sharing stories. Like Leslie Jordan (see the preface), I had to put all the ugly things under my chair and just listen to and learn from these people.

After lunch, Paige went back to his office, and Dorothy and I sat down for her interview. I had asked her to find a photograph of herself as a girl growing up in a Southern Baptist church, and she showed me one in which she was Queen Regent in Service. (More about this later. For now, suffice it to say that, for Southern Baptist girls in the mid-twentieth century, this was akin to reaching the highest level of Girl Scouts.) As I looked at that photo, I saw one of those fond memories that so many Southern Baptist girls shared, and I grieved that we had not found a way to work through our differences and hold on to those precious things we did have in common.

The Controversy among Southern Baptists began in 1979 when a group of fundamentalist leaders developed a scheme to take control of the denomination's boards, agencies, and institutions by electing a fundamentalist as president of the Southern Baptist Convention. The president of the SBC has great appointive powers, and the plan was that he would use those powers to appoint like-minded people to the committee on committees, which nominated people to the committee on boards, which in turn nominated trustees to the boards of the various denominational organizations. The motivating forces behind this power play were the fundamentalists' belief that theological liberalism had crept into the Convention and their own sense of disenfranchisement from places of power.

The work of the SBC's annual meeting is done by "messengers," people elected by their local churches to attend the convention and vote their own personal convictions. Messengers are not delegates; they do not represent their congregations. In keeping with the Baptist notion of a priesthood of believers, churches do not instruct messengers how to vote; they trust that the messengers will listen when God speaks directly to them. Each church that gives a minimum amount through the Cooperative Program, the denomination's funding mechanism, can send two messengers. For each additional incremental sum, a local church can send another messenger, up to a maximum of ten messengers per church. During the height of the Controversy, as many as 45,000 messengers attended the annual convention. The fundamentalist leadership used the rallying cry of biblical inerrancy—the notion that scripture is without error not only in theology but also in history and science (explored in more detail in chapter 2)—to rally messengers to vote for the fundamentalist candidate. They suggested that theological liberalism had to be rooted out of the denomination's agencies and institutions, and they pitted themselves—the true believers of the Bible—

against the more moderate Southern Baptists who, at the time, held most of the paid positions in the Convention and whose fidelity to scripture was open to question because they did not hold to inerrancy. For the next thirteen chaotic, hostile, and painful years, the fundamentalists controlled the Convention, and the moderates looked for ways to create alternative Baptist structures.

One of the more interesting phenomena I observed when I talked to Southern Baptist women was their puzzlement at my question about their denominational affiliation. On the demographic survey that I had the women fill out, I asked whether they were currently Southern Baptists and, if not, with what denomination they were affiliated. I also asked whether their churches were affiliated with the Cooperative Baptist Fellowship (CBF) or the Alliance of Baptists, two splinter groups founded by moderates in response to fundamentalist control of the Convention. (Some Southern Baptist churches remained within the Convention but associated with one or both of these groups. Other churches disaffiliated themselves completely from the SBC and joined one or both of these alternatives. At this point, neither the CBF nor the Alliance considers itself a separate denomination per se.) I was amazed at the consternation these questions caused. Many of the women no longer considered themselves Southern Baptist but pointed out that because the CBF and the Alliance aren't really denominations, they didn't actually have a denomination. The question for them seemed to be, "Who are we now, if we aren't Southern Baptists?" In the focus groups held at conservative and fundamentalist churches, I heard the women whispering to one another, "Are we part of the Cooperative Baptist Fellowship? Are we part of the Alliance of Baptists? What are those, anyway?" Apparently, the splintering of the SBC has created a denominational identity crisis for many women. Thirty years ago, every one of them would have said unequivocally, "We're Southern Baptist," and they would have been proud to say so. In 2005, many weren't quite sure what they were—Baptists of some sort, but to a great degree, that unwavering sense of identity that existed before the Controversy was no more.[13]

I myself face this denominational identity crisis. I earned a master's degree and a PhD at the Southern Baptist Theological Seminary in Louisville, Kentucky. I did internships at the state Baptist newspaper in Kentucky and the Woman's Missionary Union (WMU), auxiliary to the SBC, in Birmingham, Alabama. I was a full-time faculty member at a Southern Baptist college and an adjunct instructor for two Southern

Baptist seminaries. I wrote articles and devised curricular materials for WMU and the Baptist Sunday School Board. I was an ordained Southern Baptist minister. But as the Controversy raged, I found myself more and more at odds with the type of people Southern Baptists were becoming. I quit teaching for the Southern Baptist college when the personal attacks on me (I was referred to as "that woman on the religion faculty") began to take too much of a personal toll. I moved to Oregon to teach at an evangelical Quaker college, and I joined the only moderate Southern Baptist church there (there aren't many Southern Baptist churches of any stripe in Oregon); I also taught at Golden Gate Baptist Theological Seminary's extension campus in Portland. By the mid-1990s, however, the Convention had changed so radically that I felt I no longer belonged among the people who had so greatly influenced who I had become. So I left Southern Baptist life in 1995 and became a member of the United Church of Christ (UCC). I began the process of changing my ordination to the UCC—in fact, the only step left was an essay I had to write—when I realized that I just couldn't do it. Like my grandmother, I was a Baptist "teeth and toe," and though I dearly love the UCC, I couldn't change my identity. So I remain a Baptist minister in exile in the United Church of Christ.

My background provides me with a unique perspective to write a book about Southern Baptist women. Most of the other scholarly works on fundamentalist and evangelical women have been written by women who were outsiders to the groups they studied. I approached my research as both an insider and an outsider. As an insider—as someone who grew up Southern Baptist—I know the language, the practices, and the culturally constructed meanings associated with them. I also know the people, and this made my access to a wide variety of Southern Baptist women possible. As someone who left the denomination more than ten years ago, I also have the distance to approach Southern Baptists as an outside observer. I no longer have a personal stake in what happens in the Convention or in the splinter groups, although I still have a strong emotional attachment to the Convention and the many Baptist people I know and love. This research has demanded that I be highly self-reflective because of my emotional investment in the subject and because of the autobiographical content of my research. Deciding whether to use "we" or "they" when referring to Southern Baptists in this book engendered a sort of existential crisis for me, and I hope my readers will forgive my inconsistency in the use of pronouns throughout the text.

My own location in relation to this research meant that I had to be very careful to listen closely to my informants. I had to try to set aside my own issues with the denomination and hear how these women made meaning of their own lives and experiences as Southern Baptists. Sometimes this was immensely difficult for me because, as a feminist, I recognize a great deal of oppression in Southern Baptist theology and practice. Also, almost invariably, my participants assumed that I agreed with them theologically, socially, and politically about the issues at hand. At times, I felt very uncomfortable with this implicit assumption, yet I was reluctant to break the flow of the conversation or risk losing their trust in me by disagreeing. I decided that nothing was to be gained by correcting their perceptions of me, and I resolved my internal conflict by determining to write about their beliefs in a manner that was respectful and cognizant of their right to hold those beliefs and to use them to construct meaningful identities for themselves, even though I might critique them from my feminist perspective.

I worked hard to include voices that speak from a wide range of diverse perspectives and to ensure that my analysis was true to the things they told me and the meanings they made. I began with the women I knew—my mother and her closest friends (otherwise known as "the Clique"), the women with whom I had attended seminary, and the women involved in denominational work that I had met along the way. They talked to me, and they referred me to other women who might have important things to say. I logged about 30,000 frequent-flier miles traveling to Georgia, North and South Carolina, Florida, Alabama, Tennessee, Texas, and California to talk in person with as many women as possible. I shudder to think of the long-distance telephone bills for the interviews I conducted by phone. I talked to some women individually and to some in focus groups. I interviewed the Clique five times—a focus group at the beginning of the research; three separate, individual life history interviews; and a final focus group at the conclusion of the research.

There were also women who declined to talk to me. Many of them were employed by very conservative churches or denominational agencies, although other women in the same position did agree to participate. Just doing research on women raises red flags for many conservatives, and I suppose it didn't help that I was a former Southern Baptist and current director of women studies at a northwestern state university. An atmosphere of suspicion and fear is pervasive at many Southern Baptist institutions, and one participant informed me that a number of women who turned me down likely did so for fear of losing their jobs. Others may have simply mistrusted me and doubted my willingness to represent them fairly and respectfully. One pastor denied me access to women in his church for fear that I might criticize them or condemn Southern Baptists—despite my assurances that this was not my intent.

The Clique

In the early 1970s, my family attended Shorter Avenue Baptist Church in Rome, Georgia, but my mother and a couple of her friends from church began to attend a Bible study group led by a woman from another church just down the street. As a result of my mother's involvement in that group, my whole family transferred to West Rome Baptist Church in 1973. In her Bible study group, my mother reconnected with women she had known in high school and met other women with whom she had a particular affinity. Eight of them became so close that the Bible study leader nicknamed them "the Clique." Throughout the 1970s, they raised their children together, and, with the exception of my mother, in the 1980s and 1990s, they became grandmothers together. My mother had the misfortune (in her eyes) of having two daughters who opted not to have children. In fact, one year my sister and I (at the time, living in North Carolina and California, respectively)—unbeknownst to each other—sent her the same birthday card. It read: "Mom, you can have anything you want for your birthday . . . except grandchildren." Fortunately for my sister and me, one member of the Clique who has an abundance of grandchildren has loaned one to my mother.

These women who have been friends for more than thirty years gave me the central idea for this book. All my life I watched them participate in churches that taught female subordination, yet all the while, they were the ones who provided spiritual leadership in their homes, holding their families together; they were strong women who exercised power in the church, working to meet the needs of people experiencing difficult circumstances in our town. We watched the women's movement unfold on the evening news, but at the time, they didn't identify with those women's struggles; they battled daily to assert their voices and claim their agency, not realizing the extent to which their issues really did intersect with the goals of feminism.

They may cringe to hear me say it, but they gave me my first taste of feminism. By word and by example, they taught me that I was of equal value to any boy. They did not limit my aspirations. In fact, they encouraged me to excel academically. Of course, at the same time, they taught me gender roles as well. My mother tried to raise me to be a proper southern lady, but that was not to be. One of my favorite photographs from my childhood shows me at the age of four in my red velvet Christmas dress, adorned with lace, and my black patent leather shoes—wearing my cousin's new football helmet and down in three-point stance with my father.

My mother told me, "I guess I became liberated because my daughters became liberated." She reminded me of an incident from my late adolescence when she was working as a substitute schoolteacher. My father was a pretty typical patriarch, and he didn't particularly like the fact that my mother was working outside the home. He still expected her to fulfill all the traditional roles at home as well. Mom explained:

> He wanted me here, and for all those years before he retired, I *had* to get up and I *had* to cook his breakfast, and then I got him up; and I had to do all the washing, ironing, and cleaning; that was woman's work. That's what he was taught. And one time, I went off to school, and he was working second shift, and he had to pack a lunch; and he didn't take a lunch because I wasn't here to fix it. And he came in, and I said, "Did you take a lunch?" And you said, "Daddy, you mean you can't even spread peanut butter on two pieces of bread and put it in a lunch box?" [And he said], "I could if I wanted to!" And he always packed his lunch after that.

Still, Mom didn't necessarily need her liberated daughters to intervene. Another time, she got mad at Dad—again over the issue of her packing him a lunch to take to work. Dad can laugh about it now too. He said, "I told her to get over there and make me a sandwich." Mom finished the story: "I worked all the time. I had the washing and the ironing and doing the grocery shopping, preparing the Sunday school lesson because I was teaching, besides everything that [you and Karen] did all week long—and you were into everything—and I fixed his lunch. And I was so mad I put my fist right through it. And they called it the 'Knuckle Sandwich' at the mill. They said, 'She was mad, but she made it.'"

These are the contradictions that intrigued me as I began this project. How could these women be both submissive wives and self-actualized agents? How could they espouse subordination while challenging husbands, deacons, pastors, and any other man who got in their way? How could they reject the women's movement while believing in and acting on so many of its basic tenets? How could they feel empowered by churches that limited their roles based on gender? How did they construct identities as Southern Baptist women that embodied all these contradictions and complexities in a unified sense of an autonomous self?

In numerous ways, the Clique is representative of many Southern Baptist women in the South. They are conservative, family-oriented, Bible-believing, active participants in a local church. Though some of them no longer attend a Southern Baptist church for various reasons (none of which has to do with theology), they identify Southern Baptist theology and polity as central to their religious understandings—and they sometimes find themselves at odds with their current churches over these denominational differences. Even though they attend different churches now, they still interact on a regular basis. They talk on the phone; they organize outings to craft fairs all over the Southeast; they have lunch together for each person's birthday, and each woman contributes a small cash gift so the celebrant can buy herself something nice; they support one another through life's difficulties and tragedies. They tell me that they are more like sisters than their biological sisters.

So, starting with these women, I began my quest to understand how Southern Baptist women construct their identities. I decided that these women would be the heart of my study because so much could be learned from their stories as individuals and as a group. I started with a focus group involving all of them. Then, over the course of a year, I interviewed each woman individually two or three times. At the end of the year, I gathered them together again for a final focus group.

Amazingly, these women, who are all in their late sixties or early seventies, have been married to the same men for the last fifty years or so. That has required some effort on their parts, and I'll go into more detail when I discuss family, later in the book. None of them finished college, although many of their children did. I grew up with their children, and, although I haven't been close to them in many years, our mothers have made sure that we know what the others are doing. (My mother, in particular, made sure that my sister and I knew who was having children, when, and how many. I kept sending home articles, books, and photos of my trips around the world.) These women are caring, compassionate, giving, strong, and sometimes stubborn. Here is a brief introduction to each of them.

JoAnn Shaw, my mother, was born in Rome, Georgia, and has lived there all her life. For many years she was a substitute schoolteacher, and she has always been active in church leadership as a Sunday school teacher, WMU officer, or church officer. During the course of these interviews, she confessed that during the brief time she was a member of a Southern Methodist church in the 1990s, she served as a steward, the Southern Methodist version of a deacon. Mom is now a member of a small Southern Baptist church in Rome, where she leads a women's Bible study group on Sunday mornings. She told me conspiratorially that in the last deacon elections, she nominated a woman, but the (male) church leaders refused to broach the issue with the congregation.

Lidia Abrams was born in Cuba and immigrated to the United States after marrying Ralph Abrams, an American serviceman from Georgia who was stationed at Guantanamo Bay. She learned English and settled into life as a housewife, despite her mother-in-law's overt racism. She has three children, six grandchildren, and one great-grandchild. A few years ago she joined North Broad Church of God, and she has become active in its mission work in South America. During my research, she traveled to Honduras to interpret for other church members on a witnessing mission there. The first time I interviewed Lidia, we sat next to each other in the waiting room at Floyd Medical Center, where one of her family members was hospitalized, and I was reminded of her compassion and concern. Lidia is one of those women who never meets a stranger and who always has something kind to say. Again and again, in her still deeply and beautifully accented English, she told me how good it was to see me.

Doris Bailey was born in Alabama but went to school in Arkansas, where she played softball and rooted loudly for the basketball team. She moved to Georgia as an adult. She has two children and four grandchildren. The first time I interviewed Doris, I went to her house, where she had been baking. Doris was one of my Sunbeam leaders when I was a preschooler at Shorter Avenue Baptist Church. Now, with striking white hair, she devotes a lot of her time to helping her daughter raise a son with developmental issues and nursing her husband, who is recovering from a stroke.

Alicia Bennett has spent her whole life in Georgia. She has three children and two grandchildren. She loves to quilt, sew, and play tennis. During this research, she traveled with a group of women from West Rome Baptist Church to Venezuela to teach women there how to sew; they took supplies and sewing machines and distributed diaper bags donated by a local hospital. I talked to Alicia in her home while her husband, Don, puttered around outside. She told me that they had endured some difficult times when their children were young, but in recent years, Don had undergone a dramatic change—"one of my deepest blessings" she called his transformation. Alicia showed me her impressive sewing room and, at the end of the interview, gave me a beautiful kitchen towel she had sewn for me.

Kayne Carter was born in Tennessee. Her father was an alcoholic, and her mother worked long, hard hours in a textile mill to support her three children. Kayne thus learned early on that women could be strong and make it on their own. In high school, she was captain of the volleyball team and participated in the marching band as part of the "battalion" that spelled out the school's initials on the field. She moved to Rome with her husband for his job in construction. She has four children, eleven grandchildren, and one great-grandchild. In recent years, Kayne has struggled with health issues. I talked to her in her home, surrounded by pictures of her children and grandchildren. Kayne said that although she wishes she had done some things differently in life, her greatest joy is her family.

Shelby Christie has spent her entire life in Georgia. In high school, she played drums in the girls' drum and bugle corps and was involved in the square dance and drama clubs. She has three children and eight grandchildren. She's an avid doll collector; her house is full of curio cabinets filled with every kind of doll imaginable, and one entire room is devoted to her doll collection. The first time I interviewed Shelby, she was having some work done on the house, so she took me out to lunch at my favorite barbecue restaurant. The next time, however, I interviewed her in her home and got the grand tour of the doll collection, and I must say, it is most impressive. She started collecting dolls as a hobby in the early 1980s, and she's lost count of how many dolls she has now. Through the years, she's donated many of her dolls to organizations for disadvantaged children. When I asked her which doll was her favorite, she said, "I don't know. That's just like asking which is your favorite child!"

Judy Masters was born in Louisiana and moved to Rome as a teenager, where she played both basketball and the saxophone in high school. She has five children, fourteen grandchildren (one of whom, Skylar, she has loaned to my mother), and one great-grandchild. Judy, like Alicia, loves to sew, and she was part of the group from West Rome Baptist Church that traveled to Venezuela. Before leaving, she sewed a number of gowns for premature babies and donated them to a hospital in Caracas. When I interviewed Judy at her house, she showed me pictures of her children and grandchildren and gave me the grand tour of her sewing room, which was piled high with fabrics, patterns, knickknacks, and partially finished projects. Years ago, Judy sewed my sister's wedding dress. She now sews little gowns and bonnets for the tiniest premature babies—the ones who probably won't survive—and donates them to the local hospital. Making these little things, she said, is a gift the Lord has given her.

Nancy Moore is a native of Georgia. In high school she was in the glee club and worked on the yearbook. She has three children and five grandchildren. She is considered the progressive of the group. Though theologically conservative, Nancy is to the left of the rest of the Clique on social issues and politics. She's a bit of an Anglophile (she served me tea in her lovely kitchen), and she enjoys traveling, especially to Europe. Nancy lives in a wooded area, and she has created a wonderful garden. Everything in her beautiful house is in its place, yet her home feels warm and welcoming. Nancy always seems to be as put together as her house is. We talked at her kitchen table, delving more deeply into personal, theological, and social issues than in my other Clique interviews. Nancy and I have always connected because of our more liberal political bent and our love of academic study. Growing up, I was also closer to Nancy's middle daughter, Beth, than I was to the children of the other Clique members.

Other Participants

All the participants have spent some, if not most, of their lives in Southern Baptist churches, from two to seventy-eight years. They range in age from twenty-two to eighty-three. Most of them (eighty-eight) live in the South or in the Texas-Oklahoma-Missouri-Arkansas region (forty-eight). Most of them are or have been married, although a significant number are now single. More than two-thirds have children. Ten percent of the participants are women of color: eight are black, six are Latina, and three are Asian American.

Of those who identified a theological position, more than three-quarters said that they were theologically conservative or moderate. Less than 10 percent identified themselves as fundamentalist, and more than 20 percent identified themselves as theologically liberal or radical. About half have been seminary educated. Although this number is disproportionate to the number of seminary-educated women in the denomination, I believed that these women could provide a unique perspective informed both by their own experiences as Southern Baptists and by their study of Baptist history and theology. Because their experiences prior to attending seminary were very similar to those of other Southern Baptist women, I don't believe that their overrepresentation has skewed the data. Rather, it has provided additional insight and perspective to inform my interpretation.

About a quarter of the participants are involved in churches affiliated with the Cooperative Baptist Fellowship, the Alliance of Baptists, or both. Eight participants are now American Baptists, one is National Baptist, and twenty have either joined another denomination (United Church of Christ, Disciples, Episcopal, Presbyterian, or Methodist) or opted out of church life altogether, all as a result of the Controversy. I included those who've left the denomination because their experiences highlight the tensions in Southern Baptist identity that emerged during the unique historical moment when women's issues became a central dividing line. Certainly, if I had included only women who are currently affiliated with a Southern Baptist church, this would have been a very different book. Yet the women who left the denomination have spent most of their lives identifying as Southern Baptists, and they left not because they had changed but because the Convention had. Their stories, then, have as much relevance as the stories of the women who remained in Southern Baptist churches. Their choice to leave the Convention is an important part of the larger story of Southern Baptist women.

Thirty-three percent of the participants are Republicans, 40 percent are Democrats, and the rest are independents (with one Libertarian) or chose not to answer the question. (Interestingly, but perhaps not surprisingly, I found a high correlation between those who identified as theological conservatives or fundamentalists and affiliation with the Republican Party; there was a parallel correlation between those who identified as theological moderates or liberals and affiliation with the Democratic Party.)

Although these women are diverse in many ways, as I talked with them, I found an amazing number of similarities rooted in their experiences in Southern Baptist churches. These shared threads of identity are at the heart of this narrative, although the nuanced differences are also essential components of any understanding of Southern Baptist women.

Some of their responses were expected (for instance, I correctly assumed that soul competency would be an important topic), but I was occasionally surprised and perplexed by what they taught me. I knew that these women would be hospitable, but I was amazed at their graciousness, even in the face of our differences. The older women surprised me too. They're a lot more liberal on women's issues than one might think and probably a little more rebellious as well. I'm still thinking about the ways women of color negotiate Southern Baptist life; they're a lot happier with the situation than I might have expected. And, though I'm not surprised, again I find myself profoundly moved by the sense of self and the calling and faith of these women who have stood in the face of opposition, violence, disdain, apathy, and invisibility to claim their right to hear and follow the voice of God.

Making Sense of All the Stories

As I listened to the women who participated in interviews and focus groups, I heard common themes and nuanced differences emerge. These themes and differences form the core of this book. The story I tell here is one of identity and meaning—my own, my informants', and the Southern Baptist women who preceded us. My hope is that this book will foster understanding and celebration, exploration and conversation.

What intrigues me most about Southern Baptist women are these complexities and contradictions. Because Southern Baptists are not a creedal people and have historically emphasized freedom of the individual conscience before God, the diversity within the denomination is enormous, and the range of theological and social convictions moves along a continuum from fundamentalist to progressive. The women with whom I spoke represent numerous points on that continuum. Of course, this created for me the daunting task of authentically representing their commonalities within the context of their deeply felt and experienced differences. One way I manage this is by allowing them to speak for themselves as much as possible. As I analyze their comments, I draw heavily on their own words and their own interpretations of their experiences. I am especially interested in how they construct their identities as Southern Baptists and whether that construction varies in particular ways from the constructions of other conservative Protestant women as suggested in scholarly writings on the history and sociology of religion.

Of course, Baptist identity is itself a contested construct. Even the origins of Baptists are in dispute. As a product of the Southern Baptist Theological Seminary in the 1980s, however, I position myself alongside the constructions of Baptist identity suggested by E. Y. Mullins, Glenn

Hinson, and Walter Shurden,[14] focusing on the notion of freedom of the individual conscience before God. That construction informs my analysis, even as I recognize that, for other Baptists, different constructions constitute Baptist identity.[15] The Southern Baptist Theological Seminary, long considered the "mother seminary" of Southern Baptists, was founded in 1859 in Greenville, South Carolina, shortly after the founding of the Convention itself in 1845. The seminary closed for a while during the Civil War, and because of the destruction and economic hardship following the war, the seminary reopened in Louisville, Kentucky, in 1877. The seminary has never been a stranger to controversy, and through the years, it gained a reputation for serious theological scholarship among theological institutions around the country and for theological liberalism among Southern Baptists (although this so-called liberalism is relative in terms of the larger scope of theological education). When I attended the seminary from 1982 to 1987, at the height of the Controversy, its status and reputation had made it a primary target for fundamentalists. I don't think a day went by that we didn't talk about the Controversy. It affected the lives of students, faculty, and staff in profound ways that permeated the classrooms, hallway discussions, and even chapel services. Central to these discussions were our understandings of the Bible, Baptist notions of soul liberty, and the role of women. Undoubtedly, my experiences as a seminary student during this particular historical moment shaped my own identity in essential ways; they also shaped this book in terms of my understanding of who Baptists are and what has happened among them over the past half century in particular. Most importantly, my experiences affected the primacy of women in my own scholarship and teaching; my understandings of the place of women in the Controversy and the roles of women in home, church, and society; and the ways I choose to approach research and writing about women.

As I wrote this book, I paid special attention to my own voice as well as to my position in relation to the material. In preparation for writing, I read a lot of memoirs, because that was the tone I was aiming for. I wanted to tell my own story in the context of the story of a denomination and the women who have been a part of it. My story is inextricably interwoven with theirs, and despite the pain of the Controversy, my feelings for the denomination that helped raise me right and for the women who had a direct hand in that are very tender. I hope that even when I offer analysis and occasionally critique, my readers will feel the love and gratitude I have toward Southern Baptists. I hope that this book will be experienced more like the work of a daughter telling family secrets than a bitter ex-lover spilling the beans. One of the most important issues, however, is accessibility. I want this to be a book that everyone can read—especially the women who shared their time and hospitality by participating in interviews and focus groups. I strongly believe that feminist research should be accessible and relevant outside the academy, and although I give the requisite attention to the documentation of sources, theories, and research, I want this book to be easily (and enjoyably) read.

Making Meaning and Making Identity

As a feminist, I'm concerned about what is happening among Southern Baptists. The denomination claims 16 million members, and after its fifteen-year Controversy, it has reconstructed itself in a way that ideologically circumscribes women's roles. Much of the research on conservative Protestant women in general takes note of the ways women define themselves and find empowerment in churches that espouse female subordination. That is certainly an important part of the meaning-making I found among Southern Baptist women, and it suggests that denominational pronouncements hardly characterize the reality of women's lives. Instead, I found women with a strong sense of agency and autonomy rooted in their very identity as Southern Baptists. In fact, I would suggest that in Southern Baptist theology and practice lie the impetus for women's strong sense of self and agency and the key to the differences between Southern Baptist women and other conservative Protestant women. Although many of these women say that they find power in submission, they also feel perfectly free to disagree with men—whether their husbands or their pastors. And among more moderate women with feminist leanings, submission to anyone other than God is not even a part of their lexicon. After talking to these women and reading about their predecessors in Baptist history, I'm convinced that Baptist notions of independence, liberty, and individual conscience provide a powerful counteraction to the rhetoric of submission espoused by denominational leaders and many local church pastors.

My participants are largely southern women, but even those who aren't southern are influenced by the denomination's curricular materials and periodicals that come right out of Nashville, Birmingham, Atlanta, and Richmond. Therefore, they are also part of a larger story (and myth) about (white) women in the South who learned to hold their families together in the midst of war, alcoholic and abusive daddies, economic crises, and Yankee carpetbagging. From birth, most white southern women learn the subtle skills of getting what they want while making men feel like they're the ones making the decisions and ruling the home. And southern women take these skills to church with them. The rhetoric of submission is not unfamiliar to southern women; it's an assumed part of southern culture. That Southern Baptist churches would espouse submission is expected, because they are cultural products of the South. Southern Baptist women's internalization of this rhetoric is part of their birthright as southerners: women are quiet, genteel, submissive—at least on the surface.

Paralleling the rhetoric of submission, however, is the reality of resistance. In ways covert and occasionally overt, southern women challenge their subordination. It is common knowledge among conservative Southern Baptist women that they run the church; no Southern Baptist church could continue to do its work for very long without them. Among moderate Southern Baptist women there is more outright rebellion— women who claim their right to equality in the home and to leadership in the church. Of course, being southern women, they usually try to rebel as nicely as possible, with relatively few outbursts of temper or name-calling. Rather, they exhibit a quiet determination and an unshakable sense of their God-given right (as humans, as Christians, and especially as Baptists) to do whatever they feel God is leading them to do.

Raised Right

In *The Whisper of the River,* Ferrol Sams's novel about a young boy growing up Southern Baptist, the novel's protagonist, Porter Osborne Jr., explains that he was "Raised Right":

> The child who had been Raised Right was not only Saved but had spent a large part of his formative years in the House of the Lord. Attendance at piano recitals did not count, but everything else did. From Sunbeams through BYPU [Baptist Young People's Union], from Sunday school to prayer meeting, from Those Attending Preaching to Those With Prepared Lessons, everything was counted. So was everybody. In the midst of all this scorekeeping the concept of being saved by grace was a nebulous and adult bit of foolishness not to be contemplated with anything approaching the fervor accorded perfect attendance. A pin with added yearly bars swinging like a sandwich sign on an adolescent chest proclaimed indisputably to the world that its wearer had been Raised Right.[16]

I was raised right, as were the majority of the participants in my study. Most of the women I talked to grew up in Southern Baptist churches where the concept of being raised right was paramount, along with being saved, being baptized, and maybe even being called to full-time Christian service (for girls, that meant missions, music, religious education, or becoming a pastor's wife). Like many of the offspring of the Protestant Reformation, Baptists cherish the notion of salvation by faith alone, and the works that ought to accompany salvation are highly touted as evidence of true conversion. As southern girls, we were taught that we were supposed to be nice, sit still, fold our hands in our laps, cross our legs at the ankle, say "ma'am" and "sir" to every adult, never backtalk, help clear the table and wash the dishes, never call boys, and read our Bibles and pray every day. If we arrived at Sunday school early and helped the teacher set out cookies and Kool-Aid, if we remembered to say "please" and "thank you," the adult teachers would murmur approvingly among themselves, "Now that girl was raised right."

The messages from our families and southern culture came through loud and clear, backed up by the scripture verses we memorized, the hymns we sang, and the sermons we heard. Everywhere we turned, there were implicit and explicit messages about what being a Southern Baptist girl or woman means.

Sunbeams, Sword Drills, and Age-Graded Curriculum

In my travels, I often run into other Southern Baptists. Usually in less than two minutes, we are talking about the Southern Baptists we know in common. There may be 16 million of us, but I don't think there are six degrees of separation between us. Even more striking than our common acquaintances are our common experiences. To non–Southern Baptists, I'm sure it sounds like we're talking to one another in code—Sunbeams, GAs (formerly Girls' Auxiliary; now Girls in Action), RAs (Royal Ambassadors), WMU, altar calls, walking the aisle. Paula Sheridan told me this story: She had gone to see a production of Leslie Jordan's *Like a Dog on Linoleum*, a one-man show centered on his coming to terms with his conservative upbringing. The performance was so powerful that Paula wrote Jordan a letter afterward, thanking him for his work. She signed the letter "Paula M. Sheridan, Queen Regent in Service." Shortly thereafter she got a reply addressed to "Paula M. Sheridan, Queen Regent in Service," and the letter began, "Dear Queenie." Leslie thanked Paula for bringing her students to the play and then he wrote, "I want you to have this; I found it." Enclosed was a 1967 photo of his twin sisters being crown-bearers in a GA coronation. He wrote, "You of all people will enjoy this." Paula explained that, among Southern Baptists—whether current or former—"it's like there's a code." One of her colleagues at Whittier College, a professor of religion whose office is across the hall from hers, was once a Southern Baptist. "We talk in code," she emphasized, "and that is a touchstone; and we are at home with each other like no one else."

The person who transcribed the recorded interviews for this project (who has never been a Southern Baptist) e-mailed me to ask, "Susan, what's an Act Teen?" (Actually, it's "Acteen," but more about that later in the book.) Another day she called in alarm because the participants kept talking about something called "sword drills." I can only imagine what she was picturing in her mind, but in reality, a sword drill is a competition to see who can look up Bible verses the fastest.

Southern Baptist women share a common identity created by the common programs and practices of most Southern Baptist churches, the majority of which use curricular materials produced by the denomination's central publishing agencies. Lifeway, formerly known as the Baptist Sunday School Board, produces Bible study and discipleship materials. Woman's Missionary Union (WMU) produces mission-related educational materials for preschoolers, girls, and women. Other materials come from the International Mission Board (formerly the Foreign Mission Board) and the North American Mission Board (formerly the Home Mission Board). On Sunday mornings, Southern Baptists the nation over study the same Bible passages using the same lesson plans. When I was growing up, on Sunday nights we participated in Training Union (previously known as the Baptist Young People's Union, or BYPU; later known as Church Training and then Discipleship Training), studying Baptist history, theology, and polity. On Wednesday nights we had Sunbeams for preschoolers (now Mission Friends), GA for first- through sixth-grade girls, and Acteens for high school girls. Through these WMU organizations, we learned about Southern Baptist missionaries around the world and did missions in our own communities. In the summer, we'd go to GA camp and get to meet real live missionaries home on furlough from far-away places we had learned to locate on a map. So whether we were in Georgia, Kentucky, Texas, or California (yes, there are Southern Baptists in California), we read the same words, studied the same lessons, learned the same biblical principles, and prayed for the same missionaries on their birthdays.[17]

And through these materials, we also learned about gender roles. In 1978, Kay Shurden analyzed gender in curricular materials published by the Baptist Sunday School Board from 1973 to 1978 and presented her findings to the Consultation on Women in Church-Related Vocations. Not surprisingly, she discovered mostly stereotypical representations of females and males, with an occasional challenge to gender norms. She also found that as the age of the target group increased, so did the likelihood that the author of the materials would be male.[18] The drawings and photos we saw in the curricular materials reinforced traditional gender roles for women, as did the practices we observed in most Southern Baptist churches.

Few women have ever held public leadership roles in Southern Baptist churches, except in WMU. They are generally overrepresented as Sunday school teachers for children but have been forbidden to teach adult classes that include men. They have not preached nor led prayer in public worship very often. They have been ordained as deacons only occasionally and as ministers even more rarely. They have organized dinners and made sure that the little plastic communion cups were filled with Welch's grape juice for the Lord's Supper. They have taken hot meals to families who have lost loved ones, and they have given their mites to support missions.

What we witnessed in church reinforced cultural messages about gender. We learned that women's roles were supportive; we were to serve, almost always in the background, with no regard for recognition. Our works done in secret would be rewarded in heaven. But we also knew that each Southern Baptist church was ultimately dependent on us. Women were the backbone of the church, more likely to attend services and more likely to participate in its various programs. Over and over we heard the message, even from our pastors: "Women run this church." So we knew that we were powerful, but, being raised right, we also knew that we had to use that power subtly. Girls who were raised right didn't make a fuss, but we did know how to get things done, especially in the cause of Christ.

Missions are a central issue for Southern Baptists. After all, the only reason that stubbornly independent Baptists ever agreed to work together was because they realized that they could do more for missions by pooling their resources than by working alone. Key to our understanding of ourselves as Southern Baptist is our support for home and foreign missions and our involvement in missions in our own communities. We grew up making special offerings for missions, collecting toiletries to send to missionaries in poverty-stricken countries, and distributing food baskets to needy families in our own towns at Christmas. We knew that our faith demanded our action in the world, particularly if it helped us share the good news of Jesus with others.

Southern Baptists are evangelistic people. They believe that salvation comes by accepting Jesus as one's personal Lord and Savior, and they believe that their task is to carry that message to all the world. A conversion experience is another common denominator for Southern Baptists. In some way, whether at a revival, during an in-home visit by the pastor, or at a youth camp, every Southern Baptist gets "saved." This experience is usually swiftly followed by full-immersion baptism, most often in the church's baptismal pool, but occasionally in a river, lake, ocean, or swimming pool. Since the seventeenth century, baptism by immersion has been a central part of Baptist identity, and this continues to be true today, as most of my participants noted. Being Baptist means being baptized.

The reason for Southern Baptists' emphasis on issues such as salvation and baptism is their strong belief in the authority of the Bible in matters of faith and practice. In fact, Southern Baptists inevitably trace the justification for everything they do—worship, evangelism, missions, Christian education—to the Bible. And individual Southern Baptists incorporate their understanding of the Bible in their construction of self. Southern Baptist programs and materials emphasize the importance of both knowing and internalizing scripture, and this intimate relationship with the Bible provides a deep connection with the larger Christian story the Bible tells. Biblical metaphors abounded in my participants' stories, and each described the Bible as a means by which she achieved closer contact with God. Other Christian denominations also hold a high view of scripture, but Southern Baptists have emphasized the Bible in such a thoroughgoing way and produced such effective Bible curricula that scripture is as deeply integrated into the emotional and cognitive processes of devout Southern Baptists as are the ABCs and numbers. The Bible is not just a book that Southern Baptists read; it is a part of who they are.

Other characteristics of Baptist theology are also important organizing factors for Southern Baptist identity. In particular, the doctrine of the priesthood of believers is paramount, even when people don't know what to call it. Baptists believe that each person can go directly to God, without the need for any mediator. Southern Baptists also believe that each local church is autonomous, that it governs itself democratically and sets its own beliefs, practices, policies, and procedures. The Southern Baptist Convention, then, does not exercise power over local congregations. In fact, the Convention exists to empower the churches to carry out their own missions. The Convention cannot tell any local church what to do, and no real Baptist would even consider trying to coerce another person to believe anything.

Religious liberty is another principle that Baptists hold dear, although in recent years, this principle has been eroded both in the Convention and in many local churches as religion and politics have become linked. Baptists believe that the state should have no power of coercion in matters of religion. They believe that each person should be free to worship, or not worship, as she or he sees fit. Roger Williams, the first Baptist in America, fled religious persecution in New England and founded Rhode Island on the basis of religious liberty. In a sermon from the 1640s, Williams denounced religious persecution and articulated a doctrine of complete religious liberty. "It is the will and command of God," he said, "that a permission of the most paganish, Jewish, Turkish, or anti-christian consciences and worships be granted to all men in all nations and countries. . . . God requireth not a uniformity of religion to be enacted and enforced in any civil state; which enforced uniformity, sooner or later, is the greatest occasion of civil war, ravishing of conscience, persecution of Jesus Christ in his servants, and of the hypocrisy and destruction of millions of souls."[19]

Almost a century and a half later, when the founders of the Republic wrote the Constitution of the United States, they ensured that the new government would be free of religious coercion. Because of their brilliant insight, the Constitution guarantees that there is no religious test for public office. But only because of the agitation of Baptists, particularly those in Virginia, was another important sentence added to the First Amendment: "Congress shall make no law respecting an establishment of religion or prohibiting the free exercise thereof." Several years later, Thomas Jefferson wrote to the Baptists of Danbury, Connecticut, "I contemplate with sovereign reverence that act of the whole American people which declared that their legislature should make no law respecting an establishment of religion or prohibit the free exercise thereof, thus building a wall of separation between church and state."[20] Twenty years later, James Madison wrote, "I have no doubt that every new example will succeed, as every past one has done, in showing that religion and government will both exist in greater purity the less they are mixed together."[21]

Freedom is an essential strand running through Southern Baptist identity. Despite the depth and strength of their own convictions, again and again Southern Baptist women told me that belief is a matter of one's individual conscience before God. They believe that there is room for disagreement and difference among faithful Southern Baptists, although the extent to which difference is permissible depends on how conservative the women are. For most of them, certain key beliefs cannot be compromised—primarily the need for salvation, the importance of baptism by immersion, and the primacy of scripture in faith and practice. Beyond this, most of them say, there's room to disagree. "Is it okay to disagree with your pastor?" I asked them.

"Of course," they said.

"Why?" I asked.

"Because God speaks to me too," they told me.

Southern Baptist worship styles vary—from southern gospel to formal liturgical to informal contemporary. Nonetheless, the overall design of most Southern Baptist worship services is strikingly similar. The service opens with announcements, handshaking, music, testimonies, offerings, and scripture reading. But these are all preludes to the main event—the sermon. For Baptists, the preaching of the Word is central to worship; therefore, the sermon (as opposed to the Eucharist) is the primary focus of the service. The sermon is usually followed by an altar call or an invitation. During this time, as the congregation sings, people are invited to walk down the aisle of the church, take the pastor by the hand, and commit their lives to Christ, rededicate their lives to Christ if they have backslid, or join the church by baptism or by providing a statement of baptism or letter of transfer from another Southern Baptist church.

Another of the primary contributors to Southern Baptist identity is the *Baptist Hymnal.* As "contemporary" worship has moved eastward from California, the *Baptist Hymnal* has, in many congregations, taken a backseat to praise choruses projected onto a large screen. But for most of us who worshipped in a Baptist church before the last decade, the *Baptist Hymnal* provided a unifying experience of worship and theology. Although some of us sang from its southern gospel sections and others sang the more formal hymns set to music by Bach and Beethoven, to a great degree, we shared a common musical experience across the denomination. We all knew "Victory in Jesus" by heart, and thousands of us walked the aisle to "Just as I Am." When we visited other congregations on those rare Sundays we were away on vacation (vacation was no excuse for any raised-right Southern Baptist to miss church), we always knew that we would experience a sense of familiarity. Wherever we were, those Southern Baptists would be studying the same Sunday school lesson as our friends at home, and they'd be singing from the same hymnal we used. We also learned a lot of theology from the hymns—not all of it good. Certainly, the issue of inclusive language had not prevailed with the hymnal's editors at the Baptist Sunday School Board, even by the 1991 edition. Still, those hymns shaped who we were as Christians and as Southern Baptists. The hymnal of the United Church of Christ contains many of the same hymns in the *Baptist Hymnal,* with the words faithfully changed to reflect UCC theology and inclusive language. But I often find myself singing different words from the rest of the congregation because those old Baptist hymns are so deeply embedded in my memory and psyche.

One final important feature in the development of Southern Baptist identity is what I call the myth of Southern Baptists—that is, the myth of Southern Baptist superiority. The myth probably began with the Landmark controversy, when certain Baptists suggested that Baptist churches were the only true churches and that Baptists did not come out of the Reformation but have existed in continuous succession from the time of John the Baptist.[22] Baptist historian Bill Leonard explains that these Baptists "turned to an ideology that traced Baptists in an unbroken line directly to the New Testament church and enabled Baptist churches to claim a unique historical authenticity."[23] Most Southern Baptists don't believe that anymore, but many do believe that Southern Baptists are the most theologically correct, most biblically based, most missions minded, most evangelistic, and most educationally effective of all Christian denominations. Size may have something to do with the myth of Southern Baptist superiority: with 16 million members, the Southern Baptist Convention is the nation's largest Protestant denomination. All this combines to give Southern Baptists a good sense of denominational self. To be Southern Baptist is to be part of something big.

The myth per se isn't really talked about in Southern Baptist churches. Rather, the sense of success and importance is conveyed through publications and meetings and the tendency to compare Southern Baptists with other denominations. "Southern Baptists are closest to what I believe," many of my participants told me. I'm not sure that most Southern Baptists have actually looked into what other denominations believe, but they've learned from church leaders and curricular materials and programs that Southern Baptists are the best, the truest, the most correct. So, even though many participants told me that being Christian was more important than being Baptist, they were also quick to note that they were Southern Baptists because Southern Baptists are the best. What's most interesting here is that they don't seem to have any sense that such a belief is a cultural product; they tend to see themselves outside of any context that gives shape to their belief. This may be one downside of autonomous thinking. The Southern Baptist and American emphasis on individualism may well contribute to these women's thinking of their own intellectual and faith processes as outside any social and historical context that fashions them. They make their choices individually, but those choices are inevitably shaped by their social context. To a great degree, they believe what they believe because that is what they have been exposed to; it is what fits into their lives; it is what allows them to make sense of their life experiences. The myth of Southern Baptist superiority, however, suggests that their grasp on ultimate and eternal truths exists outside history and location; there is one truth, and Southern Baptists know it. This myth, like the myth of the Old South, remains a salient feature of Southern Baptist identity and plays a rather large (and mostly unconscious) role in how women construct themselves as Southern Baptists.

Race, Place, and Generation

Although Southern Baptist women share a common process of identity-making, their unique locations in time and place also have great influence on their constructions of self. Race is a primary issue of identity for Southern Baptist women. Because of its racist history, the Southern Baptist Convention is predominantly white, both in membership and in leadership. And because most Southern Baptists are southerners, their awareness of race grows out of the unique history of race relations in the South. The white women I spoke with are well aware of the privilege that comes with being white in this country, and not surprisingly, the women of color related their experiences of overt and covert racism. For the majority of Southern Baptist women, whiteness is an essential component of their identity (later in the book I explore how race has shaped who they are). By far, the majority of my participants are white women. Almost all of the women of color I spoke with participate in predominantly white congregations. My research, therefore, does not reflect to any significant degree the experiences of Southern Baptist women of color who participate in minority churches, and that is a shortcoming of this book. My inability to access these women was likely related to my own social location as a white woman, a former Southern Baptist, and a northwesterner who is geographically removed from most of these congregations, particularly black Southern Baptist churches. The book thus deals mostly with the experiences of white women, although about 10 percent of the participants are women of color. As I discuss later, for these women, identification as Southern Baptist is usually much more closely connected to theology or experiences in local churches than to issues of race.

Generational differences also emerged in my research. The women's movement seems to be one central marker for the shaping of identity. The women of my mother's generation, who were already housewives and raising children by the time the movement began, understood that their options were limited when they were growing up in the 1950s. Even if they thought about going to college, it was secondary to marrying and having a family. In the case of the Clique, they remained married to the same men all their lives; however, many of their daughters have experienced divorce and single parenthood. Although these older women don't see the women's movement as being particularly beneficial to them, they do recognize that it opened up greater opportunities for their daughters in terms of higher education and equal employment, promotion, and pay. The women of my generation, who were the first to benefit directly from the women's movement, are either decidedly feminist themselves or at least believe in and enjoy the equality won by the movement. Although many middle-aged participants see feminists as "going too far" or "being too militant," they generally recognize and appreciate the achievements of feminists.

For the subgroup of middle-aged women consisting of those in ministry, a second key event—the Controversy among Southern Baptists that raged from 1979 to 1993—is a defining part of their identities. These women went to seminary in the 1970s and 1980s with a sense that they had a calling by God and the support of Southern Baptists. Influenced by the women's movement and its emphasis on a woman's ability to hold any job, these women claimed a place in ministry and were sent to seminary by their local churches. They believed that they would be able to spend their lives serving Southern Baptists. But the Controversy, with its emphasis on women's subordination and exclusion from pastoral leadership, led most of these women to rethink their relationship with the SBC and Southern Baptist churches. For many, this became both a vocational and an identity crisis. Some resolved the crisis by focusing on their participation in autonomous local Southern Baptist churches. Others became involved in splinter groups such as the CBF and the Alliance. Still others joined other denominations. A handful left ministry and the church entirely.

Younger women, however, have had very different experiences compared with either of these older groups. Younger conservative women distance themselves much more from feminism than do older conservative women, and in many ways, they espouse much more traditional gender roles than either the middle-aged or older women in my study. They have less experience participating in Southern Baptist programs, and they identify less as Southern Baptist than as "Christian." They are more influenced by the broader evangelical and fundamentalist movements in this country than by their own Baptist history and historical Baptist practices.

Moderate young women, in contrast, have grown up in the Cooperative Baptist Fellowship and the Alliance of Baptists. Their churches transitioned to these new groups when the women were young children, so they have experienced curricular materials from a new publishing house (Smyth & Helwys) that emphasize gender equality and women's roles in the lay and pastoral ministry. Many of these young women have known female pastors, and those who have chosen to attend the new moderate Baptist seminaries (such as McAfee in Georgia and Truett in Texas) are developing identities as Baptist women with very little reference to the Southern Baptist Convention. They are much more comfortable calling themselves feminists, and they envision churches and relationships that practice equality between women and men.

Most of these women are southerners, and so their identities as women are shaped strongly by southern culture, whether they identify themselves as feminist or conservative or anything in between. Among Southern Baptists who are not southerners, regional differences play a significant role in the development of identity. For example, the older generation of California Southern Baptists who moved from places such as Oklahoma and Arkansas carried their southern culture with them. Native Californians, however, developed a Southern Baptist identity that reflects California culture. Many California churches have dropped "Baptist" from their names, preferring to be known as such-and-such community church instead. A praise band, complete with electric guitar, bass, and drum kit, leads worship. Dress is informal. Interestingly, this style has moved east, and many southern churches are now facing conflict over contemporary versus traditional worship.

Soul Competency

Despite the Convention's recent shift away from emphasizing historic Baptist distinctives such as religious liberty, local church autonomy, and the priesthood of believers, what may be most salient in Southern Baptist women's construction of identity is the idea of soul competency. And this notion may be what distinguishes Southern Baptist women from other conservative Protestant women. E. Y. Mullins, former president of the Southern Baptist Theological Seminary, claimed that soul competency is "the distinctive Baptist belief."[24] The idea of soul competency suggests that individual human freedom flows from the nature of God; therefore, the right of individual choice is sacred. Each individual is competent before God to make her or his own choices about biblical, theological, religious, moral, ethical, and social matters, and the individual alone is responsible for making those choices.[25] Although soul competency does not devalue the importance of community, it does defiantly claim that every individual must ultimately be free to choose. Christian faith, according to Baptists, is "personal, experiential, and voluntary."[26]

As I talked to Southern Baptist women, I found an unshakable belief that God speaks directly to them. Although they respect their denominational leaders and pastors and allow them to exert quite a bit of influence in their thoughts and lives, these women recognize that their beliefs and practices are ultimately their own choices under God's guidance. In relation to women's subordinate position in Southern Baptist life, the application of the concept may be revolutionary. For moderate women, heightened attention to notions of freedom and autonomy during the Controversy gave them additional motivation to claim an equal right not only to active participation in the church but also to ordination and pastoral positions. For conservative women, the persistence of the idea of soul competency allows them to negotiate gender in ways that feel empowering, and it creates the possibility for them to refuse constructions of womanhood handed down to them from male church leaders, pastors, and denominational workers. Because they believe themselves to be competent before God, these women construct identities that embrace and express their own agency and autonomy within the varying contexts of Southern Baptist life.

A comment by one of the participants exemplifies Southern Baptist women's embodiment of soul competency and the theme of this book. She works for a Southern Baptist organization that has prominently emphasized women's submission and the exclusion of women from pastoral leadership. She herself has not felt the calling to preach, and her job doesn't require her to address women's issues publicly, so she manages to both do her work and carry out her calling. But, she says, with that particular sense of graciousness and rebellion so common to Southern Baptist women, "If God calls a woman to preach, God calls her to preach." Southern Baptist women tend to "go along to get along" until they think God has told them otherwise. Their belief in their own competence to stand before God, to hear the voice of God, to interpret scripture for themselves, and to do what they feel God has called them to do is central in their construction of themselves and their willingness to resist wholesale subordination. Any submission to men, therefore, is always tentative; only God holds full sway over their loyalties and consciences, and only they have the right and the ability to determine what God says to them.

1

Just as I Am

Southern Baptist Women's Experiences of Salvation and Baptism

Just as I am, without one plea,
But that thy blood was shed for me,
And that thou bidd'st me come to thee,
O Lamb of God, I come! I come!
—Charlotte Elliott, "Just as I Am"

The beginnings of life as a Christian and as a Southern Baptist are marked by two distinct and essential experiences: conversion and believer's baptism by immersion. The first is necessary to enter the community of God; the second is necessary to become a member of a Southern Baptist church.

I was six years old when a traveling evangelist came to town to preach at an evening revival at Shorter Avenue Baptist Church. I had been in attendance pretty much every time the church doors were open since I was six weeks old, and in the language of Southern Baptists, I was a bed baby on the cradle roll. Only baptized believers can be members of Southern Baptist churches, but everyone—even infants—can be counted on the Sunday school membership roll, and I had been there to be counted. Once I started toddling around and talking, I attended worship services (this was in the days before a separate "children's church" met during adult worship services), Sunday school, Training Union, Sunbeams, and vacation Bible school. Southern Baptists had mastered age-graded curricula, so at every age they provided developmentally appropriate programs and materials to teach us to become good Christians and good Southern Baptists.[1]

Starting from the first time I heard the story of how he had been born in a stable because there was no room at the inn, I loved Jesus with every ounce of my childhood being. I also knew that Jesus loved me because every week we sang, "Jesus loves me, this I know, for the Bible tells me so." I knew that Jesus wanted me to be kind and to share with others, because my Sunday school teacher had stuck paper cutouts of Jesus, the disciples, the crowd, and the boy with a basket of bread and fish on a blue flannel board and told us the story of how Jesus used that young boy's gift to feed 5,000 hungry people. Each week, we were encouraged to memorize a verse of scripture. As a preschooler, I learned to recite "God is love," "Be ye kind one to another," and "What time I am afraid, I will trust in Thee."

But there was another side to this loving God that I was learning about. God was also wrathful. I don't think I knew the word *wrath* at the time, but I did know that I could do things that displeased God, just as the people of Israel had done when they worshipped the golden calf while Moses was on Mount Sinai receiving the Ten Commandments. My colleague Marcus Borg, who grew up in a Lutheran tradition, calls this version of deity "God the finger-shaker."[2] Looking back now, I don't imagine that I'd done a whole lot of sinning by the age of six, but in Southern Baptist thought, all people are born sinners, so it was a moot point anyway. Sooner or later, however, everyone reaches the "age of accountability" and recognizes that she or he is a sinner and is capable of making a commitment to Christ. Among Southern Baptists, despite everything we know about children's cognitive development, the age of accountability seems to have fallen drastically.

For early Baptists, conversion was an adult matter—a decision consciously and intentionally made to become a follower of Christ, a believer. After 1920, however, Southern Baptist denominational materials began to promote childhood conversion.[3] The idea was to reach children while their hearts were young and tender and thus most receptive to the Gospel. At the age of six, I was ripe for the picking.

Evangelists, whose primary task is to win people to Christ, often rely not on God's love and grace but on hellfire and damnation, among other questionable antics, to motivate people to get saved. My mother told me that the reason my grandfather didn't go to church was because one time, during the altar call at a revival, the evangelist had asked people who had not been saved to raise their hands. My grandfather did, and some well-meaning Christians tried to drag him down the aisle. He never went back to church, he said, because they had embarrassed him. My mother, however, was saved when she went to a revival in 1955 with a friend. Her friend's father, as my mother put it, "was drinking and causing a problem at home." He too went to the revival that night, walked the aisle during the invitation, and talked publicly about the life he'd lived and the change he felt when he asked Jesus into his heart. My mother was so impressed that she asked the Lord to save her that night.

Many of the women I interviewed were saved during a revival, as was I. The traveling evangelist who came to Shorter Avenue Baptist Church in 1967 was of the hellfire and damnation ilk. Night after night he paced across the stage, waving the Bible above his head as he warned of sinners' impending doom. After describing to us in graphic detail the torments of hell, he asked, "If you died tonight, where would you spend eternity?" He told the story of a group of young people at a similar revival service who had decided to wait until next time to make Jesus their Lord and Savior, only to be killed in a car accident that very night. Slowly he shook his head and wiped the sweat from his brow. Then in a tone that suggested the unnecessary tragedy of it all, he explained how they were now doomed to spend eternity in hell because they had waited, thinking they would have one more chance. I started to have nightmares. I had not walked the aisle and invited Jesus into my heart, and I knew that if I died, like those young people killed in the car crash, I would wake up in torment in hell.

Finally, on the last night of the revival, I couldn't take it anymore. I didn't want to go to hell. After the sermon, the pastor announced the time when people could walk down the aisle of the church, take him by the hand, and ask him to lead them to Christ. As the congregation stood, the choir started to sing "Just as I Am," and my knuckles turned white as I gripped the back of the pew in front of me. "Is there anyone here tonight," he asked, "who hasn't made Jesus their Lord and Savior?" I knew he was talking to me. At last, I turned to my parents and told them that I wanted to go down front to get saved. I walked the aisle and took the pastor by the hand. "I want to ask Jesus into my heart as my personal Lord and Savior," I told him, repeating the words I'd heard so often. He knelt with me and my parents on the carpeted steps leading up to the pulpit and asked me if I understood that I was a sinner and that Jesus had died for my sins. I said that I did. Then he asked me if I wanted to commit my life to Jesus and become a Christian. I did. So he led me through the "sinner's prayer," and I repeated after him. Although there's no one official version of the sinner's prayer, the prayer for salvation that's taught in most evangelistic groups has many of the same elements: a confession of sin, an acknowledgment of the atoning work of Jesus, and an acceptance of Jesus as Lord and Savior. The following sample from the Southern Baptist Convention's Web site is typical and probably very similar to the words I said that night in 1967: "Lord Jesus, I know that I am a sinner and I do not deserve eternal life. But, I believe You died and rose from the grave to purchase a place in Heaven for me. Jesus, come into my life, take control of my life, forgive my sins and save me. I am now placing my trust in You alone for my salvation and I accept your free gift of eternal life." [4]

As I look back on this event now, with a very different understanding of faith development and conversion, I am aghast at the tactics used to compel me (and millions of others) to make a profession of faith. Carolyn Hale Cubbedge told me that she was saved at a revival when she was seven years old. She explained, "My father was a preacher . . . I specifically remember talking to my father one Sunday morning about becoming a Christian, and my reason was, 'I don't want to go to hell.' I remember making a profession of faith and being baptized in a tributary of the Cumberland River." Likewise, Carolyn Weatherford Crumpler, former executive director of Woman's Missionary Union, told me that she made her profession of faith when she was twelve. "We had a revival, and I remember the cry was, 'If you don't want to go to hell, come join the church.' I joined the church." She added that despite that inauspicious beginning, the efforts of her parents, her Sunday school teachers, and the pastor's wife helped her understand what it really meant for her to accept Christ as her Savior beyond simply joining the church.

For children nurtured in the Christian faith, as I had been, conversion can be a natural, seamless progression along one's faith journey.[5] Nonetheless, many Southern Baptist congregations persist in emphasizing to children the necessity of a distinct and radical conversion. Brenda Flowers, a city government employee in Riverside, California, and a graduate of Southern Seminary, was saved when she was six years old. She told me, "I remember it was a revival, and I couldn't make it down that aisle fast enough. I was bolting down that aisle. I was totally fearful. I mean I really, seriously felt like my feet were on fire, and I could not get down that aisle fast enough."

"Were they singing 'Just as I Am'?" I asked.

"Oh, boy, were they singing 'Just as I Am'! How many times did they sing it through, with all of those verses! But I went out on the first one . . . I was bolting out of there!"

Scaring the hell out of me to propel me down the aisle to accept Christ was hardly necessary. Nonetheless, something profound happened to me that night. When I rose from those steps, I felt different. At six, I didn't have the cognitive capacity to understand the intellectual implications of conversion, but I had enough emotional intelligence to recognize that I had undergone a profoundly significant experience that marked me in a new and different way as a member of the community of faith. From that moment on, my identity as a Christian was personally and publicly sealed.

In some ways, my story is indicative of the tricky terrain of faith. As an academic, I can analyze it, and I can certainly critique the misguided (though well-intended) devices used to propel me toward a profession of faith. Yet, despite the problematic circumstances, the experience itself became a profound marker of identity. Clique member Alicia Bennett's story summarizes this paradox:

> I was a child, eight years old, and my aunt had a nervous breakdown, and Mama was keeping the children in her family and my aunt's family. She was staying there with us, and I think she got sick. I remember getting sick and thinking I was real sick. I think I was nauseated, and when I got sick I thought I was going to die. So I told Mama I wanted to get saved because I knew I hadn't, and I was afraid that I was going to die and go to hell. So I told her I wanted to be saved. That's how it came about. It might not be ideal, but. . . ."

"It might not be ideal, but. . . ." For many of us who made a profession of faith under the threat of hell, Alicia's statement sums up the ambivalence and paradox of that experience. Fear of damnation is hardly the ideal context for conversion, yet the experience of accepting Christ made a real and lasting change in many women's lives and became a central aspect of identity formation from that point on. Clique member Doris Bailey was saved during a revival when she was twelve years old. "A lot of people had been saved during the revival," she told me. "And this particular night, my brother and myself and my stepbrother, all three, prayed to receive Christ. I remember being very happy, and somebody wanted to know why I was joyous. And that was the feeling I had, a feeling of joy, and realizing I had been saved."

Phyllis Jenkins was eight years old when she attended a revival at a little country church in Louisiana. "The first or second night," she explained, "several of my friends got up and went down to accept Christ, and I followed them. My father came down and asked me why I came down, and I really couldn't tell him. So he made me go back and sit down. So I paid attention the rest of the week-long revival, and then on that Friday night I actually knew what I was coming forth for and gave my life to Christ, and he has been such a blessing in my life, and I'm so grateful to him."

Kathy Sylvest, a librarian at the Southern Baptist Historical Library and Archives, explained that she made a profession of faith on a Wednesday night when she was nine years old. "Having grown up in the church, I've been fortunate to feel like I've loved the Lord all my life," she told me. But when she was nine, she realized that she needed to get saved. "The children had a little time with the pastor before prayer meeting," she began, "and when he started taking prayer requests, one of the girls said, 'I want you to pray for my sister Maude,' who happened to be my age, 'she's not saved.' So that gave the pastor a good opportunity to open the possibility for those of us who had grown up in that church to accept the Lord, and a whole bunch of us did." Reflecting on that night, Kathy added, "I just remember crying a lot . . . I just remember knowing that I had done something very important and very personal. . . . It was a very big event to me."

Nancy Moore accepted Christ at the age of seven during vacation Bible school. A magician came and did a trick with a jug of liquid. "He put something in that, and it turned just as black as could be," Nancy explained. "And he said this was the way our hearts were before Jesus came into them. Then he poured something red into that, and that, of course, was the symbol of his blood, and that cleansed it and made it just as clear as it could be after he poured that in. And you know, that was the clearest picture to me. I knew my little heart was black, black, black. And I wanted it to be clean and pure. So he really led me to Christ in Bible school. It was a wonderful experience, really."

Southern Baptists and Conversion

For Southern Baptists, conversion is the essential step in the Christian life. For some Southern Baptists, conversion comes as a dramatic experience akin to Paul's conversion on the road to Damascus when he saw a blinding light. For many others, it is a gradual process that grows to a point of decision through years of Christian nurture. Nancy Hollomon-

Peede lived on the same dormitory floor as I did at Southern Seminary. She's now a minister for community involvement at Westwood Baptist Church in Springfield, Virginia. She told me:

> Ever since I was really young, I don't know how, but I really sensed the presence of God. So even before I went down the aisle, I guess about age six, I began noticing or sensing God's presence. And I guess I learned sometime in Sunday school to pray. So I would just talk to God and then, later on, when I could begin reading, I would read the Bible. This was before I was baptized. I was baptized at nine. But even before that, I had pretty much an active, ongoing, daily relationship with God. And my walking down the aisle to be baptized was sort of, "This is what I need to do to respond to a part of the covenant of the relationship," to join the church and be baptized and make it public, what I was already experiencing in my personal life. My conversion was a very kind of natural, casual type thing; it wasn't a mighty conversion like, "I've lived a sinful life, and now I'm converted," or something dramatic that happened. There was a previous relationship before I even went down to be baptized.

Similarly, Joyce Reed explained, "I really grew up entrenched in the church. My earliest memories are of being in church and listening to my Sunday school teachers and listening to my parents talk about Jesus. I think I was around seven or eight, and I remember saying, 'I want Jesus to come into my heart. I want to be a Christian.' So I went forward. It was almost like no big thing, no lightning bolts or anything. It was just a natural progression in my life." Beverly Howard told me that she was "born knowing church." So for her, conversion "wasn't this traumatic, dramatic turnaround that I've sinned all my life. It was just one of these things that came to me very internally, and I thought, 'I need to do something about this officially,' and so I did." Similarly, Pat Brown said, "My conversion was a child's coming to understand the love of Jesus. I was almost nine years old. It was not a dramatic conversion, but simply a child that had always heard stories and loved Jesus. I think it was a very natural, normal progression."

Angela Cofer, who now teaches music at Southwestern Seminary, was brought up in a Christian home with a very godly mother. Angela said that when she was a child, she'd sit in her Bronco Buster rocking chair and rock and sing the hymns she had learned at church. One day, as she was rocking and singing hymns, "There was a certain moment when my heart was touched; the Spirit touched me, and at that point I understood that I wanted to ask Jesus to be my Savior." She found her mother—"in the bathroom, of all places!"—and told her what had happened. "We knelt by the side of my little bed and prayed the prayer of salvation. That's what I remember about my salvation experience at that young age."

Pam Tanner's father was minister of music, and her mother played piano for the church. This meant that she had to sit in the front row during the worship service so they could keep an eye on her. At age seven, during the final service of a revival, she told me, "I just felt myself being pulled to go down and greet the minister. I thought, 'What in the world?' and went back to my seat. Then it occurred to me—I can't believe this at seven years old—that, 'Oh! I bet this is God; he's talking to me.' So I went down and said, 'I want to make my profession of faith,' and at our church, all children had a little book they had to go through with their parents asking and answering questions and filling out things to make sure we knew what was going on. So after doing that with my folks, then my dad got to baptize me because he's an ordained minister."

Theologically, for most Southern Baptists, salvation is necessitated by humanity's fallen condition and separation from God as a result of sin. By accepting Jesus as Lord, people mend their relationship with God and gain access to everlasting life. Not surprisingly, Southern Baptists differ on the nuanced points of soteriology. I remember debates when I was young about what would happen to people who had never heard the Gospel. We knew that those who did and still rejected Jesus were going to hell, but what about people in remote parts of the world who had never heard the story? What would happen to them? Years ago, a PhD student created a stir when, in her dissertation, she raised the question of postmortem opportunities to accept Christ. And while we sang hymns about a fountain filled with blood and being washed in the blood of the Lamb, we debated exactly what role the death of Jesus played in effecting salvation.

Practically all Southern Baptists believe that conversion involves a conscious, intentional decision to follow Christ, but they disagree about how this may happen. The majority of Southern Baptists rely on the more well-delineated model of conversion as a particular event that happens at a particular point in time. One minute the person is lost; the next moment she or he is saved. However, the case of Peggy Sanderford Ponder, a hospice chaplain in Birmingham, Alabama, illuminates a difficulty in this rigid way of thinking about conversion. When I asked Peggy about her conversion experience, she told me that she doesn't remember it: "For me it was just very gradual. I can't remember a moment

I invited Jesus into my life; I absolutely have no clue." Her inability to pinpoint the exact moment she became a Christian led to problems when, following graduation from Golden Gate Baptist Theological Seminary, she applied to the Foreign Mission Board for a two-year overseas appointment in what was then known as the Journeyman program. "They told me they couldn't send anybody overseas who didn't have any better grasp of what it meant to be a Christian than I do," she explained. "To me, it was just a gradual realization that there was a difference between God and me, and I needed to realize there was a difference and make a commitment. I was a sinner and all that stuff, but for me the big thing wasn't sin; it was, 'I want to be closer to God.'"

Among more progressive Southern Baptists, particularly among progressive religious educators, an alternative discourse recognizes the possibility of conversion as a process that includes an understanding of and a commitment to radical discipleship. Findley Edge suggests that a conversion that involves only saying the "sinner's prayer" is shallow and superficial if not attended by a mature commitment to living an authentic Christian life.[6] Many churches focus their entire worship service on persuading and encouraging people to come to Christ; others address the faith needs of the already converted, with sermons focused on advice for daily living rather than evangelism. Some churches encourage early childhood conversion (some as young as four years old), while others believe that children lack the cognitive ability to make an informed commitment until they are around twelve years old.

I grew up in churches that focused on conversion. In fact, my first church was so keen on winning souls to Jesus that it turned the annual Christmas pageant into an occasion for evangelism. I most vividly remember the pageant that was held the year I turned nine—because that's the year I was supposed to be a Christmas angel but ended up being a silver bell instead. The pastor's wife always directed the annual pageant, and nine-year-old girls always got to be the Christmas angels. I had just turned nine that December, right before the pageant. That year, however, the pastor's wife got sick, so another woman in the church took over the pageant. Her daughter, who was eight, should have been a silver bell, but she didn't want to be. Neither did I, but since I was the last nine-year-old to have attained that age, I was demoted, in my eyes, to a silver bell so that the director's daughter could be a Christmas angel. You may be wondering what silver bells were doing in the Christmas pageant at all. In our particular pageant, the Christmas story was framed by contemporary scenes, and the silver bells were in the first contemporary frame that led to the telling of the Christmas story. Our bell costumes were shaped from large cardboard boxes covered with what we in the South call tin foil (that's aluminum foil to the rest of you) and circled by a big red bow. We moved from side to side to simulate ringing while we sang Christmas carols (to this day, I dislike the song "Silver Bells"). After our scene, we silver bells removed our costumes and took seats in the back of the auditorium to watch the rest of the play.

The middle section of the pageant included the traditional telling of the Christmas story—Mary, Joseph, the innkeeper, the baby Jesus, shepherds and wise men from the East, and Christmas angels. The end of the pageant was truly amazing, although I don't quite remember how the story got there. It ended with the Second Coming of Christ and the Great White Throne Judgment during which the resurrected Jesus either allowed people to enter heaven or sent them off to hell. In a resounding voice, Jesus announced to the unsaved, "Depart from me. I never knew you," and waved them away. I vividly remember the pastor's son playing the devil and dragging these people off the stage begging and screaming, only to be thrown into the pits of hell that awaited them in the wings, where there was much wailing and gnashing of teeth. When the curtain came down, the pastor took the stage and warned people that without Jesus they would be like the characters in our play, thrown into hell on the Day of Judgment. He then invited people to come to the front of the auditorium to invite Jesus into their hearts and avoid the fate of those who die without Christ.

I think somewhere along the way, in their evangelistic zeal, these church leaders lost sight of the baby and the manger and "peace on earth, goodwill to all." I do believe that the motives of those who use scare tactics to propel people down the aisle are sincere. I think they truly believe that if these methods are effective in bringing people to Christ, they are legitimate. But I also agree with Edge that if conversions aren't rooted in a thorough understanding of costly discipleship, they are ultimately ineffective in bringing people into the authentic Christian living that can't be separated from conversion.[7]

Altar Call

Conversion experiences happen in many contexts. Children kneel at home with their parents beside their beds and invite Jesus into their hearts. Around the campfire at youth camp, adolescents give their lives to Christ. Conversions take place wherever a person makes the decision to accept Christ—in a restaurant, on the battlefield, in a break room. Becky Kennedy became a Christian on the sidelines of a church volleyball court when the pastor asked her if she wanted to follow Jesus. Lucy Elizalde (a pseudonym) accepted Christ at her private Christian school.

The most visible context for conversion among Southern Baptists, however, is the altar call. In most Southern Baptist churches, the altar call follows the sermon. It is a time when audience members can publicly respond to God. It usually involves walking down the aisle to the front of the sanctuary, where the pastor waits to hear the congregant's profession. Typically, during the altar call, the choir and congregation sing a hymn:

> Softly and tenderly Jesus is calling, calling for you and for me.
> See on the portals he's waiting and watching, watching for you and
>   for me.
> Come home, come home, ye who are weary come home.
> Earnestly, tenderly Jesus is calling, calling, O sinner, come home.[8]

or

> I've wandered far away from God. Now I'm coming home;
> The paths of sin too long I've trod. Lord, I'm coming home.
> Coming home, coming home, nevermore to roam.
> Open wide thine arms of love, Lord, I'm coming home.[9]

Although conversion is the primary reason for the altar call, people may also come forward to join the church by baptism, if they have previously been saved; by transfer of letter, if they are members of some other Baptist church; or by statement, if they are members of another denomination and have undergone believer's baptism by immersion. Others walk the aisle to rededicate their lives to Christ if they have fallen away ("backslidden," in Southern Baptist parlance) from a right relationship with Christ or to request a prayer for a specific issue in their lives. Others come forward to answer God's call to "full-time Christian service"—the pastorate, missions, Christian education, or music ministry.

Typically, the altar call lasts as long as it takes to sing through the specified hymn once. Sometimes, however, the pastor may extend the altar call if many people are responding or if no one is responding. Unofficially, the altar call is an assessment of the effectiveness of the pastor's sermon, and for many pastors, lack of response is an indictment to be avoided, even if that means singing all the verses of "Just as I Am" three or four times and then adding a verse or two hummed by the choir. In her ethnography of a Southern Baptist church in South Carolina, Jean Heriot observes that the altar call also allows members "to assess their own salvation and the salvation of others." The altar call demands action to substantiate belief. She explains that the altar call provides "an arena within which members [can] demonstrate commitment."[10]

Clique member Kayne Carter had always been drawn to church, even though her family didn't regularly attend the downtown Presbyterian church her mother claimed as her own. Her mother didn't drive, so they had to take two buses to get there. There was a Baptist church near their house, and at age twelve or thirteen, Kayne began to walk to it and attend services on a regular basis. She told me that one Sunday during the altar call, "I was just so drawn. I want to do this. For some reason, I started crying, and a lady came back to where I was sitting—I didn't come down; she saw me where I was sitting and came back—and started talking to me. She said, 'You want to go down?' and I said, 'Yes.' So she walked with me." For Kayne and the others who responded to an altar call, the act of walking the aisle was the physical enactment of their spiritual commitment. It represented their public profession of an inner reality and, as Nancy Hollomon-Peede put it, their public commitment to a covenant relationship with Christ and the church. In fact, for many of my participants, the act of walking the aisle during an altar call followed a conversion experience that had happened elsewhere and functioned instead as the mechanism to express their desire to be baptized.

Clique member Judy Masters grew up in a Methodist church, but as an adolescent, she attended a Baptist youth get-together. She recalled that during the service she "was just immersed in the Word that was preached that day, and I knew I was not saved. And I went forward, and this Methodist pastor that we had was there. And after church he said, 'That's the craziest thing I've ever heard. You know that you were already saved; I don't know why you'd think you weren't because you were confirmed.' And he literally made fun of me for doing that [walking the aisle]. He said, 'Why in the world did you do that?' And I said, 'Because that's what the Lord wanted me to do.' Well, from then on I loved going to the Baptist church, but I couldn't join the Baptist church because I followed under my parents; I went to the Methodist church." When she started dating Wayne, whom she would eventually marry, Judy attended her parents' Methodist church in the morning and Wayne's Baptist church in the evening. Once they married, she explained, they decided to join a Baptist church, and that was when she was baptized by immersion. "I was baptized into the Baptist church and got my baptism in order, and that's how I became a Baptist because I actually believed as a Baptist even though I grew up in a Methodist home."

Faith as a Central Aspect of Identity

For almost all these women, their faith is the means by which they make sense of the world and of themselves; it is who they are and what they do, not something they have. Cindy Johnson said, "I think the Christian faith for me is what gives meaning to my life. Jesus is for me the best understanding of God's love lived out in the world. So when I think of what does God's love look like, it is Jesus. And when I think about how to live life, it is Jesus as the model." Ginny Hickman said that she became a Christian "by default" because she was born a preacher's kid in southern Oklahoma, but, she added, "I would have to say that over the years I keep choosing it." Heather King noted, "I realized early on that my own personal walk with my Savior Jesus Christ needed to be cultivated outside the Sunday morning service. My identity cannot be found apart from the work of Jesus Christ in my life." Libo Krieg said that from the moment of her conversion, "I felt like I was walking, and he was walking to me, and he held me; and from that time he never let me go."

Many of the participants told me that they can't even imagine their lives without their faith. "I just can't imagine trying to get through life without it," Alicia Bennett said. "The demands that I have had on my life, there is no way that I could have made it without [my faith]." Kayne Carter added, "I don't see how anybody makes it without the Lord. He's my strength and my shield, and so I don't see how anybody can go through this life without the Lord." Shelby Christie noted, "I don't know how people can get along without being a Christian. I really don't, especially in hard times." She talked about her recent experiences caring for her aging parents and parents-in-law. "It would have been devastating if I hadn't known that God was in control. If I hadn't been a Christian, I just don't know how I would've made it."

Many of the participants talked about the role of prayer in their lives. Lidia Abrams said, "Without prayer, I'm nothing. When I get out of bed, it's the first thing [that] come[s] to my mind, the first thing through the day. I'm all day long praying for people, doing things for people; you know, it's my life." Judy Masters said that she relies on knowing that God hears her prayers and knowing that she can call on friends to pray for her. Cari Garrett of First Baptist Church in Hendersonville, Tennessee, said that she prays about all the big decisions in her life and asks others in her church family to pray for her. "It's a huge thing for me," she explained, "asking God to let me know—whether he tells me directly through his Word or through the counsel of other people."

Many of the women also noted the extent to which scripture is a significant part of their lives. Nancy Moore starts each day reciting verses from Psalm 143: "Cause me to hear Thy loving-kindness in the morning, for in Thee do I trust. Cause me to know the way wherein I should walk, for I lift up my soul unto Thee. Deliver me, O Lord, from my enemies; I plea to Thee to hide me. Teach me to do Thy will, for Thou art my God." "That's how I start my day," she told me, "and I try to bring him in[to] everything that's happening and acknowledge that he is here and [ask] what does he want me to do?"

These women also make conscious attempts to embody their faith in their everyday practices. Alicia Bennett told me, "I have routines of daily life, and when opportunities arise I try to behave in a way that would be pleasing to the Lord, and it's my desire to do that. And to be a witness. And I try to be encouraging and loving to people and try to be alert and aware of people's needs who I come in contact with." LaDonna Burton said, "I just try to live each day and take it a day at a time, not a week at a time or a month at a time, but just a day at a time and try to be an example to people, that they can look at me and see that I've got something different. That I can handle situations, and I can handle them in the right way—and sometimes I don't. But just try to be every day as Godlike as you can possibly be." Jennifer Wofford added, "You have to put your faith into practice. As a single mom, I feel like I'm just an inch away from any time maybe losing my house, losing things that I have; and it's just my faith—and I know it's my faith—that I have been able to do as well as I have on my own. It's because I trust that God's going to take care of me. You have to put that into practice." Candi Finch, a PhD student at Southwestern Seminary, said that one's life should be "radically different" from the point of conversion on. "Living a Christian life," she explained, "is doing those things the Lord has called you to do."

Believer's Baptism by Immersion

My very first memory is of my mother's baptism. She hadn't grown up as a Southern Baptist and hadn't experienced believer's baptism by immersion, so in order to join a Southern Baptist church, she needed to be baptized. Because baptism is considered the first step in obedience following conversion, most Southern Baptist churches have a baptismal pool in the front of the church to facilitate the process. The baptismal pool is typically about four feet deep, and converts go down into the water with the minister, who immerses them.

At the time of my mother's baptism, the baptistery at Shorter Avenue Baptist Church had a painting of a riverbank on the wall behind the baptismal pool—something that, I discovered during my research, is not uncommon. The Bible claims that Jesus was baptized by John in the Jordan River, and I guess the goal is to make the experience as true to that event as possible (of course, Jesus probably wasn't really immersed by John, but once the notion of immersion worked its way into Baptist theology, the historical facts were apparently no longer relevant). I doubt that the painting behind the baptismal pool at Shorter Avenue Baptist Church looked anything like a riverbank in the Middle East. I imagine it was much more like the banks of the Coosa, Oostanaula, and Etowah rivers that flowed around the seven hills of Rome, Georgia.

Nonetheless, I was barely out of infancy when my mother was baptized, so that painting looked real to me. I suppose, in actuality, the baptismal pool must have been unbelievably tacky. But fortunately, the sanctuary was remodeled while I was still a young child, and so I never saw the painting as an adult. I can forever remember my mother's baptism as I saw it then. Even now, the image that comes to mind is of her rising out of the baptismal pool onto the banks of the river Jordan.

Just a few years later, I was baptized in that same baptismal pool. A week after I walked the aisle during that revival, I stepped into the baptismal waters to symbolize the new life in Christ that I had begun. I don't remember the river mural from my own baptism, but I do remember getting water up my nose, and I came up coughing and sputtering, an official member of a Southern Baptist church.

Baptism in Baptist History

Baptists emerged in the seventeenth century as Reformation ideas spread throughout England. In the sixteenth century, when Pope Clement VII refused to grant King Henry VIII a divorce, the king broke with the church in Rome and reconstituted the English church with himself as its head. When Henry's daughter Mary Tudor came to the throne, she returned England to Catholicism, putting nearly 300 Protestants to death along the way. Upon her death, her half-sister Elizabeth I ascended to power and began to restore Protestantism, though she maintained some of the liturgical contributions of the Catholic Church. Some thought that she retained too many of the trappings of the Catholic Church and sought to purify the Church of England. These Puritans were persecuted by both the church and the crown, and by the time Charles I became king in 1625, a full-scale attack on dissenters led many to flee to other parts of Europe and North America. One group of Puritans known as the Separatists believed that the Church of England was beyond redemption; it was a false church, and they began a quest to establish the "true church."

Former Anglican minister John Smyth was among those who fled to Amsterdam to avoid persecution. As a Separatist, Smyth wrote a 1609 treatise called *The Character of the Beast, or the False Constitution of the Church,* which argued that because the church is made up of baptized believers, and because infants can't believe, they should not be baptized. Because he and others in his Separatist band had been baptized by a false church, Smyth decided that they should be baptized again and reconstitute the true church. Smyth baptized himself and his followers, and they formed the first Baptist church. Smyth eventually sought membership with the Mennonites, but he was excommunicated from that church and returned to London in 1612 to found the first Baptist church in England.

The first Baptists did not practice baptism by immersion. More than likely, they used the method of trine affusion, or pouring three times in the name of the Father, Son, and Holy Spirit.[11] In 1641, Edward Barber suggested that immersion, which he called "dipping," was the correct New Testament mode of baptism.[12] The influential 1644 London Confession confirmed immersion as the proper method of baptism: "The way and manner of the dispensing of this Ordinance the Scripture holds out to be dipping or plunging the whole body under water."[13] The Confession goes on to explain that immersion symbolizes the death, burial, and resurrection of Christ, as well as the washing of the convert's soul in Christ's blood and the hope for resurrection in the life to come.

For Baptists, baptism follows conversion; it is an experience reserved for believers. Smyth's 1609 treatise states, "Baptism is the external sign of the remission of sins, of dying and of being made alive, and therefore does not belong to infants."[14] Similarly, the 1644 London Confession explains, "Baptisme is an Ordinance of the New Testament, given by Christ, to be dispensed onely upon persons professing faith."[15] Baptism does not convey salvation; rather, it signifies the new life in Christ experienced by believers. For most Baptist groups, baptism is also the way into church membership. However, John Bunyan, the controversial Baptist who wrote *Pilgrim's Progress,* refused to make baptism a prerequisite to church membership. For Bunyan, faith was the only criterion for church membership; baptism was important but not essential.[16] Bunyan was certainly in the minority on this issue, but differences of opinion over baptism continued to pervade Baptist life long after the seventeenth century.

Because baptism was associated with conversion, Baptists rejected infant baptism. Of course, this left the problem of what happened to those who died in infancy or childhood. From their beginnings, Baptists differed on the theological notion of "election" and divided into the "particular" and "general" schools of thought. Particular Baptists followed a moderate Calvinism that suggested that God had elected some people to salvation (and because God had elected them, they could not fall away from grace) but nonetheless called for the preaching of the Gospel to all people. General Baptists believed that humans exercise free will in choosing to accept God's gift of salvation and therefore anyone can be saved (and because people choose salvation, they can also choose to fall away from it). On the question of children, general Baptists argued that because children don't know the difference between right and wrong, they cannot sin and are therefore still under the grace of God. The 1679 Orthodox Confession explains, "We do believe, that all children, dying in their infancy, viz. before they are capable to chuse either good or evil, whether born of believing parents, or unbelieving parents, shall be saved by the grace of God, and merit of Christ their redeemer, and work of the holy ghost, and so being made members of the invisible church, shall enjoy life everlasting."[17] Particular Baptists dealt with the question by responding, "Elect Infants dying in infancy, are regenerated and saved by Christ through the Spirit."[18]

Southern Baptists resolved these questions by adapting a modified version of both election and free will, although some fundamentalist leaders are now calling for a resurgence of Calvinism in the denomination.[19] E. Y. Mullins articulates a belief in God's election of those who freely choose salvation: "Election is not to be thought of as a bare choice of so many human units by God's action independently of man's free choice and the human means employed. God elects men to respond freely."[20] The 1963 *Baptist Faith and Message* adds that although people freely choose to believe, "all true believers endure to the end."[21] Southern Baptists have combined the general Baptist emphasis on free will with the particular Baptist belief in perseverance. In the popular rhetoric, this means "once saved, always saved." Bill Leonard explains:

> Sometime in this [the twentieth] century, popular Southern Baptist piety transformed that idea [perseverance] into "once saved, always saved," a slogan which became a theology. Evangelists and pastors explained perseverance in terms that maximized justification—entering in—and minimized sanctification—going on. While most did not explicitly deny that perseverance was essential, popular piety heard: "Once you are in, everything else is secondary." Close scrutiny suggests that perseverance of the saints was a long way from "once saved always saved." It is possible, therefore, that heterodoxy slipped into one of the Southern Baptists' most self-defining dogmas.[22]

Of course, not all Southern Baptists accept that aphorism so easily. In fact, professor Dale Moody was forced to retire from the faculty of the Southern Baptist Theological Seminary in 1983 because he questioned this simplistic understanding of perseverance, based on his reading of the book of Hebrews.

Like the general Baptists, Southern Baptists resolved the problem of childhood death by developing the notion of an "age of accountability," a point at which a child develops the cognitive and emotional capacity to differentiate between good and evil and understand the need for salvation. Nonetheless, the widespread practice of baptizing four- and five-year-olds and receiving them into church membership led one denominational leader to label the phenomenon "toddler baptism."[23] In 1993, Leonard cited this emphasis on the baptism of children as evidence of the predominance of populism over orthodoxy:

> In the 20th century Southern Baptists modified their theology of a "believers' church" to permit the baptism not simply of children but of preschoolers. Statistical analysis of current SBC baptismal statistics would indicate that anywhere from 10 to 20 percent of that number, depending on the church and the region, is composed of persons six years of age or younger. Thus the SBC has opened the door to semi-infant baptism. A believers' church that baptizes preschoolers is committing heresy against its theology of conversion and its ecclesiology.
>
> How did this happen? To some extent it was the natural outgrowth of the churches' nurturing impulse and sensitivity to children raised within the community of faith. It also developed alongside the emphasis on child evangelism and the notion of an age of accountability by which people, even children, become morally and spiritually responsible. No doubt it was linked to the desire for conversion of all people and the concern of Chris-

tian parents that their children be saved. It may also have been influenced by some congregations' desire for statistical growth. It developed, I believe, not intentionally but from the popular needs and spiritual realities of the community of faith.[24]

In 2005, Southern Baptist churches reported baptizing 4,272 children aged five years or younger and 49,683 children aged six to eight years.

For my participants, the issue of the baptism of children results in a mixed bag of feelings. For many, an early profession of faith and baptism were powerful experiences that profoundly marked their identities. For others, childhood baptism led to periods of deep doubt and the desire for rebaptism during adolescence.

Swimming around the Pool

Many of the participants, like myself, reported making a profession of faith and being baptized at a very young age. Beth Crawford, now a Presbyterian minister and a law student at the University of Oregon, was saved when she was seven. Her reason for making a profession of faith was that she wanted to participate in the Lord's Supper, an ordinance refused to those who were not baptized believers. She had begun to ask questions of her parents, and they invited the church's youth pastor to come to their home to talk to her. Beth recalled that he "opened the Bible and read me John 3:16 and said, 'Now, do you believe that if we substituted your name for "the world" that this would still be true?'" (The verse reads, "For God so loved the world He gave his only begotten son so that whosoever believeth in him shall not perish but have everlasting life" [King James Version, of course].) Beth continued, "I'm seven, and I'm like, 'Uh-huh.' That was it; that was all I needed. We prayed the prayer for Jesus to come into my heart, and I walked down the aisle the next day." When Beth was finally able to participate in the Lord's Supper, she ended up being afraid to do so. Her pastor, she explained, "rather than using some kind of scripture about the inclusivity of the table and the beauty of the whole thing, he used the Pauline passage about those who eat and drink unworthily are eating and drinking damnation on themselves. . . . So, my hands were shaking. I was like, 'Am I really worthy? I just got baptized so I could do this!'" Although that part "was a little scary," she said, "at the same time, when I came forward and told people I was planning to be baptized and join the church, this was my extended family in a lot of ways; I was down front for about half an hour as people lined up to give me a hug and welcome me to the family. So there were some really wonderful things about it, even though I carried this fear of the Lord's Supper for a while after it too."

Phyllis Rodgerson Pleasants said that she waited three months to join the church after her conversion experience at a Billy Graham crusade. One Sunday, without warning, she went forward during the invitation and presented herself for baptism and church membership. Her father's first response was to question whether she was doing it because she really believed or because she thought her Sunday school teacher wanted her to do it. She responded that she was doing it because *she* wanted to. Shortly thereafter she was baptized by her father. Phyllis told me:

> I just remember it being like one of those pivotal moments in my life, and I was just so happy I grinned all the way through it. [Daddy] didn't think I was reverent enough. But I didn't care! I was just beaming, because to me this was just the culmination of something that had started three years earlier. What I remember about it is not so much what happened, but just being so happy and thrilled that it was done. And it's interesting; I mean, I've had lots of doubt about being Baptist, but I've never questioned being Christian. So it was one of those core identity experiences.

Pamela Tanner was seven when she was baptized in her white and black polka dot Easter dress by her father. "It was just a wonderful experience," she told me. "I remember crying and saying, 'I don't know why I'm crying; I'm so happy.' And, of course, I was little, but, anyway, it was a very emotional experience for me, too. It was just a neat experience, especially to be baptized by your dad." Similarly, Kathy Sylvest remembered crying a lot. "I just remember knowing that I had done something very important and very personal." She also remembered that the baptismal waters were very cold.

Dorothy Kelley Patterson was eight years old when she was baptized at the First Baptist Church of Beaumont, Texas. Little did she know that her pastor, T. A. Patterson, who also baptized his own son Paige that same day, would eventually become her father-in-law. Dorothy told me that being baptized made her feel like she was being obedient to the Lord. She added, "I did see that as a very meaningful expression of my faith. And I think I felt, as much as a child could feel, that I was bearing a testimony for Christ just by following him in believer's baptism."

Peggy Sanderford Ponder was in the seventh grade when a Sunday School teacher asked her class, "How many of you have not been baptized?" Only two raised their hands—Peggy and the son of the chairman of the deacons. "So that made me feel a little bit okay," she admitted. She decided that since baptism was the outward sign of an inner commitment, she should go ahead and be baptized. The day of her baptism, that same Sunday school teacher wrote her a note "saying something about how special my baptism would be as I remembered Christ's death and burial and resurrection. I thought, 'That's kind of cool.'" But the actual baptism was somewhat unnerving. Peggy explained, "When the pastor baptized me and put me down and down and down [under the water]—and I'm sure what he did was go down and up, but the down felt like forever—and I remember thinking, 'I didn't know I was really going to die!' So that was my very spiritual baptism experience."

Tisa Lewis, who now works for the Association of Theological Schools, was nine years old at the time of her baptism. In her book *Faith Influences*, she tells her story this way:

> Being a water lover, the baptismal pool always intrigued me as a young child. Before I had ever seen an actual baptism, I was a bit afraid of what was behind that dark, scary curtain behind the choir loft. As young children do, I imagined all kinds of things that could be there. One of my favorite television shows at that time that had a tremendous faith influence on me was *Casper the Friendly Ghost*. Casper was such a good fellow and was always doing nice things for people, and I associated him a little bit with Jesus. All my life I had heard of the Holy Ghost and wondered if this might be Casper or at least like Casper. That was a comforting thought to me. So I got it into my head that maybe Casper the Holy Ghost lived behind that baptismal curtain.[25]

Tisa finally witnessed a baptism and understood what really went on when the dark curtain was drawn. When the time came for her baptism a few weeks after her profession of faith, she bravely entered the water and was baptized in the name of the Father, Son, and Holy Ghost (though she admits that she was still thinking a little bit about Casper) and was raised to walk in the newness of life. Afterward, she found a seat in the corner of the room where the other newly baptized children were changing into dry clothes. Tisa just sat there, dripping, in her little white baptismal robe. At last one of the women helping with the baptisms came over and told Tisa that she needed to change into dry clothes. Shivering, Tisa whispered, "That's OK. I'm going to wait until everybody is dipped, and then I'm going to get back in and swim around for a little while if that's OK."[26]

Despite her misunderstandings about Casper and swimming in the baptismal pool, Tisa says that the phrase "newness of life" stuck with her. "I was determined to be different, to be better," she explains. "Some days I was successful, and some days I wasn't, but the memory of that moment has lasted. Baptism meant something very important to me even as a 9-year-old."[27]

For both Tisa and me, our experiences of conversion and baptism were profound, even though they happened when we were young children. Immersed as we were in the nurture of Southern Baptist churches, those early commitments grew into a deeper understanding of costly discipleship. But that is not the case for all children who are baptized at such a young age.

Paula Sheridan was baptized twice. When she was in the second grade, she had the measles. As she was dozing off and on, she overheard her father asking her mother about Paula's not having been baptized. Paula thought to herself, "Oh, dear heavens; I'm going to die, and they want to baptize me so I won't go to hell." As soon as Paula was better, she talked to her pastor, and shortly thereafter she was baptized. "So," she noted drily, "I didn't die, and I didn't go to hell. I did live through the measles." Then, while she was a GA camp counselor during her college years, the camp's emphasis on having a conversion experience prompted Paula to reexamine hers, and she had some questions. After she got home, she talked to her pastor at the time, who said, "Well, I think you know the Lord."

She responded, "I'm not sure if I would die right now if I would go to heaven or hell."

The pragmatic pastor told her, "Well, being saved is like being pregnant; you either are or you aren't. There's no middle way. You sound to me like a Christian, but if it makes you feel better, I'll baptize you again."

And so she was rebaptized. Looking back, she wishes that her religious leaders had understood more about childhood development and had reassured her that, as a child, she belonged to God's family. Then, when she was older and cognitively able, she could have chosen for herself without the fear and guilt. "So," she concluded with a smile, "*when*

I was saved, I don't know; but I was baptized twice, just to make sure I would not burn in hell."

Faith Wu (a pseudonym) was about ten years old when she heard "one of those . . . hellfire, brimstone kind of messages; and . . . you obviously don't want to end up there, and you want to go to heaven, and that's why I accepted Christ. So to me, it was very worth oriented, and so there were certain things I knew I was supposed to do. They told me I was supposed to pray every day, read my Bible every day, and go to church on Sunday. And then not cuss. I don't know why that was one of the things I wasn't supposed to do." When she was in college, Faith began to explore what a real commitment to Christ meant, and she rededicated her life to Christ. "I wanted to have a believer's baptism that marked my understanding of what baptism meant," she explained, "and what accepting Christ meant, and the Lordship of Christ, and all those things combined." And so she was baptized again.

Leah McCullough's story is similar. When she was thirteen years old, her mother, worried that Leah and her brother weren't saved, prompted the pastor to talk to them. As a result, both children decided that they needed to be baptized. Yet when Leah went to college and became involved in the Baptist Student Union, she felt that her faith was missing a kind of vitality that she saw among her peers. So she walked to a friend's dorm room and said, "I think what I really need to do is accept Jesus as my Savior and be saved." When she returned home for Christmas break during her freshman year in college, she was baptized again.

Amy Mears told me that she was baptized long before she was converted. When her older brothers made their professions of faith and were baptized, Amy decided that she wanted to participate. "I'm darned if I'm gonna sit in the pew and not count," she recalled thinking at the time. "So I marched my six-year-old self down the aisle and said, 'I want to join the church.'" Her parents were taken by surprise. "They were unprepared and didn't have the ability to say, 'Let's hold off on that,'" Amy explained. "It would have been sort of a public scandal to explain, 'She just came down looking for the bathroom.' So there was no way out of it that they could see, and so I was baptized at six." A few years later, when her friends were making professions of faith and talking about the importance of following Christ, Amy realized that her own experience had been more about wanting to belong than about making an intentional commitment.

My sister was also baptized twice. Karen's first profession of faith and baptism came when she was six years old. Our family had moved from Shorter Avenue Baptist Church to West Rome Baptist Church, and when my parents and I walked the aisle to join the church, Karen had to remain seated because she had never been saved. The next week, when the associate minister came to visit our family, she asked him to explain why the rest of us got to go down front, and he said that it was because we were Christians and she wasn't. So Karen decided that she wanted to become a Christian and was baptized a few weeks later. My sister has always been very petite, and even standing on the support in the baptistery, her chin was still under water. So the pastor held her up above the water and then basically picked her up and dunked her. By the time she was in college, Karen was no longer attending our parents' church, and she realized that she hadn't actually experienced conversion as a child. She finally understood what it meant to be saved and requested to be baptized properly. Our parents were upset at the time because they thought her first experience was adequate. Now, Karen sees her second baptism as a first step away from our parents' views of religion and toward her own construction of her faith.

Alien Immersion

Of course, not all Southern Baptists grew up in Southern Baptist churches or were baptized at such young ages. Kryn Freehling-Burton was baptized in a Lutheran church as an infant, and when she decided to join a Southern Baptist church in California, she was required to be baptized as a believer by immersion. Kryn noted, "I was already baptized! And I was confirmed. And I was a little offended, like my faith was [being] questioned, that it was really real until I had [been baptized] in that church."

"So were you?" I asked.

"I was. It was the thing to do. I think it was peer pressure a little bit. . . . My mom had decided she was going to be rebaptized, and it kind of seemed the thing to do; it was a big youth group, and I was like, 'Oh, okay.' It was kind of an acceptance thing by my community."

What Kryn didn't realize (at least until she took my Baptist Life course at California Baptist College in 1990) was that her experience was typical of many members of other Christian denominations who become Southern Baptist. Unless the individual has experienced believer's baptism by immersion, Southern Baptist churches require rebaptism for church membership. In fact, a huge controversy took place over this very issue.

Landmarkism, which emerged in the mid-nineteenth century, contended that Baptist churches were the only true churches and that believer's baptism by immersion was the only true baptism. Baptism in other traditions was considered "alien immersion," because Landmarkism did not accept the validity of other churches or ministers. Landmarkism also focused on the centrality of the local church, to the point where its adherents opposed cooperation to support missions through mission boards. In the early twentieth century, the more extreme Landmarkists split from the Southern Baptist Convention to form the Baptist General Association, but Landmark ideas continue to influence Southern Baptists to some degree around the issues of baptism and ecumenism.[28] In fact, when I moved to California in 1987, I was surprised to find that Southern Baptists there (many of whom had come from Oklahoma and Arkansas in the early and mid-twentieth century) were still strongly influenced by Landmarkism (which I considered primarily a movement of the past), much more so than most churches in the South.

Take Me to the River

Not every Southern Baptist is baptized in a nice heated baptismal pool at the front of the church. Becca Gurney was baptized in a small mission church in the Northwest. "We had a baptistery in the sanctuary," she said, "but it had to be filled with a garden hose. Then boiling water was added so people didn't go into shock." Many churches had no baptismal pool at all and had to make do with whatever body of water was closest. Doris Bailey was baptized in a ditch. "My dad helped dig it," she related. "It was 'Moore's Ditch.' That was my maiden name, Moore." Gladys Peterson and Phyllis Jenkins were both baptized in ponds near their churches. Debra Owens-Hughes, the daughter of Southern Baptist missionaries, was baptized in an outdoor concrete baptismal pool in the fog and cold of Limuru, Kenya. Carolyn Weatherford Crumpler was baptized in Florida's French Lake, Carolyn Hale Cubbedge was baptized in a tributary of the Cumberland River, and Becky Kennedy was baptized in the Gulf of Mexico. Sandra Cisneros was baptized in a river in her native Guatemala. Her father, who was not a believer, told the nine-year-old convert that he would spank her if she got baptized. Nonetheless, she walked the several miles to the river where her pastor was baptizing people. Even though she was afraid of her father's reaction, she eventually approached the pastor and told him that she wanted to be baptized. Afterward, she went home and said to her father, "I'm sorry, Dad, but I got baptized." "I was ready for my spanking," she said, but fortunately, he didn't follow through on his threat.

For Southern Baptists, the practice of believer's baptism by immersion is a significant part of Baptist identity. It is a meaningful ritual that, for many of my participants, marked a significant commitment in their Christian lives. Louisa Smith (a pseudonym) said that her baptism "was a dramatic experience that I cannot really put into words. I felt something glorious as I was dipped into the waters and emerged to see the faces of a community that loved and supported me as a child." When I asked her what being Baptist means to her, she responded, "I tie it to my baptism, the community that nurtured me as a child, my own mother and grandmother." Many participants spoke of baptism as an event tied closely to community. For these women, baptism is more than an act of obedience to God; it also marks one's entrance into a special relationship with a community of faith and a long tradition of other Baptists who have undergone the same experience.

2

The B–I–B–L–E

*Southern Baptist Women and
the Bible*

*Holy Bible, Book divine
Precious treasure, thou art mine:
Mine to tell me whence I came;
Mine to teach me what I am.*
—John Burton Sr., "Holy Bible, Book Divine"

Vacation Bible school, that week or so during the summer when thousands of Southern Baptist children make macaroni art and hear stories about Daniel in the lion's den, the three Hebrew children in the fiery furnace, and David and Goliath, begins with a series of pledges—to the American flag, the Christian flag, and the Bible (not necessarily in that order). Standing with their hands over their hearts, they recite, "I pledge allegiance to the Bible, God's Holy Word. I will make it a lamp unto my feet and a light unto my path and will hide its words in my heart that I might not sin against God."

People in the South, more so than in any other region, are likely to believe that the Bible is completely accurate and should be read literally.[1] The Bible is absolutely central for Southern Baptists. It is held in the highest regard as the authority in matters of faith and practice. It provides the meta-narrative by which Southern Baptists shape their identities as Christians, and it is at the center of preaching, teaching, missions, and music. Its nature and interpretation are also hotly contested among Southern Baptists, and for women, these disputes are particularly personal. The freedoms afforded to Southern Baptist women, and the limitations placed on them, are intimately related to Southern Baptists' diverse understandings of the Bible, and when Southern Baptist women construct their sense of self, they do so in light of what they believe the Bible has to say about the status and roles of women. To understand the gendered identities of Southern Baptist women, we must understand their relationship to the Bible.

Sword Drills and Memory Verses

Nearly every Southern Baptist child has learned this song:

> The B-I-B-L-E, yes, that's the book for me.
> I stand alone on the Word of God, the B-I-B-L-E.

We'd always stand to sing it in my Sunday school class—a dozen little kids getting as much air into our diaphragms as possible so we could really shout it out when we got to the "yes" in the song. Those of us who were really being raised right had already memorized the scripture verse of the week and dutifully marked the space on our offering envelopes to account for it.

If we had a little extra time after the Sunday school lesson, which consisted of studying a Bible story in some detail, we might have a sword drill. Sword drills began in Southern Baptist churches in 1927. According to the Baptist Training Union Department's brochure, which was distributed to countless Sunday school and Training Union teachers, the sword drill gets its name from Ephesians 6:17: "And take the helmet of salvation, and the Sword of the Spirit, which is the Word of God." The brochure continued, "The Sword Drill is one of the most effective means that has been devised thus far for helping boys and girls to know their Bibles better and to be able to use them more efficiently for Him." The brochure recommended at least one sword drill a month.[2]

On our rather irregular sword drill Sundays, the teacher would have us stand with our Bibles, which we faithfully brought to church with us, and prepare to compete to be the first to find the specified verse. We'd start off holding our Bibles in one hand to our sides. "Attention," the teacher would call as we stood even straighter and readied ourselves. "Draw swords." We would raise our Bibles, Genesis down, left hand underneath, right hand on top. The tension was palpable as we waited. Then she'd tell us the verse we had to find. The first few would be easy— passages from one of the Gospels or a well-known book in the Hebrew Bible, such as Genesis or Isaiah. But then we'd move on to harder ones—Nahum or Habakkuk or Titus. Of course, those of us who were raised right had an advantage because we had already memorized the sixty-six books of the Bible (to this day, I still use the song I learned listing the books in order to find passages in the more obscure ones). The truly raised-right children—the ones who went on to participate in the associational and state-level sword drills—spent long hours practicing for these more formal, organized competitions. I was content to be the best sword driller in my Sunday school class.

"Deuteronomy 6:4–5, children," the teacher would announce. Already the raised-right children would be locating the book in their minds. "Genesis, Exodus, Leviticus, Numbers, Deuteronomy . . . okay, pretty early on, first few pages, flip there."

"Charge!" she called. Our Bibles flew open and our fingers flipped pages as fast as they could. The first child to find the passage would step forward, and when the teacher called on the apparent victor, he or she would read the verse aloud to confirm that it was the correct one. If it was, we would all return to the line, Bibles at our sides, awaiting the next verse. If it was not the right passage—say, someone turned to Numbers 6:4–5 by mistake—the rest of us would race furiously to step forward and read with all the self-righteousness a raised-right child can muster, "Hear, O Israel: The LORD our God is one LORD: And thou shalt love the LORD thy God with all thine heart, and with all thy soul, and with all thy might."

The Right to Interpret Scripture

In his 1908 treatise on soul competency, E. Y. Mullins laid out six axioms of religion.[3] One axiom is that "All Men Have an Equal Right to Direct Access to God." This means that each individual has the right to deal directly with God without the need for any human or institutional mediator. It means that no one can determine truth or the voice of God for another person, nor does any one person have greater access to God than another. In practice, this means that each person has the right to pray directly to God and to read and personally interpret scripture under the guidance of God's Spirit. No one should be coerced into accepting any interpretation that is not her or his own.

Of course, this means that different interpretations are common, hence the very heartfelt and regular disagreements among Baptists. Many Baptists perceive disagreement over biblical interpretation as a positive thing that contributes to the vitality of the faith. In the past thirty years, however, some fundamentalist leaders have sought to squelch disagreement and enforce a single view of the Bible and its interpretation (the controversy over biblical inerrancy is examined in the next section).

The right to interpret scripture for themselves has been especially empowering for Southern Baptist women. If my mother disagrees with the interpretation her pastor offers in a sermon, she feels perfectly free, if not obligated, to let him know about it shortly after the church service. For Southern Baptist women who felt called to ministry in the 1970s and 1980s, the right to interpret scripture for oneself was paramount. At the time, although many Southern Baptists read the Bible as excluding women from the ordained ministry, many others did not. In fact, they interpreted the Bible as encouraging both women and men to take active leadership roles in both the ordained and the lay ministry. They understood that the Bible taught equality between women and men in society, in church, and at home, and they often supported the burgeoning women's movement based on their own biblical understandings.

What happened in 1979 and over the next fifteen years, however, challenged what many of us had been taught about Baptist identity. Disenfranchised fundamentalists began a concerted effort to wrest control of the Southern Baptist Convention from moderates under the rallying cry of "biblical inerrancy." According to these fundamentalists, there was only one correct way to view the Bible, and from that viewpoint, only a limited range of interpretations was acceptable.[4]

Biblical Inerrancy and the Southern Baptist Controversy

The idea of biblical inerrancy emerged in the late nineteenth century in response to the growth of historical criticism. Conservative Protestants feared that this criticism would somehow undermine the authority of the Bible, so they began to argue for inerrancy in the original autographs. In 1969, W. A. Criswell, a leading fundamentalist and pastor of the First Baptist Church of Dallas, wrote *Why I Preach that the Bible Is Literally True*. In this book, published by the denomination's Broadman Press, Criswell argued, "On the original parchment, every sentence, word, line, mark, pen stroke, jot, and tittle were put there by inspiration of God."[5] He further argued that archaeology had confirmed the factuality of the Bible and that every supposed error or contradiction could be explained in such a way as to leave biblical inerrancy intact. In fact, Criswell dismissed historical criticism as an attack on the Bible's divine origins and authority. Criswell's influential rhetoric characterized the attacks that were soon leveled at Southern Baptist seminary professors who, despite their assertion of a high view of scripture, were criticized for utilizing the tools of historical criticism to interpret the biblical text and refuting the narrow claims of inerrancy as stated by Criswell and other Southern Baptist fundamentalists.

I became a professor of religion at a Baptist college in the middle of the Controversy. My training had been in religious education, but as so often happens in small liberal arts colleges, I was expected to teach classes in all the religious subdisciplines. During my first semester of teaching, I was assigned three sections of Introduction to the Old Testament. Having just finished two degrees at a seminary that valued historical criticism, I naively jumped right into teaching the Pentateuch by telling my students about the documentary hypothesis. In brief, this idea refutes the notion of Mosaic authorship of the first five books of the Bible and suggests that multiple authors and editors compiled these books over many years. Within only a few weeks of arriving on campus, I was already in trouble. Pastors and parents began to call the dean and the president to complain about my heretical teaching. That December, I returned to Southern Seminary's campus for graduation (I had finished my dissertation in late June), and I spent some time with its president Roy Honeycutt, a Hebrew Bible scholar. I told him what had happened, and he gave me this sage advice: "Let them discover the documentary hypothesis for themselves."

I went back for spring semester and devised an exercise in which I gave students a long list of passages from the Pentateuch and asked them to come up with as much information as possible by reading the passages. Many of the passages were duplicate accounts of the same stories, some with very distinctive and different writing styles. Some passages were narrative; others were lists of laws. Some showed God in one light, some in another. The students spent about half an hour working in small groups. Then we filled the chalkboard with all their observations about the passages. When we were done, I asked, "Based on what you see here, what would this lead you to think about who wrote these books?"

"Obviously, more than one person," they replied.

"Right!" I said. "And we have a name for that. It's called the documentary hypothesis, and here's how it works. . . ."

After that, the students never objected to my introducing them to the documentary hypothesis, but I can't say the same for their parents. I got in trouble once again when one of my students innocently shared what she had learned with her horrified mother, who called her pastor, who in turn called the president of the college.

Although I had solved the problem of teaching the documentary hypothesis, I continued to run into trouble at the Baptist college, especially when I dealt with passages pertaining to women. I didn't force the students to accept my views, but I did ask them to learn various interpretations of those passages, which didn't sit well with many pastors and parents. What had been happening for almost a decade at the national level had now filtered down to the state level. Professors were under attack if they didn't profess biblical inerrancy and utilize biblical literalism as a method of interpretation.

I won't rehash the entire history of the Controversy among Southern Baptists. Many books written by people on both sides of the debate offer detailed analyses beyond the scope of this book.[6] Fundamentalists claimed that the Controversy was about biblical inerrancy—the notion that the Bible is without error in history and science, as well as theology. They posited the debate in terms of those who believed the Bible (inerrantists) and those who didn't (the moderates). In reality, the disagreement was between those who believed one thing about the Bible and those who believed another. The fundamentalist rhetoric was so persuasive, however, that conservative, Bible-believing Southern Baptists voted fundamentalist leaders into power in the Convention. Once in power, the fundamentalists quickly began to eliminate those who disagreed with them from the denomination's seminaries and agencies. Historians and social scientists suggest that the Controversy was really about any number of things beyond biblical inerrancy—theology,[7] bureaucratic structure,[8] the end of segregation,[9] the continuing legacy of racism,[10] social status,[11] control versus freedom,[12] politics,[13] pluralism,[14] and culture.[15] Certainly each of these issues played a significant role in the dispute. But another interesting issue emerges in the textual record created by the Convention's resolutions and other writings since the beginnings of the Controversy—women.

Throughout the 1970s, the Convention, most notably its seminaries and publishing houses, was surprisingly supportive of women's equality. For the fundamentalists, the progress of women was glaring proof of the theological liberalism in the Convention, thus justifying their attempt to gain control.[16] The combination of the loss of white privilege in the face of the successful civil rights movement and the economic downturn of the 1970s meant that many southern white men found themselves with little social power, except that which they exercised over women in the only two institutions they still controlled—the church and the family.[17]

What Does the Bible Say about Women?

Fundamentalists say that the Bible is the inerrant, infallible Word of God and that its truths are plain, binding, and timeless, without social or historical context. According to their reading of the Bible, sin came into the world when Eve was deceived and tempted Adam. They believe that women and men are of equal worth before God but that women must submit to men. Women are not to teach men in the church nor be in authority over men in pastoral leadership. In the home, wives must submit graciously to their husbands. The difference, fundamentalists suggest, is not one of worth but one of roles. Women and men are of equal value before God, but they have different roles in the church and the home.

More moderate or progressive Baptists interpret the Bible differently. Although they view scripture as the inspired and authoritative Word of God, they do not see it as inerrant. Their method of interpretation usually involves historical criticism, a process of closely examining a text by asking questions about its authorship, audience, historical context, genre, and biblical context. Their concern is not for the historical or scientific accuracy of a text but for its meaning—both to its original audience and to contemporary Christians. They suggest that the Bible teaches the equal worth of women and men and that passages suggesting women's submission should be interpreted in light of the historical context that gave rise to them. They believe that the larger framework of grace, equality, and giftedness should guide interpretation. Therefore, they contend that the Bible supports women in all roles in the home, the church, and society.

Of course, Baptists can be found at various places on the continuum of interpretation. Every Baptist who reads scripture has a unique set of interpretations. The observations I offer here are generalizations of the typical fundamentalist and moderate approaches to interpretation, but I acknowledge that individual Baptists actually encompass a wide range of interpretive strategies and beliefs.

So, what does the Bible say? Following are the passages used most often by both fundamentalist and moderate Southern Baptists to explain their beliefs about the roles of women. I discuss their interpretation later. Unless otherwise noted, I'm using the New Revised Standard Version (which locates me in the progressive camp). First, here are the verses most often cited by fundamentalists to support their belief in the subordination of women:

> As in all the churches of the saints, women should be silent in the churches. For they are not permitted to speak, but should be subordinate, as the law also says. If there is anything they desire to know, let them ask their husbands at home. For it is shameful for a woman to speak in church. (1 Corinthians 14:33b–35)

> Wives, be subject to your husbands as you are to the Lord. For the husband is the head of the wife just as Christ is the head of the church, the body of which he is the Savior. Just as the church is subject to Christ, so also wives ought to be, in everything, to their husbands. (Ephesians 5:22–24)

> Let a woman learn in silence with full submission. I permit no woman to teach or to have authority over a man; she is to keep silent. For Adam was formed first, then Eve; and Adam was not deceived, but the woman was deceived and became a transgressor. Yet she will be saved through childbearing, provided they continue in faith and love and holiness, with modesty. (1 Timothy 2:11–14)

> Wives, in the same way, accept the authority of your husbands, so that, even if some of them do not obey the word, they may be won over without a word by their wives' conduct, when they see the purity and reverence of your lives. . . . It was in this way long ago that the holy women who hoped in God used to adorn themselves by accepting the authority of their husbands. Thus Sarah obeyed Abraham and called him lord. (1 Peter 3:1–2, 5–6a)

For the next passage, I cite the King James Version (KJV) first, followed by the New Revised Standard Version (NSRV); the latter translates the verse the way the moderates interpret it. The italics are mine to emphasize the differences.

> This is a true saying, If a man desire the office of a bishop, he desireth a good work. A bishop then must be blameless, *the husband of one wife,* vigilant, sober, of good behavior, given to hospitality, apt to teach; Not given to wine, no striker, not greedy of filthy lucre; but patient, not a brawler, not covetous; One that ruleth well his own house, having his children in subjection with all gravity; (For if a man know not how to rule his own house, how shall he take care of the church of God?) . . . Likewise must the deacons be grave, not doubletongued, not given to much wine, not greedy of filthy lucre; Holding the mystery of the faith in a pure conscience. And let these also first be proved; then let them use the office of a deacon, being

found blameless. Even so must *their wives* be grave, not slanderers, sober, faithful in all things. Let the deacons be the *husbands of one wife,* ruling their children and their own houses well. (1 Timothy 3:1–5, 8–12 [KJV])

The saying is sure: whoever aspires to the office of bishop desires a noble task. Now a bishop must be above reproach, *married only once,* temperate, sensible, respectable, hospitable, an apt teacher, not a drunkard, not violent but gentle, not quarrelsome, and not a lover of money. He must manage his own household well, keeping his children submissive and respectful in every way—for if someone does not know how to manage his own household, how can he take care of God's church? . . . Deacons likewise must be serious, not double-tongued, not indulging in much wine, not greedy for money; they must hold fast to the mystery of the faith with a clear conscience. And let them first be tested; then, if they prove themselves blameless, let them serve as deacons. *Women* likewise must be serious, not slanderers, but temperate, faithful in all things. Let deacons be *married only once,* and let them manage their children and their households well; for those who serve well as deacons gain a good standing for themselves and great boldness in the faith that is in Christ Jesus. (1 Timothy 3:1–5, 8–12 [NSRV])

The following verses reflect the broader teachings of scripture to which the moderates appeal in their support of women's equality.

There is no longer Jew or Greek, there is no longer slave or free, there is no longer male and female; for all of you are one in Christ Jesus. (Galatians 3:28)

Now there are varieties of gifts, but the same Spirit; and there are varieties of services, but the same Lord; and there are varieties of activities, but it is the same God who activates all of them in everyone. To each is given the manifestation of the Spirit for the common good. To one is given through the Spirit the utterance of wisdom, and to another the utterance of knowledge according to the same Spirit, to another faith by the same Spirit, to another gifts of healing by the one Spirit, to another the working of miracles, to another prophecy, to another the discernment of spirits, to another various kinds of tongues, to another the interpretation of tongues. All these are activated by one and the same Spirit, who allots to each one individually just as the Spirit chooses. (1 Corinthians 12:4–11)

Be subject to one another out of reverence for Christ. (Ephesians 5:21)

Moderates also cite numerous biblical women as models for contemporary Southern Baptist women in ministry.[18]

The fundamentalist interpretation of these passages is best summarized in a 2003 article by Bruce Ware, associate dean of Southern Baptist Theological Seminary. Ware argues that male headship was in the original design of creation and that the Fall led to woman's desire to usurp man's rightful place as ruler and to man's inclination to "misuse his rights of rulership." Calling himself a "complementarian," Ware argues that although men and women are of equal worth before God, God has given them different roles that involve woman's submission to man in both home and church. He writes, "Women are to submit to male leadership and teaching because Adam was created first and because Eve was deceived and sinned first." He adds that wives are to submit to their husbands because "the husband is head of the wife *as* Christ is head of the church." He also points to Peter's assertion that the woman is the "weaker vessel" for whom the husband is responsible.[19] In the same publication, Daniel Akin (then dean of Southern Seminary; now president of Southeastern Baptist Theological Seminary) reads Titus 2:1–8 as directing young women to be homemakers rather than career women.[20] It is interesting that Akin fails to include the rest of the passage in his literal reading of scripture. Verse 9 reads: "Tell slaves to be submissive to their masters and to give satisfaction in every respect."

Akin's omission highlights what the moderates see as the necessity of interpreting the Bible in its social and historical contexts. Most fundamentalists are willing to recognize the historical contexts of passages such as Titus 2:9 on slavery or other New Testament prohibitions on short hair or jewelry for women. Yet they apply these interpretations selectively, even within the same passage: they take some verses literally and argue that they represent timeless principles, yet they interpret others as referring only to the particular period in which the words were penned.

Moderates, in contrast, argue that the social and historical contexts of the writer and the original audience and the social and historical contexts of contemporary readers must be factored in to biblical interpretation. Rather than reading texts literally, moderate interpreters of scripture search for the meaning of the text as it can be understood in contemporary life. They recognize that the Bible was written over hundreds of years in different languages by people who lived in various nations with diverse customs. Therefore, its specifics cannot be taken out of their historical context and dropped into twenty-first-century American life as if the social forces of that time and ours play no role in the meaning of the text.

Fundamentalists believe that the Bible is inerrant. They argue that a perfect God must give rise to a perfect book. They are willing to use some of the tools of historical criticism, but only if they do not challenge fundamentalist assumptions about inerrancy. Moderates believe that God worked through the Bible's authors to create a book that is unique in its place and authority in Christian life, but they acknowledge that the process involved a complex interaction of divine inspiration and human cognition. In other words, the Bible is both a divinely inspired sacred text and a human product that reflects the personalities and histories of its writers.

In this light, moderates read the Bible to support the equality of women both in worth and in roles. They reject notions of male headship and female submission and argue that God can use women in the same ways he uses men in the home and in the church. On the whole, moderates understand that the more prohibitive passages addressed specific problems in specific churches in the first century B.C.E., during a time when women were essentially property with no civil rights. In that sense, exhortations for husbands to love and respect their wives likely served as a means to improve women's lives. But, given women's completely subordinate status in the first century, why did the biblical writers feel compelled to tell them to be submissive? Is it possible that women had heard something revolutionary in the Gospel that called them to freedom and caused them to begin to rebel against their cultural constraints? Given Christianity's marginalized status in the first century, were the biblical writers simply afraid that free and independent women might cause non-Christians to question this new religion and further marginalize it? Were women and their newfound freedom being disruptive in the church? Or were the writers simply struggling with their own issues about women? These writers had been raised in a culture that accepted female subordination, yet they often pronounced submission on the one hand and announced liberation on the other. The apostle Paul wrote that in Christ there is neither male nor female. In the book of Romans, he commended Phoebe, a deacon, and Junia, an apostle.

For every passage that suggests female subordination, another passage can be cited that articulates women's equality. Fundamentalists believe that the Bible must speak in a unified voice—no one passage can contradict another; because both passages must be accurate and true, and if they seem not to be, the problem is with the reader. Moderates accept the diversity of voices and experiences in scripture and recognize that this diversity inevitably leads to different ideas. Unlike fundamentalists, however, they do not see this diversity as incompatible with the divine inspiration of scripture; in fact, they see it as evidence of divine inspiration because of the larger message that comes through these diverse voices—that of love, grace, freedom, justice, and acceptance. A verse-by-verse exegesis of each passage pertaining to women is beyond the scope of this book, but there are a number of good books that offer alternative interpretations of the Bible's comments on women.[21]

Years ago, I developed a role-play activity designed to help students recognize the various ways to interpret scripture in relation to women. In the activity, I role-play six different religious thinkers: C. I. Scofield, Rudolph Bultmann, Elizabeth Achtemeier, Elisabeth Schüssler Fiorenza, Delores Williams, and Mary Daly. If you're not familiar with these folks, trust me, they cover the full spectrum of possible ways to understand the Bible. As each of the six characters (I wear a different hat for each one), I talk about what the Bible is, how it should be interpreted, and what it says about women. Once I've finished my short spiel, I interact in character with the students, who are encouraged to ask questions and engage in discussion with each religious thinker. What students get from this experience is a new understanding of how many ways there are to read and interpret the Bible and the close connection between that biblical interpretation and the social location of the interpreter. The experience is enlightening, I think, for both conservative Christian students and those who've never experienced a religious service of any kind. Almost across the board, they are surprised that so many different interpretations are possible and that these interpretations result in so many different readings of what the Bible says about women.

What Do Women Say about the Bible?

When I was growing up, I had a dark blue hardback Scofield Reference Bible. The Scofield Reference Bible was first published in 1909 and revised in 1917. It offered an annotated King James Version of scripture that promoted fundamentalist notions of creationism and dispensationalism. Although C. I. Scofield was not a Baptist, his reference Bible became highly influential among fundamentalist Southern Baptists; thus, it was the Bible of choice during my youth. I faithfully took it to church with me every Sunday morning, Sunday night, and Wednesday night, and I dutifully made notes in the margins when teachers or preachers would make some profound observation about the text. I underlined passages that spoke to me in my adolescent angst: "The good that I would, I do not, and that which I would not, I do"; "What time I am afraid, I will trust in thee"; "Trust in the Lord with all thine heart and lean not unto thine own understanding. In all thy ways acknowledge him, and he shall direct thy paths." I read my Bible every night; I read it in its entirety—cover to cover, Genesis through Revelation—every year. Soon it was so worn out that I had to use duct tape on the spine to hold it together.

By my midteens, however, I had begun to keep a secret list on a piece of paper that I kept stuck in my Bible. On that secret list were passages I had discovered that seemed to contradict other passages or conflict with history or science, accounts that I couldn't harmonize, questions I couldn't deny. I was a fairly astute reader. My tenth-grade English teacher, Jim Moss, had pinpointed me as a future English major and had me writing literary analyses of *Of Human Bondage* and *The Grapes of Wrath*. So I was confident that I knew how to read and make sense of a text. But I never asked those questions or raised those issues in church. I already knew the answer I would get: "You're not reading the text right. There aren't any contradictions or errors in scripture. The problem is with you." But I knew a contradiction when I saw one (such as all the differing accounts of the same event in the Hebrew Bible), and I kept adding to that list all through college, where I did indeed major in English.

I even took that Scofield Reference Bible and my list to seminary with me. After the first meeting of my New Testament class, I went to the bookstore and bought an Oxford Annotated Revised Standard Version, and when I read my Bible devotionally or for class, I read those notes instead of Scofield's. As I listened to my professor, Jim Blevins, offer new (at least to me) ways to interpret scripture, I realized that my secret list was not the threat to my faith that I had been led to believe by all those preachers who said that to question scripture was to put oneself on the slippery slope to nonbelief. I quit worrying about becoming a heretic and dove into historical criticism with unbridled enthusiasm. For me, historical criticism opened up new avenues of understanding; it made scripture make sense and come alive in a way that was both relevant and believable. I remembered the moment in the novel *The Whisper of the River* when the entire Baptist college campus is embroiled in a raging debate about evolution and the Bible. Porter Osborne Jr. climbs an old magnolia tree outside the president's home to listen through an open window as the president and three religion faculty members are accused of heresy. While sitting in the tree, Porter remembers these lines from Tennyson: "By faith and faith alone embrace, / Believing where we cannot prove"; and "There lives more faith in honest doubt, / Believe me, than in half the creeds." At that moment, Porter realizes that he can have both faith and science. He can believe the geologists, the archaeologists, the scientists, and the book of Genesis.[22]

Probably the most liberating moment of my seminary experience came during my first semester. Because I started midyear, I took the second half of the course on the New Testament first. One of Blevins's areas of expertise was the book of Revelation. In fact, he had written a little book called *Revelation as Drama* that was about to change my life. I had grown up on premillennial dispensationalism. I could draw the timeline of the Rapture, Tribulation, Great Tribulation, Millennium, and Great White Throne Judgment. I had watched *A Thief in the Night* over and over throughout my adolescence and had sung "I Wish We'd All Been Ready" with all the earnest enthusiasm of youth. Yet somehow, the whole idea had always bothered me. I remember the day that Blevins introduced us to the ideas of apocalyptic literature and the codes of the book of Revelation. He told us that the idea of a rapture had been introduced in the nineteenth century by a man named John Darby who had had a vision that it would happen. Until that time, the notion of the Rapture *had never been part of Christian thinking.* In fact, Darby's idea was met with great skepticism and resistance at the time, and Darby had to go through extreme exegetical gymnastics to create biblical support for the notion. Still, the idea was picked up by Scofield and included in his reference Bible, which popularized it among evangelical and fundamentalist Christians. I felt as though scales had fallen from my eyes. In that moment, something clicked. Perhaps this was the biblical parallel to the feminist "click"—that moment when one first becomes aware of the operation of gender in women's lives. It changed my life and opened up new and liberating ways of interpreting the Bible for me.

The Controversy among Southern Baptists had started only a few years before I enrolled at Southern Seminary. In fact, I remember my pastor preaching to my home congregation about how we needed to send all ten of our messengers to the Southern Baptist Convention in 1979 to vote the "liberals who teach that the Bible isn't true" out of our seminaries. After that first semester at Southern, I no longer subscribed to the fundamentalists' argument that to question scripture's scientific or historical accuracy was tantamount to disbelief. Instead, I discovered a more credible (for me) way of studying scripture and allowing God to speak to me through it without having to pretend that I hadn't noticed the two very different creation stories or the four very different resurrection accounts (and by the way, in my five and a half years at Southern Seminary, I never heard a single professor say that the Bible isn't true). I threw away my secret list, packed up my Scofield Reference Bible, and embraced the study of scripture in a new and more meaningful way.

In my research, I have found that Southern Baptist women, whether fundamentalist, conservative, moderate, or liberal, hold the Bible in high regard. Though they may interpret it very differently, practically all of them see the Bible as a central aspect of their faith and a guiding light in their relationship with God and their responsibilities in the world. Comments by Heather King, director of women's ministries at Southern Seminary at the time of her interview, and three students at one of the newer, more moderate seminaries represent the range of women's views on scripture. Heather explained to me, "Scripture is God's Holy Word, both inerrant and infallible. It is literally God-breathed; sufficient for doctrine, reproof, correction, and instruction for holy living. The presupposition that scripture is God-breathed dictates how I interact and interpret scripture. I cannot interpret God's Word based on feelings and emotions or on my personal experiences. To do so puts 'me' at the center; my feelings, my opinions, my experiences become the measuring rod for scripture when the reverse should always take place. Personal experiences and feelings should be filtered through the grid of scripture." The conversation among the moderate seminary students, by contrast, went like this:

> STUDENT 1: At times, it's hard to dissect the Bible so much; it's hard to keep it at its holy status . . . and to remember that this is an inspired and holy book because we pick it apart so much. So that's kind of a tension: you question, "Well, Paul didn't really write all these things, and Jonah is really just a story," . . . [yet you] hold it at a high esteem. . . . I value it as God's Word, as a way of living, as a way to know God, as a way to learn more about myself, all those things.

> STUDENT 2: I wouldn't say that the Bible is God's Word; maybe some of it is from God, but I think some of it is not from God: the parts that are oppressive and degrading to women and to humanity, I don't think that's of God. But I do value it as the faith tradition. It's amazing that it has come from so long ago, and it's been preserved, and so many people have studied

it. I think about it as a collective memory. I think it's really amazing. I do value the Bible, but I have a hard time saying that it's holy. But I do respect it, and I can use it for devotional material.

STUDENT 3: I value scripture. It definitely holds a high place. I think it mediates to us the Word of God. I think truth follows through it too. There are parts of it that don't do that much for me, and I think that I do hold it in such high regard because it is a tradition of the church, the tradition of the community I claim to be a part of. They say, that community, "This is holy scripture. These texts help us understand God, understand what truth is," and so I say, "Okay. If you say that, then I can go with that too." I guess that's what scripture is for me. I guess that just says that I have a high view of community and tradition.

These examples tend to represent the extremes of Southern Baptist women's understanding of the Bible. Most of the participants fall somewhere in the middle. They are generally not rigid biblical inerrantists (though some are), but they do believe the Bible to be a unique text, inspired by God and central to their experience of faith. Many would be uncomfortable with these students' challenge to the equal inspiration of each part of the text, but many would not. Most tend toward the more conservative understandings of inspiration, but some, especially those who are seminary educated, both hold the Bible in high regard and understand it as a cultural product that reflects the ideologies and social mores of the times in which it was written. Nonetheless, most are less concerned with the how and why of inspiration than with the way God speaks to them in the here and now through scripture.

Dorothy Patterson told me, "Scripture is to me the most important thing. Without any apology, I can say with Martin Luther, *sola scriptura*." She went on to explain that for her, the Bible is also the final authority. "I may not agree with it; I may wrestle with it; I may feel it's not appropriate; I don't see how I can teach this. But the point is, if it's going to be God's Word in my life, then it has to be God's Word across the board."

WMU's Sheryl Churchill said, the Bible "is the written Word of God; I believe it to be true. It is the place where I learn many things about Jesus Christ and his teachings, but I also see it as the history. . . . it reveals God in history and salvation." To most of my participants, the Bible is the "Word of God." By this, they mean that the Bible is inspired by God, and through it, God speaks to them. Lisa Vang explained, "The Bible is a way of communication with God and from God. I gain knowledge and wisdom from reading the scriptures." Likewise, Debra Hochgraber, director of women's ministries for the Baptist General Convention of Texas, noted, "The Bible is God's Word, the tool that he gave us to be able to know him. I read scripture. I study scripture. I pray scripture. I learn from scripture, often changing my attitude and behavior concerning matters because of what I learned. I gain insight into every aspect of my life." Debbie Williams, a member of Second Ponce de Leon Baptist Church in Atlanta, stated, "The Bible is a source of great knowledge and wisdom." Nancy Moore declared, "I revere it; I respect it; I know that in it is everything we need to live the Christian life. It's the guide. I love it. I love to study it; I love to be near it. I always have it near me; it's always there when I sit down. The Bible is in reach." Debra Owens-Hughes added, "God directs me in my life through the scriptures. Sometimes it may be just a gift of peace for a day of turmoil; sometimes a reminder to repent of the things in my life that are hindering love, joy, peace, patience, and kindness towards others and within myself." Doris Bailey said, "The Bible is the Word of God. It's my foundation. It's strength. It's power. It's encouragement. It's faithfulness." Carolyn Matthews declared, "The Bible is the guide, a guide for living, a guide for understanding who God is, yeah, and for shaping who I am and how I view people and how I view life and different situations."

For these women, their experience with the Bible is an intensely personal one in which God deals directly with them. When Kayne Carter sits down to read the Bible, she asks "the Lord first to enlighten me, to put the Holy Spirit through to guide me and teach me. . . . God speaks to everyone, but you still get it personally." Shelby Christie concurred: "The Bible is the Word of God; it's just like God speaking to you, all the time, to me, and it means everything to me, more than any other book. I like to read other books sometimes, but it's the first book, it's the only book that really means life and death to you." Sarah Shelton, pastor of Baptist Church of the Covenant in Birmingham, told me, "The Bible kind of roughs me up all the time. I think just those issues of justice, you know. Jesus just confronts this over and over again. And we just don't seem to get it, you know? The Bible is an inspired message, continually inspiring, just a wonderful guide. If I had to pinpoint my ministry, I'd say it's in terms of relationships, and the scriptures just constantly kind of stir you up to make your relationships what they ought to be. It challenges me and gets my attention." Debra Owens-Hughes noted, "Many times the Word calls me into specific ministry or action and counsels me when I need to know what to do in various situations. But it also is simply a source of joy for me as I read it and it reminds me of the very presence of Christ right now, within my present moment." Dorothy Patterson said, "I love the fact that God speaks to me through his Word, and I firmly believe that there is no decision I will ever face that I cannot find the principles in his Word."

Most of the women with whom I spoke turn to the Bible for comfort, wisdom, and guidance. Millie Culp of Mount Alto Baptist Church in Rome, Georgia, said that the Bible is her "daily guide. What you need, if you have a question, you can find the answer." Judy Masters called the Bible "a handbook for life." Likewise, Beth Cox of North Broad Baptist Church in Rome, Georgia, told me that the Bible "is a guidebook of the way I should conduct my life," and Minerva Escobedo of Fresno, California, said, "It's God's Word to us, to help us lead a life that is fulfilling if we learn to use it and study it and be open to God speaking to us and letting him guide our life daily." Lidia Abrams said, "It's like a map of life. You have to find your way. It's where we been; it's where we going." Sheryl Churchill called the Bible "a teacher; it is a prodder; it's one of those things that sometimes when I read it, I will say, 'Ouch!' Or it is often a surprise because of what's there. It encourages me to go deeper because I know there is something else there I'm not seeing. So I guess it's a treasure chest, things that are waiting to be explored." Mitzi Sayler of First Baptist Church in Hendersonville, Tennessee, said that when she has to make a decision, she goes to the Bible. She explained, "In major decisions that I've had to make in my life, I've gone back to scripture. Because sometimes, me myself, the judgments and things I want to do right now and the decisions I want to make right now aren't quite sound. So the Bible is the biggest part of making my big decisions in life."

Many participants cited Southern Baptists' emphasis on scripture as a significant reason for their own affiliation with the denomination. In one focus group, Nancy Moore explained, "I feel that it was important, from the standpoint of our own spiritual development, because the Baptists, especially the Southern Baptists, in our experience, emphasized the Word, and you had a better opportunity to grow spiritually in a denomination where the Word of God was exalted. I just think that if I had not come up Southern Baptist, I would not appreciate or know as much about the Bible as I do." Alicia Bennett agreed, noting that when she was growing up, Southern Baptists felt that it was their responsibility to make sure their children knew the Bible. "It wasn't enough just to 'have it once over lightly,'" she pointed out. "There was a lot of memory work." Phyllis Jenkins, who has been a Baptist all her life, said, "I can only tell you that it's through being a Baptist that I have learned God's Word at an early age. We were taught scriptures, and we had to memorize them through the Sunday school and what we called Baptist Training Union; so I would say that Baptist, to me, has meant my foundation in the Word of God."

Elaine Richards grew up Baptist but became Episcopalian when she was twenty. When her son was old enough, however, her church didn't have a Sunday school class for him, so his aunt and uncle took him to Sunday school at Travis Avenue Baptist Church, and Elaine decided to join them. "The teaching," she pointed out, "you just get so much more of true biblical teaching; you really get the Word of God here." Pam Boucher of Magnolia Avenue Baptist Church in Riverside, California, pointed out that she participates in a Southern Baptist church primarily because her understandings of the Bible "match up" with the statements of Southern Baptists. Likewise, Leigh Ann Grubbs and Brenda Faulkner of First Baptist Church in Orlando, Florida, remarked that Southern Baptists follow scripture. Leigh Ann pointed out, "We follow scripture, and we try the best we can to follow the Lord." Brenda added, "Being a Baptist, to me, really brings to my mind the firm, strong conviction based on what we believe to be the inspired, inerrant Word of God. And because of that, we aren't swayed by culture. We aren't tossed to and fro." Amanda Lake of First Baptist Church in Hendersonville, Tennessee, noted that "the Bible being taught is what I love." Janet Dickerson of Atlanta's Second Ponce de Leon Baptist Church said, "Other people just go on Sundays, and that's it. And they can't even find their Bible. They dust it off, and it's not underlined, and it's just like brand new. I've known people, older women, who have had to replace their Bibles because they wore them out. And that doesn't happen in some denominations." Joanne Parker grew up Catholic and chose to go to a Southern Baptist church as an adult because of its Bible studies. She said, "It is not denominational politics or anything like that that . . . connects me to the Southern Baptist denomination; it is the Bible study."

Studying the Bible together is an important aspect of Southern Baptist women's experiences with scripture. As noted earlier, the Clique got together through a women's Bible study group. Debbie Williams stated, "Women's Bible study in a Southern Baptist church is practically sure to give me an instant place of comfort and belonging." These women generally allow for differences in interpretation, although the breadth of allowable differences varies. For the most part, the women agree that if the Bible says something, they are obligated to believe it. Chris Ritter from Travis Avenue Baptist Church in Fort Worth explained, "I think it's important that if it says it in the Bible, then that's it . . . if the Bible says it, Southern Baptists need to do it." How they discern what the Bible says, however, depends on the extent to which they have been introduced to the tools of historical criticism and whether their churches are basically fundamentalist, conservative, or moderate. Women in moderate churches, women who attended Southern Baptist seminaries before the mid-1990s, and women who attended moderate seminaries are much less likely to be literalists or inerrantists and much more likely to read the Bible with the tools of historical criticism. Two women from North Broad Baptist Church in Rome, Georgia, explained how they interpret scripture. Nancy Echols said, "I think our different experiences help us to interpret it in a different way, and I learn from other people." She gave her parents' divorce as an example of how experience had challenged her to rethink her interpretation of the Bible. Carla Moldavan agreed. She said that one pastor had told the congregation, "We read the Bible for information and for formation"— to learn the facts and context of the passage and to allow the Bible to speak personally and devotionally.

More conservative women tended to identify themselves as inerrantists and literalists, but even they recognized that individuals' interpretations of scripture would inevitably vary. A group of women from Mount Alto Baptist Church in Rome, Georgia, exemplifies conservative women's approach to scripture. When I asked whether they believe that there's room for disagreement in churches, one replied, "Yes, but not when it comes to scripture." She went on to explain that although people might differ in their interpretations of scripture, within the church they had to agree that their beliefs and practices come from the Bible. When I asked the others whether people can have different interpretations of scripture and still remain in the church, they cited my mother, who happens to be their Sunday school teacher. "She does all the time. We have a prime example right here," they insisted.

In her study of two fundamentalist congregations, Brenda Brasher found that women's study of the Bible was simultaneously empowering and disempowering. She writes, "Women are empowered because they embrace the Bible as something accessible to them and not as a text understood by an erudite few and intelligible only if a pastor explains it." The problem, she says, is that women do not utilize the tools of historical criticism, including feminist studies, "that disclose the patriarchal social context of these writings." In other words, women are not introduced to the information that might undermine literalist readings of the text, especially those passages that seem to advance women's subordination.[23] In many ways, since the end of the Controversy, this is true of the majority of Southern Baptist women. Their primary resources for Bible study are often SBC curricular materials, which are written from a very conservative perspective, or commentaries and other works by conservative or fundamentalist writers. Rarely do the typical resources utilized by these women, by their pastors, or by their Bible study leaders present the findings of historical criticism in a positive light and as a legitimate way to interpret scripture. In contrast, women in churches utilizing CBF resources are much more likely to find the influence of historical criticism in the works they use to study and interpret the Bible.

As might be expected, most of the seminary-educated women offered a more nuanced view of the Bible and biblical interpretation than did non-seminary-educated women, although they were no less passionate about the significance of the Bible in their lives. The majority of seminary-educated women I spoke with are not biblical inerrantists (though some are), but most of them have a very high view of scripture. Most of these women attended seminary prior to the Controversy, at a time when higher criticism was an integral part of their education. Judy Baker told me, "I love the Bible, and I also am very careful with it because of the power that it has." She added that the biblical themes of love, compassion, forgiveness, and mercy are her yardstick for measuring other biblical passages. She referred to the Bible as a living, breathing document "that should always be interpreted in light of the revelation of God in Jesus Christ, the suffering servant." Rosalie Beck said, "The Bible does what the Bible is intended to do, [which is] explain God to the world. And to teach God's characteristics, to help people understand the absolute love of God for humanity." She added, "I'm real serious about the Bible. I have personal devotion daily, and I take the Bible very, very seriously." Doris Borchert told me that she has always been "very grateful that Baptists have been a people of the Book," but she is saddened "when the Book is taken over for God rather than as a guide."

Many of the seminary-educated women focus on biblical teachings about justice and equality. Julie Pennington-Russell said that until she went to seminary, she saw the Bible as being about "how to be a righteous person." But after seminary, she began to look at the Bible as "a picture of the kind of heart God has, and that has a whole lot to do with justice and the poor and a whole lot to do with helping us see how we really miss the point in so many ways." She now sees the Bible as being about both personal righteousness and social justice.

A few of the seminary-educated women are much more left-leaning in their understanding of the Bible, but they aren't typical. They see the Bible as one tool through which God is revealed. For them, the Bible is central to Christian faith because of its long and important role in the history of the church. Although God speaks through the Bible, they contend, the Bible is not the Word of God. Rather, it becomes the Word of God as the Spirit of God speaks through it in contemporary situations. As one seminary-educated woman put it, "Is it holy? Sure, I'd say it's holy; it's one way we know God. Is it inspirational? Yes, it is. Is it part of what gives my faith tradition identity and roots? Yes. But the Word of God? No, it is not." Leah McCullough, now a UCC campus minister, explained that the Bible "is a part of my tradition. I choose the Christian path to God, and so I read scripture. I read scripture critically as well as devotionally. But the Bible is only one aspect that informs me. . . . It is a way that I am able to learn more about how these kinds of human communities throughout time and throughout history have understood God. And I read the Bible, not literally—it's not inerrant—but kind of metaphorically. That's how I would gain the most from it."

The women who now teach at Southern Baptist seminaries and those currently being educated at these seminaries are most likely to be biblical inerrantists. As Sheri Klouda, at the time a teacher at Southwestern Seminary, told me, the Bible is "inerrant in the sense that everything it says is true."

Across the theological spectrum, Southern Baptist women value the Bible. Some are biblical inerrantists, and some are classical liberals, but most Southern Baptist women fall somewhere in the middle. They believe that God speaks through the Bible; more importantly, they believe that God speaks directly to them through the Bible. They believe that they are competent to interpret the Bible for themselves, and they try to live by what they believe the Bible teaches. Because the Bible is so highly emphasized in Southern Baptist life, Southern Baptist women know the biblical text very well; in fact, in many ways, they know the text so intimately that the Bible becomes an important part of their own identities.

The Bible and Women's Sense of Self

For most Southern Baptist women, the Bible is a significant aspect of the self. From childhood, they have hidden its words in their hearts as the psalmist suggests, and it has become an integral part of who they are. Carolyn Hale Cubbedge explained, "I came up at the time when you memorized your memory verse for Sunday school and another one for Training Union; you did sword drills, and all that kind of stuff. You did your daily Bible reading. I had a minor in Bible when I was in college and then a seminary degree; so it's been part of my life as long as I can remember. I think there are times when I'm getting ready to do something, and Bible verses just pop into my head and remind you of who you are and what you're about."

To this day, scriptural allusions populate my speech. I don't even think about it; they just come out. The other day I was talking to the Women Studies staff about turning the other cheek when a couple of nasty editorials about our program appeared in the campus newspaper and on the Web. I find myself telling the story of the widow's mite to encourage my students to participate in feminist activism, even when they feel like their small efforts don't make a difference. I'm employed in a state school, and I'm not trying to proselytize. The words are just a part of me. I have indeed hidden them in my heart.

In various ways, most of the women in my study find self-affirmation in the Bible. Clique member Doris Bailey told me, "I think the Bible teaches that women are on the same level ground as men, as all people; according to the cross, according to the Bible, we are all equal." Lidia Abrams pointed to Phoebe and Lydia in the New Testament as women who had a hand in starting the church.

Despite their differing opinions about the nature of the Bible and how it should be interpreted, all the women I talked to felt competent to read and understand the Bible for themselves. Many of them, particularly the laywomen, recognize the limitations of trying to interpret an ancient document, but they all believe that God is still able to speak to them through scripture, and although they appreciate the insights of pastors and biblical scholars, ultimately, only they can decide for themselves what the Bible is, what it says, and what it means. Wanda Lee, executive director of WMU, even suggested that the Controversy has been helpful, because it forced her to figure out for herself what the Bible says. She observed, the Controversy "has given me an opportunity to decide for myself what do I believe, why do I believe it. Often those difficulties and controversies have driven me to examine scripture for myself, and probably one of the strongest things has been to realize that I have to know what I believe in relationship to Christ and what the Bible teaches, and not what other people tell me I'm supposed to believe."

3

Casseroles and Covered Dishes

Southern Baptist Women, Hospitality, and Friendship

Out in the highways and byways of life, Many are weary and sad;
Carry the sunshine where darkness is rife, Making the sorrowing glad.
Make me a blessing, make me a blessing, Out of my life, may Jesus shine;
Make me a blessing, O Savior, I pray, Make me a blessing to someone
today.
—Ira B. Wilson, "Make Me a Blessing"

I found this joke on the Internet: While working on a lesson in world religions, a kindergarten teacher asked her students to bring something related to their families' faith to class. At the appropriate time, she asked the students to come forward and share with the rest of the students.

The first child said, "I am Muslim, and this is my prayer rug."

The second child said, "I am Jewish, and this is my Star of David."

The third child said, "I am Catholic, and this is my rosary."

The final child said, "I am Southern Baptist, and this is my casserole dish."[1]

Casserole dishes are ubiquitous in Southern Baptist life. From dinner on the grounds to fellowship suppers to funerals, those homemade concoctions of meat and potatoes, chicken and rice, or tuna and noodles show up all over. To a great extent, the phenomenon is rooted in southern culture (Baptist or not). Casseroles have been around for centuries across a wide variety of cultures. The term refers to foods cooked slowly together in an oven or to the dish in which they're cooked. What we think of as casseroles became part of American cuisine in the nineteenth century, but their popularity increased during the Depression, when they became an economical way to stretch scarce food resources.

The 1940 edition of *The American Women's Cook Book* notes these advantages to casseroles:

> THE CASSEROLE SAVES DISH-WASHING, because it makes it possible to bring food to the table in the dish in which it was cooked. Frequently, also, it contains a "one-dish meal" which eliminates all but the one cooking dish. THE CASSEROLE MAKES IT POSSIBLE TO USE LEFT-OVERS in attractive, palatable combinations, to cook tough meats tender, and to prepare vegetables in an almost unlimited variety of ways. Any vegetable may be boiled, steamed, baked, scalloped or creamed, and cabbage, cucumbers, eggplant, onions, peppers, potatoes or tomatoes may be stuffed and cooked in the casserole. FOOD COOKED IN THIS WAY NEEDS LITTLE WATCHING, it may be kept warm and still attractive if the meal is delayed, and there is no loss of vegetable or meat juices. These juices contain a valuable part of the food which is often thrown away, especially in the case of vegetables that are boiled. A WHOLE MEAL MAY BE COOKING IN THE OVEN in the casserole while the oven is being used for some other purpose, such as baking cookies.[2]

Women all over the country made casseroles, but this economical and convenient dish became embedded in southern culture. Deborah Knott, the protagonist in the mystery novels of North Carolinian Margaret Maron (who is not a Baptist), always keeps a casserole or two in the freezer in case of an emergency requiring her to take a dish to someone who is sick or to the family of someone who has died. One group of food scholars writes, "The things we eat can say a great deal about us—who we are, where we came from, our current social, cultural, economic, and religious circumstances, and what our aspirations might be."[3]

In the South, women are still the ones who make casseroles. They are the ones who organize meals for the family when someone is ill, and they are the ones who drop off covered dishes whenever there's a death in the family. For the women in my research, the activity of preparing and providing food is a ministry. It is a way to nourish soul as well as body. Anthropologist Sidney W. Mintz explains, "Eating is never a 'purely biological' activity. . . . The foods eaten have histories associated with the pasts of those who eat them; the techniques employed to find, process, prepare, serve, and consume the foods are all culturally variable, with histories of their own. Nor is the food ever simply eaten; its consumption is always conditioned by meaning."[4] Daniel Sack asks why American Protestants have used so many resources to feed their own members, "most of whom were perfectly capable of feeding themselves?"

He answers his own question: "It's because Americans go to church for more than teaching and prayer. They go looking for community." He explains that although food-centered social events are not religious in themselves, "the meals are a place where religious identity is shaped, community is built, and memories are created. They may not be religious, but they're not just another meal."[5]

Kate Campbell, a folk musician and daughter of a Southern Baptist preacher, grew up in Nashville during the civil rights movement. Her music reflects her concerns with social justice and faith as well as her southern roots. Influenced by southern writers Eudora Welty and Flannery O'Connor, Kate's spin on life in the South includes the slightly odd and the often humorous. To a great extent, her song "Funeral Food" captures the significance of something so seemingly insignificant as casserole dishes:

Aunt Fidelia brought the rolls
With her green bean casserole
The widow Smith down the street
Dropped by a bowl of butter beans
Plastic cups and silverware
Lime green Tupperware everywhere
Pass the chicken, pass the pie
We sure eat good when someone dies

Funeral food
It's so good for the soul
Funeral food
Fills you up down to your toes
Funeral food
Funeral food

There sits mean ole Uncle Bob
Gnawing on a corn on the cob
And who's that walking through the door
I don't think I've ever seen him before
Isn't it a shame she passed away
She made the best chocolate cake
Let's hit the line a second time
We sure eat good when someone dies

Everybody's here for the feast
But come next week where will they be?[6]

As I was finishing this book, I experienced the importance of funeral food personally. My friend Tisa Lewis's daddy died unexpectedly, late on a Sunday night in September 2006. Her family has been my adopted family since 1982, when Tisa and I were in seminary together. I immediately booked a flight to South Carolina and arrived early Tuesday morning. By the time I got there, the women of Batesburg had already gone into action. Tisa's mother, Joan Lewis, was surrounded by women friends and relatives, most of whom were in her Sunday school class or WMU group. For three solid days, a steady procession of women came to the house, each bearing food. Out in the gazebo sat a loaner refrigerator sent over by the funeral home. It was as crammed full as the refrigerator in the kitchen. Fried chicken, green beans, potato salad, creamed corn, macaroni and cheese, coconut cake, banana pudding—all homemade southern comfort foods—provided real comfort through those first days of grief. Each dish represented the community's care and concern for the Lewis family. Women also pitched in to help in other ways, doing whatever had to be done. The woman who lived next door mowed Joan's grass and swept her sidewalks. Joan's sister-in-law Cindy kept the kitchen clean. Other women dropped off paper plates and napkins. All the women sat and talked with Joan and the rest of the family, listening to their grief and their stories. Again and again Joan said, "Bobby always did for others, and now they're doing for me." By Tuesday evening, the house and the funeral home were full of flowers, symbolizing support, community, and friendship. I watched, astounded, as the women just came in and took control. They created a place of safety and support to give Joan time and space to grieve. Without waiting to be told or asked, they did what needed to be done.

For Southern Baptist women, being aware of the daily physical needs of the people in their community is as important as any of the other tasks of church members. They take seriously the Bible's injunctions to feed the hungry, clothe the naked, and care for the sick. Interestingly, most of the women I talked to didn't necessarily see these as women's tasks; men, they explained to me, just wouldn't think to do such things. Most of my participants firmly believe that women and men are different—essentially, inherently different. They emphatically do not believe that this makes women less than men; in fact, they acknowledge that women are just better at some things than men are. However, the things they identify as women's strong suits generally fall into the traditional categories of feminine traits—nurturing, caring, listening, performing the emotional work of human existence. But the women like being good at these things. They highly value their nurturing abilities, and they know that the work of nurturance is essential to human physical, emotional, and spiritual well-being. Laura Gene York, a member of Travis Avenue Baptist Church in Fort Worth, told me how women took care of her family when she fell ill as a child. Her father was not a Christian at the time, she explained, "but he saw the people bringing the things in when I was so sick, and he couldn't believe it. For about two weeks, somebody was bringing food to our house every day, and he'd say, 'Why, I just can't believe they'd do this,' and so that was an inspiration to him."

Providing meals and other forms of nurture is an important part of how these women embody gender and express their complex identities as Southern Baptist women. Deborah Lupton explains, "Food and other eating habits are banal practices of everyday life. . . . This apparent banality, however, is deceptive. Food and eating habits and preferences are not simply matters of 'fueling' ourselves. . . . Food and eating are central to our subjectivity, or sense of self."[7] Kim Heath, a student at McAfee School of Theology, said, "It seems to me to be a very southern thing that all of our activities revolve around food. We plan church events, and there's got to be Dessert Fellowship or something; there has to be some kind of food involved because that's what brings people. And it goes into forming my identity as well, I think, just like manners and way of life, and it's completely shaped who I am." Homemaker Elaine Richards offered this explanation:

> I was raised in a small, small country church, and being raised in a small Baptist church you're raised to know how to treat people and how to give to other people. You're raised knowing what to do for people. And you're raised knowing to always be a servant to other people. You grow up knowing what casseroles to cook. When somebody dies, this is what you're supposed to do, and this is a part of your heritage and part of your culture; it's just second nature. Nobody can take care of anybody better than Southern Baptist women. And I have friends here in Fort Worth that weren't raised in small Southern Baptist churches, and when there's a death they will call and say, "Okay, what do Southern Baptist women do?" because they need to know how you're supposed to move in and help the family during a tragedy. And I think that's something we just all know, naturally. You just know what it is you're supposed to do to comfort and to help people, and it's just like breathing.

Southern Womanhood

The South and Southern Baptists are intimately connected. Sarah Frances Anders told me, "I definitely think there's a lot of southern in Southern Baptist." Similarly, Amy Mears said, "It's very difficult to separate southern culture and Southern Baptist culture." Likewise, Leah McCullough said, "You didn't separate 'southern' and 'Baptist.' It was just a way of life." Even Southern Baptists who live outside the South are affected by southern culture to a certain extent, since it permeates the programs and curricular materials of Southern Baptists. These people, however, tend to think of themselves as Christians who just happen to be Southern Baptists but could easily be some other denomination. In fact, Melodie Yocum, a drama professor at California Baptist University, became a Southern Baptist when she married one. She grew up in a nondenominational church in California and found that Southern Baptist churches weren't all that different from the ones of her childhood—except for limiting women's roles a bit more. She believes that Southern Baptist women in California may be less constrained by gender roles than women in the South. "You don't have nearly that stigma that the pastor's wife has to fit into a certain mold, and the women are always responsible for the food," she explained. Melodie appreciates Southern Baptists but still doesn't feel a "strong denominational allegiance." She said that people in California don't necessarily look for a church of a particular denomination; they look for a church that's a good fit for them, and if happens to be Baptist, so be it. Mary Key, another native Californian who became a Southern Baptist at age twelve, agreed. "I'm not the born and bred [Southern Baptist with a] diehard allegiance." She laughed when she told me that she often feels like Southern Baptists in the South still think of California as a "pioneer" or "frontier" area for Southern Baptist work.

For Baptists in the South, however, southern culture and Southern Baptist identity are thoroughly intertwined. Julie Pennington-Russell grew up in the South, attended seminary and pastored in California, and is now a pastor in Waco, Texas. Julie told me, "I think that in southern culture, often Christianity is sort of in the water; you know, it's in the air. I almost want to go as far as to say that it's not really something that you have to work hard to choose. It's just, everything is painted with a Christian brush, a Baptist brush." She added, "I think southern culture has really aided and abetted this Baptist notion of biggest and best." Peggy Sanderford Ponder said something similar: "To be a Christian in the South is a cultural thing. You go to church not because you believe, but because that's the thing to do." Being Southern Baptist and being southern are not quite synonymous, but they're close. Certainly, Southern Baptist culture and southern culture both leave their mark on Southern Baptist women.

Sometimes my Oregonian friends don't understand me. Even though I left the South almost twenty-five years ago (and I made a concerted effort to leave behind some its more problematic gender ideals), I still feel compelled to wait on my guests hand and foot. And I'm mortified if someone drops by and my house isn't spotless. I still wait until everyone has food before I begin eating, and when I invite people over for a meal on my deck, it's to cook out, not to barbecue (I have often tried to explain to them that *barbecue* is a noun, not a verb, consisting of meat—preferably pulled pork—that is smoked and slathered in sauce). I still say things like, "Is anyone else a little cool in here?" when what I really mean is, "I'm freezing and I'd like to shut that window." When people ask me a question, I usually answer with a story. As Paula Sheridan told me, southerners' use of the language is "not only our consonants and vowels; it is the way we think, in metaphor and story."

My favorite television show of all time was *Designing Women*. I wanted to be Julia Sugarbaker—the thoroughly classy, thoroughly graceful southern lady meets the liberated feminist. She could slice up a foolish man trying to pick her up, and he wouldn't know what hit him until twenty minutes later. Her elegant tirades led her more reticent friends to label her "the Terminator." In many ways, Julia embodied the paradoxes of contemporary southern women, and although some feminists criticized the show for not going far enough in its critique of white patriarchy, for many of us, the show represented a form of feminism that made sense in that context. To me, Julia Sugarbaker was exactly what I expected a southern feminist to look like—Scarlett O'Hara meets Gloria Steinem.

A Tool in the Tool Kit

Understanding southern womanhood begins in the Old South of the colonial period. Constructed around notions of gentility, hospitality, and separate spheres for women and men, colonial ideals of elite, white southern womanhood continue to shape modern-day concepts. When I asked my participants how southern culture has shaped their identities, many spoke of the culture's emphasis on women's submissiveness. For example, Beth Duke explained, "I think the submissiveness is in some way ingrained, even though you can be a little bit sassy. That's kind of ingrained in being a southern woman; you just smile, and you're just always charming." Of course, corollary to that submissiveness is women's ability to get what they want. Some see that ability as a form of manipulation; others see it as an act of resourcefulness.

Carolyn Blevins, a professor of religion at Carson-Newman College, told me about a neighbor of hers who expressed a willingness to obey her husband even if he told her not to go to church. When Carolyn asked if she would obey her husband rather than obey God, the woman replied that if she obeyed her husband, she believed that God would hold her husband responsible, not her. Carolyn was shocked by the response, but it helped her realize that some women hide behind submissiveness as a way to avoid responsibility. "I think there are some women," she said, "who are very comfortable when the church makes the decisions, when the men make the decisions; they're very comfortable with that, and it kind of lets them off the hook." Unfortunately, I also saw evidence of that in some of my interviews. Some participants were only too happy to have men take on the responsibility of decision making, freeing the women from any accountability for situations occurring in their lives, their families, and their churches.

Nonetheless, many of these women find ways to work around male control, often espousing submissiveness all the while. Nancy Ammerman explained that when she was working on her dissertation, she witnessed explicit teachings in one church about women's submission. "But," she added, "what I also watched was women very explicitly teaching each other how to get around that."

"Was that occurring through informal things, or was it Sunday school?" I asked.

She replied, "It was Wednesday night prayer circle: how to pray your husband into the right decision."

Kate Campbell asserted, "Southern women actually are very powerful. On one side, it looks like they are accepting a certain system—which they are—but they know how to use that system much more effectively, I think, than women outside the South. And have used that for years to get what they want because they can say, 'Well, sure honey, I'll get you a drink.' And then, 'Will you buy me a fur coat?'"

Paula Sheridan has observed this phenomenon too. She said of her own family, "Everybody acted like the men were in charge, but everybody knew the women really ran the show, and you didn't mess with them." She referred to the scene in *My Big Fat Greek Wedding* where the women "get the daddy in the booth in the restaurant, and they manipulate him into something. . . . Well, the women planned the conversation, but they all acted like it was his idea, and then they turned around and applauded him for being so bright. And I've said to my students, because we've watched it together, 'I've seen that story a hundred times in my own family.'" But, Paula added, "that's one of the by-products of oppression." For these women, using manipulative tactics becomes "a way of carving out their own agency."

Amy Mears struggles with "the patterns of southern womanhood that achieve big things, but without . . . much integrity." For example, she asked, "Do I risk shunning southern grace and forthrightly demanding what needs to happen or asking for what I want, knowing that the odds are much lower that I'll get them that way; or do I play the southern game, and do the ends justify the means?" Amy is a pastor, but she wonders whether she also needs to do all the things expected of a pastor's wife, since she's female. "I was raised to come and bring a dish and stay until the party's over and help clean up," she explained. That's what she watched her mother—a pastor's wife—do, and she wonders whether she should do the same. Judy Baker worries that southern faith may be built more on politeness than on justice. "It's one thing to be polite," she explained, "but you can dismiss people while being polite, and justice calls on us not to dismiss people."

The tension of Southern Baptist women's cultural situation creates an interesting and sometimes frustrating dilemma, as Amy Mears expressed. Because women are expected to be nice and submissive, being confrontational or demanding is a cultural faux pas that is unlikely to result in a positive outcome. (As I discuss in chapter 7, this disdain for confrontation is a primary reason why Southern Baptist women distance themselves from feminism.) The other option, which is more effective but more manipulative, may also be a form of competency developed in an oppressive situation to provide southern women with the space in which to exercise agency. I certainly experience this ability as a tool in my tool kit, at the ready should other options fail.

Scarlett O'Hara with a Different Dress

Many participants also discussed the importance of being ladylike in the South. Nancy Moore noted these rules of southern culture: "Keeping your dress over your knees, and your legs together, all those little things that we were taught, had to do with being a real southern lady." She went on to parallel those lessons with Ibsen's *A Doll's House*. Peggy

Sanderford Ponder pointed out, "You dress up on Sundays because it's the thing to do; it's not because you want to. You dress up to do whatever because it's a very southern thing. Scarlett O'Hara—we just wear different dresses." Karrie Oertli once perceived southern women as very cultured. They "were models that gave me a sense of propriety and manners and dress; and a model, in a way, of being cultured. Of course, now I think very differently about that, but that was very appealing to me. I think it offered a kind of solace and a boundaried existence. I knew the rules, and if I knew the rules, I could be in this group, and belonging was really very much a part of my experience. It also became the bane of my existence, because I found myself not wanting to be bound by those rules, and there I was, bound by those rules." Sara Wisdom, who directed the Northwest WMU for many years, pointed out obvious differences in southern and northwestern cultures. For instance, when she went back to Birmingham, Alabama, for WMU meetings, proper attire was an issue. Before one meeting, she was told that the dress would be casual. But "what does casual mean?" she asked. "To us [northwesterners], casual means jeans and a T-shirt! But to them, casual dress means they come in business casual, which means nice pantsuits, not warmups." Charla Milligan frets that she's expected to be the perfect wife, mother, and minister—"and look pretty while you're doing it."

Karen Massey pointed out how the southern emphasis on being ladylike played out for Southern Baptist girls: "Women in southern culture, when you're a teenager you know that the greatest thing you can do as a female is be a cheerleader and win a beauty pageant. You're not told that explicitly; you just know it. So, like Acteens, you're queen, and queen with a scepter, and queen regent, and it was like a pageant with all the girls walking around and parading across the front of the church."

"I took a charm class at church," I added.

"Oh, that's good," Karen replied, laughing.

"It turned out well," I noted with some sarcasm.

Pastor Sarah Shelton talked about the difficulty of attending associational meetings. Some of her church members offered to accompany her to provide moral support, but she realized that she needed to go alone and stand up for herself.

"We haven't been taught to do that," I said, stating the obvious.

"We haven't," Sarah concurred, "In fact, [standing up for oneself] was considered to be rude and not socially acceptable. I think trying to find out how to do that, and how to do it with some grace, is pretty exhausting sometimes."

"Do you consider yourself a feminist?" I asked.

"I don't think I did, just because [the term] 'feminist' was so angry and militant. I'm probably too southern and genteel."

Lynda Weaver-Williams noted that being taught to be "nice" (which, in her southern drawl, she exaggerated—and the transcriptionist spelled as *nass*) can be detrimental. "We have confused being nice with being honest, truthful, and kind," she explained. "I think that being raised in the South, taught to try to look pretty and be nice and don't make trouble and those kind of things, sometimes got wrapped up with 'Go to church, look nice, don't get dirty, don't be loud, don't run up and down the aisles,' you know. Not that I didn't do all those things—we all did, or most of us probably did. But I think the message of Jesus could become simply, 'Be nice.'"

Southern Hospitality

The participants noted that the providing of hospitality is another important characteristic of southern women. Priscilla Denham grew up loving the graciousness of the South. "That you are hospitable to strangers made all the sense in the world to me," she declared. Drawing from her study of antebellum history, Cynthia A. Kierner argues, "Domestic hospitality—the offering of food, drink, lodging, and entertainment to unknown and familiar persons of varying status—was common among southerners."[8] She explains that hospitality in the southern colonies was a particular obligation of the elite, used to reinforce their class status and cause others to be indebted to them. In addition, because of the great distances between farms and plantations, family and friends had to travel far to visit, so they would likely stay for several days once they arrived. Kierner notes that writings of the time indicate a lack of inns in the South because southerners' hospitality made them unnecessary.

The role of southern women in hospitality was rooted in their connection to the domestic sphere. They were responsible for food and housekeeping, while the men were responsible for earning the income that maintained the home financially. Hospitality was also closely connected with notions of Christian virtue, which was typically characterized as a feminine attribute.[9] Consequently, the expectation arose that because women were the moral guardians of the home, they could act as a regenerative force in society as well. Kierner notes that in contrast to this image of genteel white womanhood, pejorative images of women of color were common in the eighteenth century.[10]

The ideals of southern hospitality and southern womanhood persist, having made their way into other social classes and other races following the dismantling of the plantation system. On the whole, however, hospitality remains a gendered system, with women retaining responsibility for food and the household, along with providing a positive moral influence in the private and public spheres. Again and again, my southern participants connected their concerns for hospitality, nurture, and kindness to their roots in southern culture.

As I conducted my research, I was struck by the expansiveness of southern women's hospitality. Everywhere I went, I was made to feel welcome—and I was fed! Though personally touched, even overwhelmed, by their outpouring of generosity, as a researcher, I had to step back and examine these acts as part of the material realities of their lives. When I did that, I could see that their kindness to me (in many cases, a total stranger) was a result of the way they have constructed their identities. They have taken the expectation that women nurture and turned it into a calling.

My journey into this research began in Batesburg, South Carolina, Tisa's hometown. I asked her mother, Joan, if she would organize a group of women from her church, the First Baptist Church of Batesburg, for a focus group. What happened next was indicative of the response I would receive from many women when I requested their help. Joan invited women from her Woman's Missionary Union group to her house for a focus group and dessert. Joan's house is always spotless, but on the day of the focus group, she used extra vigilance in making sure that every surface was dusted and every fixture gleamed. Ten women showed up, and as we sat in Joan's living room (with lavalier microphone cords running all over the place), they told me about being Southern Baptist. Afterward, Joan (who is a fabulous cook) brought out her peanut butter pie—a frozen confection of chocolate ice cream and peanut butter in a chocolate crust—with coffee or iced tea. (In the South, to say "iced tea" is redundant. Tea is always iced tea, and it's very, very sweet. I realized the extent to which I'd become an Oregonian when I recently ordered tea in a Georgia restaurant and, without thinking, proceeded to empty a packet of artificial sweetener into it. The face I made when I tasted it made my mother laugh. I had forgotten that, in the South, tea is, by definition, sweet.)

In J. D. Salinger's *Franny and Zooey,* Franny is a brilliant college student who returns home to face a spiritual crisis. Her very average mother, Bessie, doesn't know what to do with her, so she keeps trying to feed her chicken soup, which Franny rejects with all the weighty angst of young adulthood. At last, Franny's older brother Zooey confronts her and tells her that she doesn't even recognize the religious action that's going on around her. "You don't even have sense enough to drink when somebody brings you a cup of consecrated chicken soup—which is the only kind of chicken soup Bessie ever brings to anybody around this madhouse. . . . How in hell are you going to recognize a legitimate holy man when you see one if you don't even know a cup of consecrated chicken soup when it's right in front of your face?"[11] I thought about Zooey's words as the women who participated in my research fed me. I was the recipient of consecrated peanut butter pie, and thanks to having read Salinger, I was aware of it.

During my quest for women to interview, I talked to one of my former professors, John Hendrix, who had recently retired from a pastorate in Mississippi. When he learned that I was going to be in Nashville, he recommended that I call Pat Brown, the librarian at what's now known as Lifeway. Pat gave me the name and number of another woman at Lifeway, who in turn put me in touch with Tammy Hayes, a member of First Baptist Church in Hendersonville, Tennessee. Tammy graciously volunteered to help me set up a focus group and even offered to invite the women over to her house and make dessert for them. A few days before I left for Nashville, Tammy called me back. "Why don't you come on over early," she suggested, "and I'll make dinner for both of us." We ate spaghetti and salad and French bread in her lovely kitchen and discovered that one of her bridesmaids had been a friend of mine in seminary.

Julie Pennington-Russell is pastor of Calvary Baptist Church in Waco, Texas, a large Cooperative Baptist Fellowship congregation. I met Julie when I was teaching at California Baptist College and she was pastor of Nineteenth Avenue Baptist Church in San Francisco. A lot of female students from Truett Seminary attend Julie's church (Truett is one of the relatively new moderate seminaries that opened after the fundamentalists took control of the six Southern Baptist seminaries), so she invited a group of them over to her house for a focus group. I went to Julie's house early so we could catch up, and I stood at her kitchen counter chatting with her as she made consecrated pigs in a blanket and cut up carrot and celery sticks.

A number of women in Fort Worth, Texas, made me feel welcome. Shirley Powell made sure that cookies and drinks were available when I interviewed women at Travis Avenue Baptist Church. Lilla Schmelte-kopf made pies to serve the women from Broadway Baptist Church when I interviewed them in her home. Jorene Swift, minister of congregational care at Broadway, is part of a group of women who gather once a month for a birthday celebration. After our interview, she invited me to join them for dinner (she even paid) at a fabulous Italian restaurant. I'm not particularly outgoing among people I don't know, but these women made me feel like part of the group from the moment we sat down at the table.

I was going to Orlando, Florida, for the annual meeting of the National Women's Studies Association, so I decided to do a focus group while I was there. I called Kate Campbell, whose father, Jim Henry, is pastor of a 12,000-member Southern Baptist church there. Kate put me in touch with Jennifer Adamson, director of women's ministries at the church, who agreed to organize a lunch for some of the women congregants. When I got to the church, Jennifer met me at the door and took me back to a small, beautiful dining room. The table was elegantly set, and a gracious wait staff served us tasty grilled chicken salad, delicious rolls, and iced tea (of course), followed by key lime pie—the real thing!

The Clique, in particular, took me in, as they have throughout my life. Nancy Moore made lemon bars, and we sipped English Breakfast in china teacups. In the afternoon, Alicia Bennett offered me a nice, cold glass of lemonade. Shelby Christie couldn't entertain me at her home because she was having some work done, so she took me out to lunch instead. The first focus group met at Judy Masters's house after enjoying lunch at Red Lobster to celebrate Kayne Carter's and Lidia Abrams's birthdays. The next trip, I started my interviews at Doris Bailey's house. She tried to feed me, but since I'd already promised Shelby that I'd have lunch at her house, Doris insisted that I take a slice of homemade coconut cake for Shelby and me for dessert. She didn't have to ask twice, and I wasn't really surprised when the "slice" turned out to be about a third of the cake.

Most recently, at her invitation, I traveled to Fort Worth to interview Dorothy Patterson, author, speaker, professor, and wife of Southwestern Baptist Theological Seminary president Paige Patterson. Dorothy provided lodging for me in the presidential suite of the seminary's guest housing and invited me to lunch before our interview. Paige joined us as well, along with Candi Finch, Dorothy's assistant and a PhD student in systematic theology at the seminary. Even though we stand at very different points along the theological and social spectrums, we enjoyed talking with one another and connecting at a very basic human level over a meal. I felt welcomed and cared for, just as I had in all my other encounters with Southern Baptist women.

Why are these stories important? They speak to how these women construct their identities. Feeding me and ensuring my comfort weren't simply acts of hospitality. They were statements about the kind of people these women want to be—people who give priority to relationships, care, and nurture. Most interesting is the fact that theology doesn't matter. Whether their churches or their personal views are fundamentalist, conservative, moderate, or liberal, all these women opened their arms and their lives to me. I was particularly struck by the amount of trust they vested in me. They told their stories, and they trusted me not to make them look foolish or naive or victimized. Their willingness to feed me and to talk to me indicates the extent to which they have developed a strong sense of self that is reflected in their way of being in the world.

Community and Women's Friendships

When I read *The Divine Secrets of the Ya-Ya Sisterhood*, I thought of the Clique. They are Ya-Yas with a Southern Baptist twist. Part Red Hat Society and part women's missionary organization, they are a tight-knit group of women bound by love, geography, social class, and faith. When Janet Lockhart transcribed their second focus group interview, she e-mailed me and wrote, "Wow! I wish I had a group like this!"

Friendship is a form of social organization that meets a variety of emotional, social, cognitive, and material needs and takes on a reality that is greater than the individuals involved in it.[12] For women, friendships are located in the broader social and political contexts of power and patriarchy, which give shape to friendships in relation to marital status, economic dependence or independence, and social class. Additionally, women with similar social and cultural locations are likely to share values that bind them in friendship. For the women I spoke with, relationships are absolutely essential to their understanding of self and their sense of themselves as Christians. Friendships are a vehicle through which Christian life is nurtured and lived. For many of the participants, this sense of relational faith began in childhood with their own mothers.

Godly Mothers

When I asked my participants about Southern Baptist women who had influenced or inspired them, many of them told me stories of mothers and grandmothers who had introduced them to Christian faith by word and by example. These women formed close connections with their mothers and grandmothers, who represented their first experiences of Christian community.

Becca Gurney's mother was a big influence in her life. "She never finished college," Becca related, "certainly didn't go to seminary, and hasn't been ordained, but [she] was a partner minister with my dad all along, and appointed by the mission board, but not ever paid. And her perseverance and her sense of calling has been an influence, definitely, in my life." Heather King said, "My own mother's imprint on my spiritual walk and journey is immeasurable. Her spiritual walk and testimony make her one of those 'unknown' giants in the faith." Zana Kizzee said, "I have a godly mother who led each one of us, when it was our time, to the Lord."

In the Latino churches that Lucy Elizalde attended, pastors often didn't have seminary degrees. Neither did Lucy's mother, who was on the church staff, but when Lucy felt called to ministry, her mother supported her decision. Her mother told her, "I dedicated you to the Lord when you were a little girl, and I always knew that he had great things for you; but it's a little scary to see you going into ministry. Kind of exciting at the same time!" Lucy's mother believes that she's grown herself through Lucy's experiences.

Debra Owens-Hughes called her mother truly inspiring. "She came from a family that had nothing, very little love, and no faith. A WMUer from a SBC church was their neighbor and began taking my mom to church when she was young. My mom became a believer, worked her way through a master's in nursing and through seminary so that she could serve the Lord in Africa. She loves WMU and helped start many women's groups in Africa, groups that were very mission-minded. My mother's love of the Lord was evident in her practice and in her daily life."

Jean Cullen's mother held leadership positions in the church while Jean was growing up. "When I was in seventh grade," she recalled, her mother went back to school and "got her doctorate. We graduated at the same time; and to see a woman in her forties go and get her doctorate when her kids were teenagers said a lot to me about being a Christian woman." Jean's mother showed her that a woman "can continue to grow and live out her calling and be whatever she wanted to be."

When asked whether Southern Baptist women had influenced or inspired her, Louisa Smith replied, "Certainly my mother, grandmother, and the women who taught GAs, Acteens, and Sunday school. They represented Southern Baptist life to me, at least as a young girl growing up."

Church as Community

Christian educator John Westerhoff claims that to be Christian is to be part of a community. One cannot be Christian alone, he contends.[13] Most of what I remember about my childhood in Southern Baptist churches is connected to that sense of community, of belonging. When I was a preschooler, the pastor would enter the church from the back and walk down the aisle to the podium, shaking hands with people in the pews as he passed. I always waited anxiously at the end of our pew near the back of the sanctuary to shake the pastor's hand, but one Sunday he missed me; he didn't shake my hand. I was distraught. As far as I was concerned, church could not begin until the pastor shook my hand. I must have made a fuss, because my father (who I'm sure was mortified) carried me down the aisle, marched up the stairs to where the pastor sat in his chair, and essentially thrust me toward the pastor. I held out my hand and, smiling, the pastor shook it. I was then content to return to our pew, secure in my knowledge of my affirmed place in the faith community.

As I grew, I developed most of my closest friendships at church. After all, I spent a lot of time with these people—Sunday mornings, Sunday nights, Wednesday nights, youth camp, youth events. By the time I was in high school, a group of us had formed a traveling evangelism team: David preached, Greg led the choir (which was the rest of us), and we traveled to tiny churches all over north Georgia leading revival services (at the time, I must admit, it didn't occur to me to think about the gender arrangements of the team). I looked forward to church, probably as much for the social needs it met as for the spiritual ones. As a raised-right adolescent, I didn't dance; I didn't go to R-rated movies; I didn't stay out late. Church was the safe venue that both my parents and I could agree on, and since my church friends were the daughters of my mother's friends, they were a safe bet not to lead me into temptation.

For Southern Baptist women, friendships are an integral part of their experience of faith and church. For many women, amidst the demands of marriage, motherhood, housework, and career, church provides a necessary site for the development of and participation in a sense of community. A number of participants told me that they attend church because of the community they find there. Karrie Oertli said, "[The church] provided a sense of community and security for me during a very, very lonely and insecure time in my life." Travis Avenue Baptist Church member Elaine Richards explained, "I love my church. It keeps me grounded. Because the world is so crazy and so wild, and this is where I come for peace." Fellow member Shirley Powell added, "I feel happy here. Travis is a warm and welcoming family church. It just welcomes you in the door, just like if you were having a homecoming and you walked in the door of your extended family. You're welcome there, and that's the way our church is." Missy Loper of First Baptist Church in Hendersonville, Tennessee, said, "My church is my family." Melissa Ashley, also of Hendersonville, agreed, "I always thought of [my church] as a home away from home."

On my second visit to Fort Worth, I sat down with the Broadway Baptist Church birthday group at Lilla Schmeltekopf's beautiful home. I asked the women what their church means to them. Ginny Hickman said that church means community to her. "It's a support system," she continued, "within a context of shared values, but also a community where there's a pretty good respect for values that are different. It's the place that helps me keep my perspective." Cindy Johnson added, "I think it's both a place that supports me as I try to live a life of faith and one that challenges me to do the same." Lilla pointed out, "For me, it's a place that calls me to worship regularly, reminds me to worship in my life all that time. That's important." Then I asked what they gain from participating in their church. Jimmie Nell Galbraith responded, "Strength and comfort. Shared friendships. Encouragement." When I asked what their church gains from their participation in it, Ginny laughed and said, "That's a question for someone else!" Pat Smith answered, "I think that whatever we receive is also what we give, and that's why it's shared, because of the sharing of values and the encouragement and the camaraderie.

In another group, seminary student Kim Heath explained, "There's a community to rely on, a community to be a part of, a community to learn with, all those things." Candice Christian reported that First Baptist Church of Orlando, Florida, has become "a wonderful place of community" for her. She appreciates that the women in the church don't judge her in any way. She was drawn to the church by the "very warm, caring, growing atmosphere," and having other women around her who are seeking the same spiritual life has "just been wonderful." Jennifer Adamson, who is on the staff of First Baptist, added that her most memorable experience in Southern Baptist churches is "the richness of the community. We've been in several churches through my lifetime, but I've found it to be very consistent, just the community and the encouragement for Christian growth."

Likewise, members of the First Baptist Church in Batesburg, South Carolina, consider the community they experience in church as absolutely essential. Joan Lewis explained, "When I don't go to church, my whole week does not go right. And I always like to go to church, and I tell my children to go to church, and I enjoy Sunday school. I enjoy the friends at church, the people." Sara Fox added, "I'm never happier than when I am in church. It is my life, really." Several members recounted the centrality of church in their social lives as children growing up in the rural South. Jean Gaston recalled, "We lived out in the country, worked on a farm, and the only place we ever went was church, our social life, everything." Annie Cockrell, too, was raised in the country. "Like Jean, we went to church on Wednesday night and Sunday, and the preacher came home periodically to eat with individuals, and that was just the life of our week. I love the Lord, and that's why." Grace Geddes especially enjoyed Sundays because her mother made fried chicken and cake for lunch after church. Helen Winstead added, "I grew up in the church, and that church was our social life. I went to a small school, a one-teacher school, and when you go to church on the weekends, that's where you get your spiritual support." Paige Trotter noted the importance of being at church: "For anyone to say, 'It's not important. They're not going to miss me if I'm not there,' is just incorrect thinking. We're many members, one body. We need to be there; we need to support each other; we need to worship the Lord together. We need to do this together; being a Christian is not a Lone Ranger thing; it takes everybody. So everyone is important."

I met with some of the women of Second Ponce de Leon Baptist Church, located in an affluent area of Atlanta. We gathered in one of the Sunday school classrooms, where we sat in a circle. The six white women range in age from twenty-eight to sixty-five; five are married, and one is a widow. They are theological moderates and political conservatives (the church itself was decidedly moderate during the Controversy). All of them are college graduates. Only one of them currently works outside the home, although two have done so in the past, and one manages a home office for her husband. They had the following conversation about the importance of the church as community:

PATTY LAMB: [Church] is my stabilizing force. It keeps me grounded.

DANIELLE MONGIN: It's my whole life. You take this away, and I don't know who my friends are, what I'm supposed to be doing this week.

JANET DICKERSON: When I say "my church," I feel it way down in here. Passionate.

MELISSA HELLEM: I've been here since I was six months of age, so it's pretty much the backbone of me. It's where my great-aunt and my great-uncle, my grandmother, my parents still attend here and were married here. My Catholic husband was baptized here, and we have dedicated three children here. We had, at one point, four generations of us under this steeple.

"What do you gain from participating in the church?" I asked the others.

ANGELYN TURNER: I get a real peak, a feeling of belonging. I had that in the church I grew up in, and when I came here, the first Sunday I was here—I was twenty-two years old at the time—and I bet I had six or eight people around me speak to me, and somebody called me on Sunday afternoon. A week later, I was in the singles group; they welcomed me with open arms. Just a feeling of belonging.

The Intimidating Women

My experiences at Southern Baptist Theological Seminary were at the other end of the spectrum. Women were a minority in most seminary classes, and we bonded in solidarity through our common experiences. Fortunately, the numbers of women enrolling in theological education had increased dramatically, and we constituted about one-third of the student body at Southern. I lived on the fourth floor of Mullins Hall with twenty-nine other women. Most of us had grown up in Southern Baptist churches and had experienced a call to ministry in those churches. We were idealistic, committed, and probably a more than a little naive. We believed that because God had called us, Southern Baptists would welcome our ministry. So when we arrived at Southern Seminary during the very early days of the Controversy, we never dreamed that the denomination would change so much in just a few short years. We embraced the seminary experience with gusto, convinced of our right to be there. And, living in such close quarters, we embraced one another as friends and colleagues.

On the fourth floor, we shared a bathroom with three shower stalls and a single kitchen in which each of us had one-third of a refrigerator shelf and one-third of a cabinet shelf. Of course, when all you can afford is macaroni and cheese, you don't need a lot of food storage space. Tisa and I often say that more of our seminary education took place around the kitchen table than in the classroom. The intensity of theological education can be daunting, even in the most supportive environment. For us women, the added burden of being female in a traditionally male academic environment was palpable. But at the end of a day of classes in biblical studies, church history, Christian education, systematic theology, and ethics, we gathered in the kitchen and argued theology and biblical interpretation, lamented the latest dating fiasco, and shared our dreams of ministry. We usually ate in three shifts, because we couldn't all fit in the kitchen at the same time. I remember Micki Davis would start out with the first group at around 5:00, but she ate so slowly that she'd still be there when the third group came in.

We celebrated everybody's birthday in that kitchen too. Usually the roommate would arrange the party, and we'd try to make it a surprise by hiding in a closet or throwing the party a week early. I was there for Tisa's twenty-sixth birthday party in that kitchen, and just last week I threw her a fiftieth birthday party at my house in Oregon. During seminary days, no one had much money, so Tisa and I would save all week so that on Friday we could ride our bicycles to Burger King for a ninety-nine-cent Whopper, followed by a dollar movie at the Uptown Theater. In the span of a couple of months, several of us were dumped by the seminary men we'd been dating because, as they put it, we were "too intimidating." After that, we became known as "The Intimidating Women of Fourth Floor Mullins." In those two to three years, we built a web of relationships that has lasted, in different forms, for twenty-five years. We now live all over the country, but through various channels, many of us still stay in touch. For a while, one of us even published a newsletter for the group, the *Intimidator*.

These seminary friendships were forged in a unique time and place, at a crossroads between the women's movement and the Controversy; at no time before or since has there been the same degree of openness to

Southern Baptist women in ministry. As we struggled with the complexities of theological education, and as the Controversy and its attendant focus on women intensified, these friendships helped sharpen our identities and reinforce our sense of self and our calling in the face of fierce opposition. In many ways, these women shaped who I am today as much as any other force in my life. Other researchers have also found that clergywomen (and, to a lesser extent, clergymen) "value the fact that their seminary experience gave them networks that continue to provide them with informal but important friendships and support long after they have left seminary."[14] Joye Durham told me, "Tons of people from my seminary days will be friends for my lifetime. . . . [Southern Seminary] gave me so many friends, so many wonderful people."

They Are My Sisters

For my first focus group interview with the Clique, we met at Judy's house. Everyone was dressed nicely for the occasion in the sort of comfortable, casual, wash-and-wear style of women who have learned that stiff fabrics and ironing are overrated. I put lavalier microphones on everyone, and the entire living room was a tangle of cords connecting the women in a web that seemed to symbolize their relationships. Once I had them hooked up, they were talking and laughing so loudly that I had a hard time getting the focus group started. At first they were a little intimidated by the prospect of being recorded, but they got over that quickly, and I listened as they wove the stories of their lives, friendships, and beliefs.

At the end of my year of interviews, I sat down again with the Clique, after taking photographs at West Rome Baptist Church. Back in Judy's living room, they were old pros by now and clipped on their microphones with no prodding from me. When I got them to quiet down (some things never change), I asked them what the interview process had been like for them, and I asked whether they thought other people would be interested in what they had to say. They surprised me when they identified their friendship as the one thing they thought would be most interesting for my readers.

Shelby said, "This group of ladies is like my sisters. My two sisters, we don't have that closeness, although I love them dearly, and I know that they love me. But we don't get together and go places and do things together. This [the Clique] is my family." The others concurred. "I don't have no sister here; so they are my sisters," Lidia said. "It's wonderful to have such Christian friends," Alicia explained. "I think it's because one spirit, one mind; we have the same Holy Spirit," Kayne offered, "I think the Lord put us together." "It's a remarkable friendship," Nancy added. Lidia noted, "We know about each other's children, pray for each other; when something bad is going on, we all hurt, when something good, we [are] all happy. We share in that." She continued, "I tell my [other] friends. They say, 'Oh, I wish I could have that.' Because we started so long ago." The women pointed out that even when some of them moved out of Rome for a short time, they remained in the Clique and continued to drive back to Rome for birthday gatherings and other excursions. "That didn't break us up," one of them noted. "That's because I threatened them all," my mother interjected.

I asked them to tell me about some of the things they've done together through the years. A lot of that recording is unintelligible because they were all talking at once and laughing so hard that the transcriptionist couldn't make out what they were saying. Through the years, the Clique has taken many trips together, all piled into my mother's van, with her driving. They've been to Callaway Gardens, the little White House in Warm Springs, Georgia, the Birmingham Botanical Gardens, and the Southeastern Flower Show in Atlanta. They've toured Charleston and Charlotte; they've shopped in outlet malls and antique stores in just about every small town in the Southeast. Each year, they take a drive in the Blue Ridge Mountains and go to the Apple Festival in Ellijay, Georgia. They may go to some little town just to try out a new restaurant. On one of their trips, they stayed overnight in a cabin, and Judy had sewn them all long nightgowns to wear to bed. Although someone suggested that a group photo of them all in their nightgowns did exist, I never saw one, and nobody offered to let me use one in the book.

My mother is the de facto leader of the group. Lidia explained, "I got to tell you something on your mother. She been the captain of the group since we started. And whatever she say, we have got to do it." In the transcript, Janet notes the hilarious laughter at this point. Having grown up with my mother, I can only nod in agreement. Lidia continued, "She say none of the rest of us can drive, none of us can find the directions. She got a lotta laws." This led to more laughter and general agreement. Then Lidia offered this example: "One time [JoAnn] said [after some Clique members, including Lidia, had missed some of their outings], 'All right, this Clique now, we not gonna be out anymore. And from now on, if one say she sick, we not gonna believe it. If Lidia die and Ralph call and say, "She not going today,"' she says, 'Show me the corpse in the front yard.' That's how serious she was, honey."

Mom interjected, "That's because Lidia had missed like three times."

"Of course, I was sick," Lidia explained.

Mom pointed out, however, that after her ultimatum, Lidia's husband, Ralph, called to say that Lidia would be going on their next trip, even though she had "been sick as a mule."

Lidia added, "She [JoAnn] taking care of me; she see that I get the shade, that I didn't walk too much. They [the Clique] are watching over me. They are my precious."

"Nobody else would take the job," Mom concluded to more raucous laughter from the group.

With a history that spans thirty-five years for the entire group and more than fifty years for some members, the Clique has developed a web of relationships that are central to their lives and to their identities. Although common experiences and a common geography largely define the group, they perceive their faith as a key element of their friendship. They are Christian friends, and that shared faith allows them a deeper connection than they find in other friendships. Mom said, "I think that's what's held us together for lo these thirty years . . . our shared faith."

They disagree and take on roles, like all sisters do, but their relationships remain vital because of their active commitment to the group, its activities, and their prayers and care for one another. Research indicates that, for older women in particular, continuity and ongoing significance characterize their friendships.[15] Also, affective qualities—"having similar attitudes/values, feelings of belonging, discussing personal problems, and expressing intense feelings"—may well be the most important facets of ongoing friendships for older women.[16] Judy wants younger generations of women to understand the importance of friendship. "The older you get, the children are grown and gone," she explained, but "you still have your lady friends that you can do things with, share things with. Hopefully, if we all go to the nursing home, it'll be the same one."

Influence and Inspiration

Many participants pointed to specific women who had a profound impact on their lives. For the Clique, Elizabeth Robertson was the driving force who brought them all together. Elizabeth is a devout Christian woman with severe rheumatoid arthritis. In the early 1970s she taught a women's Bible study class at West Rome Baptist Church, and one by one, the members of the Clique (who were not yet the Clique) found her class. Lidia was amazed the first time she heard Elizabeth teach, and she immediately decided to join the class. At the time, only four women attended, but that number soon grew to more than seventy. Lidia said the class grew so quickly that people asked, "Does she give Green Stamps over there?" All the members of the Clique told me that Elizabeth had profoundly shaped their lives through her teaching and the witness of her own life, living with a disability. The members of the Clique also pointed to one another as sources of influence and inspiration.

When Debra Hochgraber was a young pastor's wife, a former associational WMU director befriended her and became her mentor. "We didn't ever name or define the relationship. She simply cared, listened, encouraged, prayed, and shared from her experience." A state WMU staff member also encouraged Debra to take on leadership roles, which, she said, "was a far stretch from what I had envisioned in my future when I was a self-conscious little girl with a low self-esteem. But her encouragement, the training she made available, and the opportunities she created launched what turned into a lifelong ministry with women."

Likewise, Wanda Lee, now executive director of WMU, SBC, was influenced by a state WMU staff member. Wanda's church in Florida didn't have WMU children's programs, and this WMU leader trained her in her very first job as an Acteens leader. In turn, Libo Krieg mentioned Wanda Lee as one of the Southern Baptist women who have inspired her. She was impressed by Wanda's willingness to leave nursing and become executive director of WMU in response to God's call.

Eva Buford, a Truett student, also credits a WMU leader with fostering her participation in ministry. Eva explained, "She calls [me] and says, 'You go to seminary. You get your work done. You can do it.' She's almost like a grandmother figure to me; she's very encouraging." Eva's supporter told her, "'These are some of the things I couldn't do because of the age and era I grew up in, but these are things that you can and you will do.'" She doesn't give Eva a chance to back out.

In fact, many of my participants mentioned GA, Acteens, and WMU leaders, as well as Sunday school teachers, as significant influences in their lives. Women in leadership positions in Southern Baptist churches and denominational organizations provide important role models and offer needed mentoring to younger women. To a great degree, these relationships are built into the programmatic structure of Southern Baptist life, which relies on women's leadership for the education of children. But these programs and roles are animated by the personal commitments and energies of these women, who see their relationships with others, especially children, as a reflection of their Christian faith. By teaching and mentoring others, they are carrying out a ministry to help others grow as Christians.

Heather King also noted the importance of the "faithfulness of elderly women who taught children's Sunday school classes [and] first shared Bible stories and the Gospel with me." She said that during her junior high years, "several women actively discipled me, requiring homework assignments and scripture memorization." Tisa Lewis was influenced less directly by one of her Sunday school teachers. "I don't remember anything she really said to us," Tisa explained. "I just remember the way she treated us." Candi Finch recalled that the wives of her pastor and youth pastor made a huge investment in her life. Miss Jean, as she called the pastor's wife, helped Candi get involved in speakers' tournaments and missions projects. "Miss Jean worked me hard!" Candi noted. She also benefited from the more formal mentorship of the youth pastor's wife, who provided her with spiritual guidance. "How they invested in me," she concluded, "is what I want to do for girls now."

Amy Mears was deeply influenced by "the women that worked their behinds off in the churches I grew up in, in every way except preaching and ordained ministry." They're still having an impact, she added, because "they're still working their behinds off." The church she grew up in sent a bus to a retirement home every Sunday to pick up all the retired missionary ladies and bring them to church. "They taught our Sunday school classes," she added. "They spoke, and they did the mission studies, and they prayed, and they sanctified the whole place."

Brenda Flowers credits "the women from the WMU" with inspiring her. If you had asked them pointedly what they thought the role of a woman was, she said, they would have responded, "Women are supposed to support." But, Brenda observed, "their actions told me everything but that. They were the ones who ran the church. And I don't mean that by putting the men down; they were the ones who were there and doing the work. So it was their actions that taught me so much about things."

Many women also mentioned college and seminary professors—from Molly Marshall to Dorothy Patterson. Others mentioned women ministers, such as Nancy Sehested and Susan Lockwood Wright and Sarah Jackson Shelton. These women were emblematic of the possibilities available to young women, and they offered significant mentoring opportunities. However, the response I received from Julie Pennington-

Russell was more typical: "Honestly, probably most of the women who have influenced me are people whose name nobody would know; they were just folks who said, 'Go fight the good fight,' or women doing their thing in their Sunday school classes."

Jesus Was a Friend of Women

Another hymn we all learned to sing in those Southern Baptist churches went like this: "What a friend we have in Jesus, all our sins and griefs to bear! What a privilege to carry everything to God in prayer. . . . Can we find a friend so faithful who will all our sorrows share? Jesus knows our every weakness, Take it to the Lord in prayer."[17] As Southern Baptists, we were taught to believe in an ever-present, living Jesus who was our personal friend and companion along the journey. Jesus was the friend for sinners, the lover of our souls, the one who walked and talked with us in the dewy morning garden. Our relationship with Jesus was not some abstract belief or cognitive assent to a particular Christology. Rather, it was an actual, day-to-day, moment-by-moment friendship with our personal Lord and Savior, whose love for us both in the present and for eternity brought us salvation. We also sang:

> I have found a friend in Jesus, he's everything to me,
> He's the fairest of ten thousand to my soul;
> The Lily of the Valley, in him alone I see
> All I need to cleanse and make me fully whole.
> In sorrow he's my comfort, in trouble he's my stay;
> He tells me every care on him to roll:
> He's the Lily of the Valley, the Bright and Morning Star,
> He's the fairest of ten thousand to my soul.
>
> He will never, never leave me, nor yet forsake me here,
> While I live by faith and do his blessed will;
> A wall of fire about me, I've nothing now to fear,
> With his manna he my hungry soul shall fill.
> Then sweeping up to glory to see his blessed face,
> Where rivers of delight shall ever roll:
> He's the Lily of the Valley, the Bright and Morning Star,
> He's the fairest of ten thousand to my soul.[18]

When I asked Shelby Christie how she thought Jesus treated women, she replied, "I think he treated them very well. He was a friend of the women." Again and again, the women I interviewed emphasized

Jesus's close relationship with women. "Jesus elevated women," they explained. Alicia Bennett told me, "I think [Jesus] treated women the way they should be treated. I think he treated women, I will say equally, with equal consideration." Judy Masters believes that Jesus "treated [women] with utmost respect and loving kindness," and one member of Fort Worth's Travis Avenue Baptist Church declared, "[Jesus] was so much a gentleman to the women when he would speak to them in the Bible." Lidia Abrams said, "They was his dear friends. I think he was good to everyone and kind, men and women. I think he treated everybody the same. He loved everyone. He died for all of us. So I think he treated everybody equal."

For Southern Baptist women, Jesus provides a model for relationships, and, through his relationships with women, he elevated women's status socially and politically.[19] My mother explained, "In the Old Testament, women were nothing more than a possession. They were treated by men as something that they owned, and they were only to do the work and bear the children. But Jesus elevated women. Jesus changed the thoughts about women. You could tell that because at the cross, he wasn't concerned that he was up there suffering; he wanted his mother to be looked after." Nancy Moore asserted, "Women were benefited so much by the ministry of Christ. It took Christ, really, to raise the status of women. . . . Women, just worldwide, have not had the chance that men have had. And I think that's one of the reasons we find women so much closer to Christ, because they needed him so. And they found in him that respect and love and acceptance that the world didn't offer." Linda McKinnish Bridges specifically chose to do her PhD in the New Testament so that she could understand the Bible's teachings on women. Through her studies, she came to believe that the Bible supported women's ministry. That understanding, she explained, gave her "internal authority." She continued, "I found in myself that the Bible gave me permission and that Jesus blessed women, even though the denomination had not blessed me."

Across the theological continuum, these women believe that Jesus perceived and treated women as equals with men. They draw a great sense of worth from this belief, which is enhanced by their own personal friendship or relationship with Jesus. Their relationship with Jesus, in turn, mediates their relationships with their friends. From Jesus, they learn and feel empowered to treat other people in ways that are consistent with who they understand Jesus to be and how they believe Jesus would behave. Shelby Christie immediately connected her Christian faith with her personal relationships. "I know I'm a Christian, and I know I love God most of all. I have a lot of friends. I love all my friends. I try to be a friend to other people. I try to help other people when I see a need there, the things I can do. When I can't do, I pray about it and pray to God to send someone else to fill that need because I can't." Along those lines, in discussing the church's responsibility to women subjected to domestic violence, Joanne Parker lamented that many churches expect women to stay in such situations and just "submit more." But, she noted, "if we read the Gospel of Luke, we see Jesus repeatedly helping women. Repeatedly. We are not being followers of Christ if we do not help these women."

4

Red and Yellow, Black and White

The Dynamics of Race in the Lives of Southern Baptist Women

In Christ there is no East or West,
In Him no South or North;
But one great fellowship of love
Throughout the whole wide earth.
—John Oxenham, "In Christ There Is No East or West"

Any discussion of Southern Baptist identity necessitates a discussion of race. By far, the majority of Southern Baptists are white, and to a great extent, whiteness is an assumed norm of Southern Baptist identity. Although women of color do participate in Southern Baptist churches, they do so mostly as part of ethnic or language minority congregations. Rarely are Southern Baptist churches fully integrated, and women of color who participate in predominantly white congregations often acculturate to the prevailing norms in the church. For Southern Baptist women, gender and race intersect in a variety of ways that shape their lives and experiences. At times, these intersections are painfully obvious; at other times, they are subtle or practically invisible, yet their effects are profound.

Southern Baptists have a troubling history with regard to race. As a preschooler in the early 1960s, I learned to sing the following:

Jesus loves the little children
All the children of the world
Red and yellow, black and white
They are precious in His sight
Jesus loves the little children of the world.

In Sunbeams and later GAs, we learned about people from all over the world, and we gave to the Lottie Moon Offering for Foreign Missions to support missionaries in Africa, Asia, and South America. In Sunday school we learned that God loves everybody and that everybody is the same in the sight of God. By then, the public schools in Rome, Georgia, were desegregated, but our congregations were not. I don't think I saw a black person in my church until I was in high school in the mid-1970s, and when he did show up and ask to be baptized, there was some consternation among some of the adults in the church. Another black man, a student at the local Baptist college, started to attend church with the white female student he was dating, but her parents took her out of college.

When I was growing up, racial slurs and jokes were an accepted part of everyday conversation. Many of the same people who taught me that Jesus loves the little children of the world also taught me that using ugly words to describe others was okay. People who frowned on such overt racism often espoused a more benevolent paternalism: black people were naturally inferior, so we had to take pity on them. As a child, I wasn't aware of the disconnect, but as an adolescent, I had an experience that forever changed me. In fact, only the theological language of conversion can come close to capturing the power of that moment. I clearly remember the day in high school when I told the last racist joke I would ever tell. The words were still hanging in the air like a cartoon bubble when I was struck by a lightning bolt of conviction that racism is wrong. Like Paul on the road to Damascus, I was overcome by the wrong I had done. I was shaken to the core by the realization of what my words and attitudes really meant, and on the spot, I vowed to overcome my racist upbringing. Somewhere along the way, I imagine, the notion that Jesus did indeed love all the children of the world overrode those conflicting messages about white superiority, and in that flash of insight and conviction, God's radical inclusiveness became clear to me.

The Southern Baptist Convention itself professes to have had a conversion experience around race. In 1995 the Convention issued a long-overdue apology for its history of racism. Certainly, some Southern Baptist congregations and individuals had been standing up for equality all along. Even the Convention decried lynching, racial prejudice, and antisemitism. Nonetheless, most Southern Baptists, embedded in a culture of racism, have participated in supporting and maintaining—either consciously or unconsciously, actively or passively—a system of racism. The white participants in my study certainly acknowledge that segregation and racism are wrong, although racist notions are so deeply entrenched in the cultural fabric that some of these women still hold on to misinformation or stereotypes about people of color. They are what feminist Gloria Yamato calls "unaware/unintentional" racists. These women are often very compassionate toward the plight of disadvantaged people of color, but they still think or act in ways that betray the racial stereotypes or presumptions they hold. Yamato writes, "With the best of intentions, the best of educations, and the greatest generosity of heart, whites, operating on the misinformation fed to them from day one, will behave in ways that are racist, will perpetuate racism by being 'nice' the way we're taught to be nice. You can just 'nice' somebody to death with naïveté and lack of awareness of privilege."[1]

Examining one's unaware or unintentional racism is very difficult for white people, myself included. We know that racism is wrong, and we want to think of ourselves as people who are not racist. We would never intentionally make a racist comment or do something on purpose to harm someone because of her or his race. Across my two decades of teaching, whether at California Baptist College, George Fox College, or Oregon State University, I've found that white students are often resistant to naming and examining contemporary racism. I've finally figured out that their resistance is based on the misunderstanding that to acknowledge our unearned privilege and the misinformation we have learned about others suggests that we are not good people. So I now begin discussions of racism by assuring my students that no one is suggesting that they are not good people. Rather, I explain, they are embedded in a system of racism that imparts misinformation to everyone, and as good people, we should be willing to examine how the system of racism has affected us, how it privileges us, and what we can do to change it. Because the charge of racism is so volatile and painful, most people will do just about anything to avoid it, including denying that the system of racism affects them at all. Many of my white participants see racism as a system that limits and disadvantages people of color, but they don't acknowledge its profound impact on their own construction of identity. Or perhaps talking about their own deeply held stereotypes and misinformation is so painful that they must deny they even possess such attitudes.

Many of my white participants have begun to examine the impact of racism in their lives, and they have made conscious choices to work actively to challenge and change the social structures of racism. They have been willing to address privilege and acknowledge how racism has shaped their identities. And they have chosen to act on the knowledge they have gained from such self-examination and social reflection. Not all white southerners were explicitly taught racism in their families; in fact, many of them heard a message of tolerance and even acceptance as a Christian response to racial issues. Still, they recognize the systemic advantages they have been accorded by virtue of their whiteness.

In particular, current and former white missionaries have deep convictions about racial equality. Their experiences in other countries have made them acutely aware of the equality of all people, while at the same time giving them a true appreciation for the diversity of cultures. Carolyn Goodman Plampin, who was a missionary in Brazil for many years, said that churches in Brazil teach parishioners that they are all brothers and sisters, no matter the color of their skin. She went to Brazil during the height of racial tensions in the United States, but when she got there, "everybody, white and black and honey-colored ones, are all in the same church; we just became friends." Wanda Lee was a missionary in St. Vincent, an almost completely black island off the cost of Venezuela. She was shocked when the islanders assumed that she was rich simply because she was a white American. "So that was really one of my first encounters with what does it mean to be white in a world that is predominantly other cultures and other races, and [with the] great disparity between those who have and those who don't."

Many white participants also credited GAs with introducing them to the value of differences. Beth Crawford told me about Miss Annie, a retired home missionary who worked with the GAs in her church and led them in putting on a carnival for Latino migrant children. "I remember," Beth said, "when I went out and actually did this, I was just blown away by the fact that there were these kids, my age, whose skin color was different and they spoke a different language. Obviously their lives were really, really different from mine. I didn't have the language for 'economic oppression' at that time, but I look back, and that's what I was recognizing, that my lily-white church wasn't necessarily the only way that people were."

That women of color participate significantly in Southern Baptist churches and in the SBC itself raises interesting questions, given the denomination's long history of racism. Although the proportion of people of color in the SBC is relatively small, many women of color are active in Southern Baptist churches and in the denomination's agencies.

Their occasional experiences of overt racism are not unexpected, but, surprisingly, they make few connections between race and their identity as Southern Baptists.

Although Americans on the whole still tend to frame racial issues as black and white, thinkers and activists within other racial or ethnic groups remind us that race in the United States is a much more complex and complicated picture. Nonetheless, because of the particular history of race in the South, my participants' understandings of race, racism, and racial identity still tend to revolve around white and black. The Latina and Asian American participants offer a more complete picture of race within the denomination, but the primary racial emphases in Southern Baptist life remain the tensions between blacks and whites that began with Baptist participation in and support of slavery and continued through the era of Jim Crow and the civil rights movement.

I Never Knew Any Different

Many of the white participants who are now in their sixties and seventies were born into segregation. Clique member Judy Masters grew up in a small town where the water fountains were marked "White" and "Colored." She pointed out the irony of being taught that "God loved them just like God loved us—they were just a different color," while also being taught that "we didn't drink out of their water fountains; they didn't drink out of ours. We didn't go to their houses; they didn't go to ours. . . . I always went to a segregated school; I never knew any different." Her grandchildren now ask her if blacks really had to use separate bathrooms. "Yes, they did," she tells them. "But why?" they ask. "Because we didn't know better," she explains. "But you do know better."

Pat Brown told me this story: She lived on a farm, but her parents worked in town and hired a black man to do the farming. He had a little boy the same age as Pat, and Charlie Bill often accompanied his father to the farm. Pat had a Red Flyer wagon that she took everywhere. One day when she was playing with Charlie Bill, they climbed into the wagon and opened up a box of vanilla wafers. Pat would get a wafer out, and then Charlie Bill would get one out. "About that time," Pat said, "I heard my grandmother calling me from the back door to come inside. And it was explained that black and white people did not eat together. I remember at the time being so heartbroken and thinking, 'But, why?' And she couldn't tell me why. It was, 'Well, it's just not done.'"

Clique member Nancy Moore added, "We took it for granted that when we got on the bus, they went to the back and sat on the back seat. It was just accepted by both races; you know, they had to accept it, and we just accepted it; we didn't even think about it, you know? It was separate movies, and they didn't even have a swimming pool. There were separate water fountains, and nobody ever seemed to question anything." Doris Bailey, too, noted that segregation "was not our choice, but it was just an accepted thing, because it was what was done at the time. And really I don't think I ever had an opinion of it being right or wrong because it was just the way you did things." Alicia Bennett stated, "We didn't harbor any hatred for blacks, but there was a big dividing line because, well, there just was." When she saw a drinking fountain with a "Whites Only" sign, Kayne Carter remembered thinking "that [it] wasn't right. But I didn't go much beyond thinking. That's just the way it was, and you just went on."

Mixed Messages

Many of my white participants talked about the mixed messages they received about race. On the one hand, their families and churches taught them that God loves all people equally; on the other hand, these same institutions taught them that segregation was God's will. Many of these women said that their families explicitly told them not to treat blacks badly. "We were never taught to discriminate," Judy Masters explained.

Many of these women express an understanding of racism that is fairly typical in contemporary society. They see racism as an individual issue—one's own attitudes and behaviors—rather than as a system that includes ideologies and institutions. Therefore, they can be taught not to discriminate as individuals, yet maintain a system of segregation that is inherently discriminatory.

Many participants suggested that even as children they had a vague, niggling sense of the contradictions inherent in segregation. Judy Masters explained that segregation "was expected, but I used to feel like that wasn't quite right, because God loved them as well as he loved me; but back then, you better not say that." Annie Cockrell from Batesburg, South Carolina, explained the situation: "We all accepted that the Lord loves them, there's no difference in color, race, creed, anything. So we had to accept that. But again, as southerners, you know how we are here. We do accept it, but then we think everybody's happier in 'their own place.'" Nancy Moore noted, "On the train, we didn't sit in the same car as the black people did, and yet there were wonderful Christians among them, and we acknowledged their Christianity. It was like we were blinded; we thought we were 'good to them.'"

Sheri Adams noted this disparity as well. She explained, "If you had asked people if black people should be treated like human beings, they would have said, 'yes.' What they didn't see was that they weren't treating them like human beings." She offered this example: "I was telling a class the other day, my grandmother had a black woman named Mary who worked for her 24/7, you know? She was there every Christmas Day to wash our dishes. And it never dawned on me, or I don't think any of us, that she may have preferred to spend Christmas with her family."

We Would Play with the Children

Another common theme among the older white participants was their childhood friendships with black children, usually the offspring of the black women and men who worked for their families. Of course, as Nancy Moore explained, segregation meant that these friendships had their limitations: "When I was growing up, we always had black ladies who came and worked for Mother. Mother, like I said, was nervous and frail. They would bring their children, and we would play with the children. We never considered inviting them to a birthday party or anything like that. And I can remember a couple of little boys that were in Victoria's family, and they got their feelings hurt because I had a birthday party, and they weren't invited. And I felt bad about it too."

When my mother was a child, her aunt, who lived next door, had a black maid who was "just like a mother" to my mother and her cousin. "She just did anything for us; but I remember that if she ate with them, she had separate dishes, and she didn't come to the table and eat with them." Mom also remembered that she and her brother played with the children of a black family who lived nearby. But, echoing what my other participants had been taught, she "knew that they had their place, and we had our place."

Doris Bailey's family hired a black woman to help out when Doris's mother became ill. The woman often brought her daughter to Doris's house, and the two girls played together. Doris would naively ask the little girl if she'd like to spend the night, and of course, the little girl always turned her down. Joan Lewis also played with the black maid's children when she was growing up. Annie Cockrell added that the only other children she had to play with were black, "and they were our best friends, and we loved them." Still, she said, she couldn't understand why "Mama had to feed them on the back porch" whenever they ate with her family. Alicia Bennett's family had a black woman who came every week to do the wash, and her father hired several black men to help with the garden. "We just loved them," Alicia remembered. "They were kind of like—I won't say part of the family—but they were considered good friends."

We All Realized that It Was Wrong

When I asked my mother why she thought segregation existed, she explained that southern whites didn't believe that blacks "were as good as white people. They were supposed to be the servants; they were supposed to do the jobs the white people didn't want to do." I asked her whether her opinions on racial issues had changed over the years. "Of course," she told me. "I think everybody has." She cited the example of a former governor of Georgia who had sold his restaurant rather than allow blacks to eat in it. "In his latter years," she explained, "he said he realized that it was wrong; and we all realized that it was wrong." Historian Mark Newman points out that the Georgia Baptist Convention "often condemned racial prejudice and discrimination. Although the Convention did not criticize segregation, it promoted acceptance of desegregation by appealing to the primary commitments Baptists held to law and order, public education, and evangelism." He concludes that although the majority of Southern Baptists preferred segregation, "most Baptists accepted the end of de jure segregation when its maintenance conflicted with their primary commitments. Few Baptists sought integration, but by the late 1970s most Baptists rejected forced segregation as discriminatory and unchristian."[2]

Doris Bailey grew up with a grandfather who was overtly racist, but she tried not to be influenced by him. She said, "I never condoned what he thought, and I know that over the years as I have grown in my faith, I have also realized and accepted all races. I don't feel that I am bigoted in any way, but I might be. It's hard for us to evaluate ourselves sometimes." Kayne Carter believes that she has developed more tolerance through the years. "I feel like they are equal," she said. "I've been liberated in that view."

Shelby Christie's parents didn't teach her to be racist, "but you just got it from the neighborhood. They'd make jokes or they'd say things about blacks, but I got over it. My mother and dad never taught me to be racist, and they never were themselves; you just hear it, you know? But I don't, now. I got over it because I can think for myself anyway."

Of course, segregation didn't exist without resistance. Gladys Peterson remembered having two drinking fountains in a local store, one for "colored" and one for "white." Her sister Beulah would deliberately drink from the "colored" water fountain.

I asked Nancy Moore about the civil rights movement. "We were for it," she said. "We were not activists, but we certainly spoke our minds on it, and we knew that segregation was wrong and that this should be righted." Earline Durst of Batesburg, South Carolina, said that through the years she had learned "that race shouldn't make any difference, or we don't want it to make any difference. We've become educated to the fact." But, she acknowledged, "we have had an advantage."

Lidia Abrams moved to Rome, Georgia, from Cuba in 1960, after she married a U.S. serviceman who had been stationed there. Lidia was only the fourth Cuban to move to Rome, and although most people treated her well, including those in the Southern Baptist church she attended, her mother-in-law did not. "She thought I was black," Lidia explained. "I almost went back home because she treat me bad." Her husband, Ralph, was still in the military, so Lidia lived in Rome without him for a while, dealing with her mother-in-law's meanness. "But I already have the Lord," Lidia noted, "so that made it easier. If I didn't have that, I don't believe I could have made it." Lidia also found her church to be a welcoming and accepting place for a young, Spanish-speaking bride from Cuba.

Many participants who were young during the civil rights years pointed out that while all this was going on in society, nothing was being discussed in church. Lynda Weaver-Williams complained that the civil rights movement, Vietnam, and Watergate were all happening, but "we weren't talking about that stuff in BSU [Baptist Student Union]." She was paying attention to these issues and being profoundly affected by them, yet the church seemed disconnected and silent. In Carol Woodfin's church, "race issues were not discussed one way or the other," she said. "I don't think anything negative was said about black people, but nothing was said about us needing to change things in society." Amy Mears is ashamed of Southern Baptists' lack of participation in the civil rights movement. She never even heard about civil rights until she started paying attention to the television news. "I'm old enough to remember when Martin Luther King was assassinated," she lamented, "but I have absolutely no recollection of that. It wasn't talked about in my home; it was not a factor in my growing up." That was certainly true of many of us who were very young during the 1960s and 1970s. We knew what was going on in the larger world, but when we went to church, it was often as if these issues didn't exist. At the Convention level, however, that was hardly the case.

Keeping the Cars Coupled

Throughout the Southern Baptist Convention, racial tensions were high during the 1950s and 1960s. Although many Southern Baptist leaders embraced civil rights and pushed other Southern Baptists to do so as well, some people adamantly resisted integration and full equality for blacks. WMU executive secretary Alma Hunt felt that it was her job to "keep the cars from being uncoupled from the train" when WMU forcefully addressed racial issues against the pushback of segregationists.[3] WMU took a proactive stance against racism, offering numerous articles on race in its publications and dealing with the angry letters and subscription cancellations that resulted.[4]

The problem of race was especially salient for Southern Baptist missionaries and mission boards. As Alan Scot Willis notes, mission leaders recognized that racism hindered their work both at home and abroad, and they became active in promoting racial understanding and equality.[5] To them, the Christian belief in God's inclusive love and Christ's redeeming act was at odds with southern racism; they believed that the solution was education and the winning of individuals to Christ. According to Willis, their efforts at challenging Southern Baptist theology and social mores made an important contribution to social change in the South and in Southern Baptist churches.

The Christian Life Commission also played an extremely important role in changing Southern Baptist attitudes about race. The commission came into being in the middle of the twentieth century expressly to deal with social and racial issues. Its publications and recommendations were often at odds with Southern Baptists' commitment to segregation and discrimination. In 1965 the Christian Life Commission and the Home Mission Board created Race Relations Sunday to encourage churches to explore ways to achieve racial reconciliation. As might be expected, the response was mixed. Holly Reed Harrison suggests that the commission's advocacy of racial equality and reconciliation made it the most controversial SBC agency.[6] It retained that distinction as it addressed other social concerns until the late 1980s, when conservatives took control.

Looking at the written record of the Southern Baptist Convention, one finds a progressive stance on race, but as Andy Manis argues, the vast majority of individual Southern Baptists supported segregation.[7] They saw integration as a direct threat to the social order and what they perceived as God's divinely ordained plan for the separation of the races.[8]

Nonetheless, some progressive Southern Baptist congregations embraced racial reconciliation as a goal. In 1958 Pullen Memorial Baptist Church in Raleigh, North Carolina, adopted a new constitution that affirmed its acceptance of all people regardless of race. Oakhurst Baptist Church in Decatur, Georgia, and Prescott Memorial Baptist Church in Memphis, Tennessee, admitted blacks into membership beginning in 1968. Birmingham's Baptist Church of the Covenant was founded in 1970 in response to racial issues among Southern Baptists. In 1971 the pastor of Glendale Baptist Church in Nashville publicly supported the city's desegregation of the public schools. Interestingly, these same churches (affiliated with the Alliance of Baptists) were also among the first to ordain women and to call women to positions of pastoral leadership.

Tandy McConnell argues that Southern Baptists' "Grand Compromise"—the downplaying of theological differences in order to support the denomination's ideological commitment to missions—is what held the Convention together during the civil rights period. According to McConnell, the civil rights movement divided the Convention into three camps—segregationists, integrationists, and moderates; the last group just wanted to keep the denomination out of the conflict altogether. McConnell also points out that this Grand Compromise ultimately failed in the 1980s, when fundamentalists attacked the purported liberalism among seminary professors, and the professors' appeal to the shared ideology of missions failed to persuade voters at annual meetings of the Convention.[9]

Our Relation to Persons of African Descent Has Been Less than Ideal

Upon the occasion of its sesquicentennial meeting in 1995, the Southern Baptist Convention both passed a resolution and offered a declaration about the Convention's history of racism. The resolution reads as follows:

WHEREAS, Since its founding in 1845, the Southern Baptist Convention has been an effective instrument of God in missions, evangelism, and social ministry; and

WHEREAS, The Scriptures teach that Eve is the mother of all living (Genesis 3:20), and that God shows no partiality, but in every nation whoever fears him and works righteousness is accepted by him (Acts 10:34–35), and that God has made from one blood every nation of men to dwell on the face of the earth (Acts 17:26); and

WHEREAS, Our relationship to African-Americans has been hindered from the beginning by the role that slavery played in the formation of the Southern Baptist Convention; and

WHEREAS, Many of our Southern Baptist forbears defended the right to own slaves, and either participated in, supported, or acquiesced in the particularly inhumane nature of American slavery; and

WHEREAS, In later years Southern Baptists failed, in many cases, to support, and in some cases opposed, legitimate initiatives to secure the civil rights of African-Americans; and

WHEREAS, Racism has led to discrimination, oppression, injustice, and violence, both in the Civil War and throughout the history of our nation; and

WHEREAS, Racism has divided the body of Christ and Southern Baptists in particular, and separated us from our African-American brothers and sisters; and

WHEREAS, Many of our congregations have intentionally and/or unintentionally excluded African-Americans from worship, membership, and leadership; and

WHEREAS, Racism profoundly distorts our understanding of Christian morality, leading some Southern Baptists to believe that racial prejudice and discrimination are compatible with the Gospel; and

WHEREAS, Jesus performed the ministry of reconciliation to restore sinners to a right relationship with the Heavenly Father, and to establish right relations among all human beings, especially within the family of faith.

Therefore, be it RESOLVED, That we, the messengers to the Sesquicentennial meeting of the Southern Baptist Convention, assembled in Atlanta,

Georgia, June 20–22, 1995, unwaveringly denounce racism, in all its forms, as deplorable sin; and

Be it further RESOLVED, That we affirm the Bible's teaching that every human life is sacred, and is of equal and immeasurable worth, made in God's image, regardless of race or ethnicity (Genesis 1:27), and that, with respect to salvation through Christ, there is neither Jew nor Greek, there is neither slave nor free, there is neither male nor female, for (we) are all one in Christ Jesus (Galatians 3:28); and

Be it further RESOLVED, That we lament and repudiate historic acts of evil such as slavery from which we continue to reap a bitter harvest, and we recognize that the racism which yet plagues our culture today is inextricably tied to the past; and

Be it further RESOLVED, That we apologize to all African-Americans for condoning and/or perpetuating individual and systemic racism in our lifetime; and we genuinely repent of racism of which we have been guilty, whether consciously (Psalm 19:13) or unconsciously (Leviticus 4:27); and

Be it further RESOLVED, That we ask forgiveness from our African-American brothers and sisters, acknowledging that our own healing is at stake; and

Be it further RESOLVED, That we hereby commit ourselves to eradicate racism in all its forms from Southern Baptist life and ministry; and

Be it further RESOLVED, That we commit ourselves to be doers of the Word (James 1:22) by pursuing racial reconciliation in all our relationships, especially with our brothers and sisters in Christ (1 John 2:6), to the end that our light would so shine before others, that they may see (our) good works and glorify (our) Father in heaven (Matthew 5:16); and

Be it finally RESOLVED, That we pledge our commitment to the Great Commission task of making disciples of all people (Matthew 28:19), confessing that in the church God is calling together one people from every tribe and nation (Revelation 5:9), and proclaiming that the Gospel of our Lord Jesus Christ is the only certain and sufficient ground upon which redeemed persons will stand together in restored family union as joint-heirs with Christ (Romans 8:17).[10]

The apology reflects conservatives' understanding of racial reconciliation as a matter of biblical faithfulness and stands in contrast to the driving social ideals that have traditionally propelled progressive Christian churches to be involved in racial activism.[11] Although many people, both black and white, welcomed the long-overdue apology, others questioned its timing and sincerity. Following the Controversy, many moderate churches stopped participating in the SBC and began to send funds to the newly formed Cooperative Baptist Fellowship. Some cynical moderates saw the SBC's outreach to blacks as a way to rebuild participation and fill in the gaps left by moderates who had fled the Convention. Many black leaders also questioned the apology, calling for the Convention to show "'the fruits of repentance.'"[12] Others worried about the implications of a large, wealthy, white denomination inserting itself into the lives of black churches and communities.[13]

Of course, despite the Convention's apologies, few people of color hold positions of power in the Convention. Very few churches are truly integrated beyond a handful of people of color. Nor are ethnic and language minority churches integrated, because whites don't go to those churches. Theologically progressive congregations have been no more successful than conservative ones in attaining full integration. Amy Mears noted the irony that her church, "whose defining moment was in favor of integration," has not integrated. "Our minds and our hearts are very, very welcoming," she said, "but our practice, we continue to segregate ourselves in churches. I don't understand the sociology behind that, and I don't know how to change it, but I'm still ashamed of that too." Amy's comment points to a larger social problem that persists in almost all Protestant churches: they remain segregated. Certainly, if nothing else, this suggests that race continues to be a salient issue in Christian and Southern Baptist identity.

Paula Sheridan grew up in Louisiana during the civil rights movement. Her grandmother was the registrar of voters in their parish, and Paula used to go to work with her grandmother and hang out at the courthouse. Before the Voting Rights Act, she remembered watching poor black farmers trying to fill out the registration application "that I could complete by the time I was eight years old," she said. "I remember sitting in the chair—and I had to be very quiet, and I couldn't interfere because my grandmother was quite a professional—as they struggled and as they failed these voter application tests because they couldn't read or write." When the FBI investigated registration practices after passage of the Voting Rights Act, Paula's grandmother was one of the few registrars not indicted. "I wish I could say it was because she was progressive and believed that everyone should have the opportunity to vote, because in her own lifetime, she was born during a time when women weren't able to vote. . . . She was an avid segregationist, but she believed in following the law. So, she followed a law that violated her own personal belief system, that, in effect, in spite of her—and because of her—African American people were able to register to vote. And so I became very aware as a young child that being white meant something."

In most ways, being Southern Baptist means being white—or at least acculturating to whiteness. To Barbara Elder, being white and Southern Baptist has meant that she's been in the majority all her life. Because most Southern Baptists are white, "and that's what I am," she explained, "it reinforces being Anglo." When people go to church with people who look just like them, as Barbara suggests, their sense of normalcy and dominance is reinforced. In particular, given the historical fact that Southern Baptist identity is intimately linked with whiteness, to attend a Southern Baptist church as a white person is to have whiteness affirmed as the dominant way of being. From there, making white ways of doing things normative is an easy step.

When I asked my white participants how race influenced their identities as Southern Baptists, most of them didn't know how to answer. They have not been taught to examine how whiteness shapes their experiences and the ways they see the world; on the contrary, they have been taught to assume that whiteness is neutral, that its viewpoint is "normal." Given southerners' heightened awareness of race, the lack of examination of whiteness as a formative factor in identity is especially interesting and illustrative. Whiteness is so assumed, so normative, that the examination of its construction doesn't even arise as a question. As Debra Owens-Hughes put it, "Being Caucasian, I simply fit into their basic image of a Southern Baptist. So it has not affected my identity, other than being status quo."

The prevalence of racial issues in the South, however, means that my white participants are aware of the advantages they have by virtue of their racial identification. They often responded to my question about race by saying, "I think I've had more advantages because I'm white" or "My life has been easier because I'm white." Julie Pennington-Russell explained, "Being a white woman probably gave me some open doors that I might not have had had I been a woman of color. I think being a white anybody in America probably gives you a very different vantage point." Nearly all the white participants understand that being white situates them differently in relation to social and economic advantages than people of color. Rhonda Reeves admitted, "Well, certainly being

Caucasian has been a bonus. Certainly, African Americans have had their fights through the centuries, and I definitely recognize that. Or any other race, for that matter. Being upper middle class, brought up that way, of course, it's easier."

Rhonda's comment about class is important. In recent decades, the majority of Southern Baptists have moved into a fairly secure level of economic privilege and access. Many are very wealthy; most are stable in the middle class. The women I interviewed overwhelmingly accept the myth of a largely classless United States, because on the demographic questionnaire I asked them to fill out, almost all of them responded that they are middle class. On the form, I identified the various classes by characteristics rather than income. For example, poverty was identified as "those below the poverty line, AFDC [Aid to Families with Dependent Children] recipients, etc." Working class was defined as "craft and service occupations," and middle class was defined as "professional, technical, managerial, sales, and clerical occupations." Upper class was characterized as "listing in social registers, attendance at elite secondary private schools, membership in elite private clubs, inherited wealth, etc." Not surprisingly, few women marked "upper class" or "poverty," and that is probably true of the majority of Southern Baptists. Very few, however, marked "working class," despite the fact that the primary breadwinner in the family performed craft or service work. I think this points to the ways the working class has been obscured in American thinking and the success of the myth of the middle class. Together, these two phenomena work to maintain systems of economic advantage and privilege by denying the economic divides among Americans.

Becoming Antiracist

Nancy Ammerman noted the irony that in the 1960s she could study the evils of apartheid in church but not the evils of segregation. By 1968, she was very clear about which side of the civil rights movement was the right one. She added, "It's also really clear to me that I did grow up in a white denomination and a white *racist* denomination and a white racist culture. And it's just really hard to shed that. Those . . . deep-seated, knee-jerk expectations about how the world looks, and how people are going to act, are so deeply ingrained in my psyche that they will never go away." Nancy's awareness of the long-term effects of racism is an essential step in becoming antiracist, and it has led her to ongoing associations and work with black Baptists.

Priscilla Denham's minister father was asked to leave their church in Houston because he was an advocate of integration and civil rights. "That was a pretty difficult realization," she acknowledged, "that this body, which is supposed to be the body of Christ, and the Christ who believed in compassion and justice for all people, this body in earth, could get rid of my father because he was saying that black people were also children of God and should be able to come to church with us— which made sense to me. I grew up singing, 'Black and yellow, red and white, all are precious in His sight,' but it was not the way the grownups in this church thought."

One of the most profound stories I heard about challenging racism came from Kate Campbell. Kate is the daughter of Jim Henry, the very conservative pastor of the very large First Baptist Church in Orlando, Florida. Theologically, most would identify Henry as a fundamentalist, yet this same theology led him to stand up against racism in the 1960s. As a young pastor in Mississippi and Nashville, Henry landed himself in a lot of trouble because he refused to close the doors of the church to blacks. When I asked Kate about race, she said that her convictions and identity had been profoundly shaped by her father. As a child, she often spent time at her father's church after school and accompanied him when he visited people in the community. "That's probably the thing that shaped my life more than anything," she noted, "because my father did take the stance; my father believed that [the church] should be open for everyone, no matter what color you were, what you wore to church, what your economic level was. And I think for me that was huge in my life." When the family moved to Nashville, Kate was among the first white children chosen to be bused to school to enforce integration. Many white parents pulled their children out of public schools, but the Henrys supported integration and sent Kate on that bus. In her song "Bus 109," she sings about the profound impact of that experience: "You know my life was changed forever / All because of bus 109." Reflecting on her Southern Baptist upbringing, Kate mused, "You want to feel good about where you come from; that place has shaped you immensely [and], in my case, I believe, shaped me generally for the good and has been a positive experience for me. Up against that, though, are the negatives: slavery, racial tension . . . what is good can also vary into bad. There is a very fine line between all those things, in southern culture and in Southern Baptist life."

Likewise, April Baker commented on the effects of being a "child of integration." She attended an integrated school in a small town in

South Carolina in the late 1960s and early 1970s. She became good friends with one of the black girls in her class, but they couldn't have a relationship outside of school because of the persisting racism in the community. But, she says, the experience of attending an integrated school showed her how social change can come about through personal relationships. She explained, "Because we had to learn how to be in school together, we had to learn how to be friends; we had to recognize that they weren't quite so different as we thought they were. We could study the same things and play the same things at recess, and we could play on the seesaw together and get to know one another."

For Peggy Sanderford Ponder, her experience of growing up Southern Baptist in Alabama meant "being part of the biggest denomination, the biggest race." She added, "People of different races were people we ministered *to*, not people we ministered with." I asked how she came to resist racism. "Maybe part[ly by] identifying with the oppressed," she suggested, "feeling oppressed as a Baptist woman." Likewise, Judy Baker noted that she equates whiteness with privilege and tries to empathize with people of color based on her own experiences of oppression as a woman. She said, "I have this real strong identity with minorities. I think that comes from my biblical understanding. Jesus always identified with the minority, the people who had less voice."

While I was in seminary, my sense of Jesus's identification with the oppressed grew so strong that I became disenchanted with the overwhelmingly white, middle-class church in the suburbs I was attending. I decided to look for an integrated church, and through Wes and Jane Lites, whom I met during a travel course to New York City and Washington, D.C., I found Shalom Baptist Church in downtown Louisville, Kentucky. Shalom had recently come into being, following the demise of Twenty-third and Broadway Baptist Church. The latter church, which occupied a large building downtown, had fallen victim to "white flight," and the small, interracial congregation could no longer support the building and the staff. The church disbanded, but a small number of its members decided to start a new church with racial reconciliation as its focus. I found Shalom during my last year in seminary, and although it was a very small congregation, it showed me the possibilities of racial harmony and love. When I moved west, I had a hard time finding another truly multiracial Southern Baptist congregation. When I finally left the Southern Baptists, I continued my quest for a diverse congregation and found Ainsworth United Church of Christ in Portland, Oregon.

People offer a lot of explanations as to why Sunday morning is still the most segregated hour in America. They say, "They have their ways, and we have ours," or "I wouldn't be comfortable in their church, and they probably wouldn't be comfortable in ours." Most of the differences are written off to worship styles, but I think that these excuses are just that—justifications for refusing to take the Gospel's message of inclusivity seriously enough to do something about it. By hiding behind differences in style, white congregations can refuse to examine the hidden ways that whiteness and white privilege shape their identities, both individually and as a congregation. The multiracial churches I have participated in spend a lot of time in intentional conversation about how to conceive of church as a diverse group of people. People make compromises; they learn from one another; they come to embrace differences. And that's not always easy, but it comes from a commitment to inclusiveness and to antiracism.

My Identity Is in Christ

Given the Southern Baptist Convention's history of racism, one might wonder why women of color are involved with Southern Baptists at all. I think their connections to the denomination can best be explained by the ways they prioritize various factors in their identities. For many Southern Baptist women of color, their primary identity is based on their faith rather than their race. As Debbie Williams, a member of Second Ponce de Leon Baptist Church in Atlanta, explained, part of being Baptist is "to have my identity in Christ define me more than race, gender, geographic location." Many women of color may be comfortable in predominantly white Southern Baptist congregations because they feel more kinship with the church's emphasis on evangelism, the authority of scripture, Bible study, missions, or spiritual development than with other churches' emphasis on issues of race. Debbie told me, "Race does not seem to be a great factor since we joined Second Ponce de Leon Baptist based on the substantive Bible teaching available there." She's often asked why she joined this church rather than one of the many black churches in the area. "In each such instance," she continued, "we explain that we are attracted by the strength of the Christian education to be received, coupled with the community 'feel' of the church." Similarly, Dorcas Pérez, who immigrated from the Dominican Republic, explained that she fell in love with First Baptist Church of

Orlando partly because it offered so many programs for her children. Libo Krieg, likewise, feels a great affinity with Southern Baptist teachings and mission work. When she speaks in churches or at other meetings, she introduces herself as follows: "I'm from Costa Rica. I have two children. I'm a grandma. I'm married to an Anglo, but I'm Hispanic." She doesn't have any problems with people of other ethnicities. "I imagine," she suggested, "when everybody's gonna be in heaven, it's gonna be so awesome."

On the whole, the openness to other races professed by Southern Baptists—as a denomination and as local churches—seems to rely on the willingness of people of color to acculturate to white congregations and the white SBC. The women of color who are members of predominantly white Southern Baptist churches are comfortable in that context. Many Southern Baptist women of color, however, are part of racial or ethnic Southern Baptist churches, and these churches are not integrated either. Lisa Vang, for example, attends the Hmong Baptist Community Church in Allen, Texas. Her own racial identity has encouraged her to work with the Hmong population both in the United States and overseas. She said, "This has strengthened my faith because I participate and support missionary work."

In particular, black churches may be attracted to the SBC because of its conservative theological and social stances, and in recent years, the SBC has intentionally reached out to black churches and communities. Because Southern Baptist churches are autonomous, black churches remain free to develop their own practices that are appropriate for their communities.[14] Of course, progressive black Baptists find themselves uncomfortable in the SBC, and many have become part of the Cooperative Baptist Fellowship. Some observers have even suggested that the overriding division between conservatives and moderates may mask issues of race and differences of opinion about how to achieve black progress.[15]

Despite improvements in race relations among Southern Baptists, cultural assumptions and barriers remain. Lucy Elizalde lamented the lack of Latina role models in the curricular materials provided by Southern Baptists. She loved reading the story of Lottie Moon (for details, see chapter 5) but wishes there were more stories about women of color doing mission work. Mostly, she added, Latinos are depicted as the recipients of missions.[16] She never even met a Latino missionary until she was an adult, and until then, she couldn't imagine Latino missionaries in places like India or Russia. She pointed out that even now, as a Latina in ministry, she has a hard time finding others like herself. "There aren't very many role models that have come before me," she observed. "So, at times, even though I know that I'm not alone, I'm very aware that I'm breaking new ground."

Although few participants offered much analysis of the larger issues of race within the SBC, many told me about their personal experiences of overt acts of racism in Southern Baptist churches. Zana Kizzee faced resistance as a black woman called to the music ministry. For instance, when she took her résumé to the seminary placement office, the director told her that he wouldn't be able to send it out because no church would have her. She took her frustrations to the dean of the music school, who offered his support and encouraged her to stay in school. But as she looked for a Southern Baptist church willing to use her gifts in music, she became depressed by rejection after rejection and eventually gave up seeking a ministry position. "How can a denomination do this to people who are called, who are committed to loving and serving the Lord and his people?" she asked. She no longer attends a Southern Baptist church.

Eva Buford, a student at Truett Seminary, told me of her experiences as an undergraduate at Baylor University in Waco, Texas. When she first moved to Waco and was looking for a new church, she went to one of the Southern Baptist churches in town and was approached by an older couple. The husband asked her, "What are you doing here?" The wife pushed him aside and said, "Honey, that's not what he meant. What he meant was the church of your people is down the street." In the Baylor cafeteria, Eva invited two white students to sit with her. "Sit next to a nigger?" one responded. "I don't think so." Eva feels that, through it all, she's grown closer to God. Racism, she explained, "definitely shapes the way you view God and . . . your call to ministry, without a doubt. I know that if I wasn't secure in God, and if I wasn't secure in his love for me, there probably would have been some angry words spoken at both the church and the cafeteria; I probably could have had some severe identity issues, not minor ones."

Faith Wu, a Chinese American, grew up in California but moved to the South to teach. She's often approached by people who say, "Wow! Your English is so good," assuming that English is not her first language just because she looks Asian. She feels that being Chinese in the South makes her somewhat of a puzzle, and white southerners often don't know what to make of her. She has been shocked by some instances of overt racism, but she has seen it directed more toward blacks than toward Asians.

When Carolyn Matthews worked as the minister of education at a primarily white Southern Baptist church in California, one of the Sunday school teachers refused to ask her for help; she always went to the white pastor instead. One time, Carolyn was standing in the vestibule of the church talking with a white parishioner, and a woman looking for the minister of education assumed that the white woman was the church staff member, rather than Carolyn. For Carolyn, issues of race are a primary concern. "I believe from the bottom of my heart," she explained, "until we get it right, nobody else is going to get it right. Of all people in the world, we as children of God, who have been forgiven, should be accepting. That's pretty much where my thinking is: how are we going to do that; how are we going to go about it; how will we do? You can pass laws, and you can tell people they have to do whatever, but that isn't going to change anybody's heart."

5

We've a Story to Tell

Southern Baptist Women and Ministry

We've a story to tell to the nations
That shall turn their hearts to the right,
A story of truth and mercy
A story of peace and light.
—H. Ernest Nichol, "We've a Story to Tell"

"You can be anything God calls you to be." Women learned that refrain as children and adolescents in Southern Baptist churches, and they repeated it to me during our interviews. The history of women's ministering among Southern Baptists turns on their appropriation and embodiment of that one sentence. It is their calling, their mission, their driving force. It has led them to take on traditional responsibilities of nurturing and educating, and it has compelled them to challenge gender norms and traditional roles that have excluded women from ordained ministry and the pastorate.

Probably the most influential Southern Baptist programs for girls came from Woman's Missionary Union (WMU), Auxiliary to the Southern Baptist Convention. WMU organizations provide mission education for preschoolers, girls, and women. Girls' Auxiliary (later Girls in Action) was founded in 1913. Its watchword was taken from Isaiah 60:1: "Arise, shine, for thy light is come." Its hymn was "We've a Story to Tell." In GAs, more than anywhere else, we were told, "You can be anything God calls you to be." Our pledge of allegiance was this: "Knowing that countless people grope in darkness and giving attention to his commands, I assert my allegiance to Jesus Christ, to his church and its activities, attempting with God's help to abide in him through prayer, to advance in wisdom by Bible study, to acknowledge my stewardship of time, money, and personality, to adorn myself with good works, and to accept the challenge of the Great Commission." The Great Commission, by the way, is found in the book of Acts: "Go ye therefore and teach all nations, baptizing them in the name of the Father, the Son, and the Holy Ghost, teaching them to observe all things whatsoever I have commanded you. And, lo, I am with you always, even unto the end of the world."

Joyce Reed, who once worked for WMU in Birmingham, told me, "Being a GA was probably the most influential on my life as far as what it means to be a Christian, what it means to serve God." Pamela Tanner, who is a high school choir director, said, "When I was a GA and went to GA camp in the fifth grade, our missionary was from Uganda. So, of course, I surrendered to be a missionary to Uganda. Then as I got a little older, I realized that I was maybe not going to be a missionary to Uganda, but, wherever God called, I'd go." In an oral history interview, Nancy Sehested, now a chaplain and formerly pastor of Prescott Memorial Baptist Church in Memphis, said, "I had learned very early, especially in GAs, that we are all called and that once the hand of God is on you and you are baptized and you have the claim of Christ in your life, then your job is to listen for God's unique call to you."[1]

The workings of gender were quite apparent in our experiences as GAs. Boys were in a parallel organization, Royal Ambassadors (RAs). But while the girls were studying missions and putting together "Christmas in August" packages for poor people in Rhodesia, the boys were out playing basketball in the church parking lot. According to Tisa Lewis, RA projects in her part of South Carolina included making race cars and having soapbox derbies.

"What were you doing in GAs?" I asked.

"We were making boxes with toothbrushes and toothpaste and washcloths to send to people in other countries," she told me. "And we were visiting folks at the nursing home, and the boys were making their little cars for soapbox derbies and playing sports. I didn't quite make the connection. What does a soapbox derby have to do with church? What does a soapbox derby have to do with God? It never made any sense to me; it still doesn't."

Each week in GAs, we read the prayer calendar out loud—naming the missionaries, the countries where they were serving, and their assigned duties—and then prayed for the missionaries who were having birthdays that week. At the time, it didn't occur to us to question why so many of the women were listed as "church and home." That was (and still is) the title given to the wives of male missionaries who had the primary appointments as evangelists, church planters, seminary administrators, or physicians. Single women got their own titles.

GAs also taught us about the rest of the world—their cultures, their languages, their histories. Tisa said, "You know, we joke around that Southern Baptist girls knew geography better than anybody because of our involvement in GAs and prayer calendar and pointing out where Brazil is [on a world map]. I learned much more [geography] in GAs than I did in school." Dorothy Patterson recalled working on a cross-stitch map of the world for GAs. "And what God did in my heart with just every stitch I took!" she exclaimed, adding, "I learned more geography and more about nations and people and culture through [GAs] than I did through any college or university class." Joye Smith, a WMU staff member, said, GAs "gave me a worldview that is broad, even though I grew up in a church that was all white folk." Kristy Carr, another WMU staff member, began to feel her call to ministry when she was a GA. She grew up in a small town where "everyone knew everyone." Kristy said, "Not having computers, Internet access, [GAs] was my only window to the world, other than maybe geography and Alabama history—which was so limited—but boy, [GAs], that's where you could learn about missions in Africa and Asia, and even to this day I'd like to go to Ethiopia because I heard of so many things going on there, and the famines, and just realized that the world was bigger than Minor Heights. It was bigger than Birmingham. It was bigger than Alabama, or even the U.S."

Lottie Moon and Annie Armstrong

Every December, GAs constructed little cardboard banks where they saved their money to give to the Lottie Moon Christmas Offering for Foreign Missions. If Southern Baptists had a saint, Lottie Moon would be it.[2] She was one of the first single women to be appointed as a Southern Baptist missionary, going to China in 1873. In GAs we learned all the important things Moon did in China. As folk singer Kate Campbell noted, "You were educated about this from the time you were little; it started with the missions groups, with Lottie Moon and Annie Armstrong, who were women! The whole missions thing, to me, I understood it to be women. I cannot overemphasize to you that my understanding of missions was all about Lottie Moon and Annie Armstrong. I didn't even know really that there were the Baptist men. I mean, I knew they had RAs and it was called Royal Ambassadors, but still, I mean, who were their missionaries?"

Lottie Moon was a petite woman (some sources suggest that she stood only four feet three inches tall), but she exercised influence and power well beyond her stature. We didn't necessarily learn this in GAs, but in China, Moon had the audacity to demand an equal role for women in the governance of the missions. Kristy Carr speculated that Moon was "probably the kind of person that you say, 'Oh, Lottie Moon—grrr.' And others would go, 'Oh, but if you just get to know her!'" As Kristy explained, Moon was "so focused on what she was called to do . . . and didn't let politics, didn't let anything else get in her way." Karrie Oertli, who is now a pastoral care administrator, wondered, "How did we get from Lottie Moon the rebel to Lottie Moon the pansy?" In contemporary Southern Baptist life, Lottie Moon's legacy has been domesticated in many ways. She is held up as the self-sacrificing model for missions, but her unwillingness to be subordinate to male missionaries is omitted in the reciting of her story in many churches.

The story I didn't learn until I went to seminary is this: In 1883 Lottie Moon wrote a piece on the plight of female missionaries for a publication called *Woman's Work in China*. In this article she complained that women were relegated to the "petty work of teaching a few girls" when they had come to China intent on "ever-broadening activities." She also insisted that single women had the right to their own homes, their own mission work, and their own voice in decisions about the work of the missions. She wrote, "Simple justice demands that women should have equal rights with men in mission meetings and in the conduct of their work."[3] The Foreign Mission Board used Moon's article in its 1885 report on women's work, but it didn't cite her by name. Though the board was, on the whole, relatively progressive on women's issues at the time, it added the following statement to the report: "This is not endorsed by the committee but is reproduced to show what some others think."[4] Moon was so incensed that she wrote a fiery letter to the corresponding secretary of the Foreign Mission Board. She concluded by requesting that the board send her $550 to purchase her return passage to Virginia, at which time she would submit her resignation. The board didn't send the money, and Moon stayed in China and became Southern Baptists' most beloved missionary. In fact, when I asked participants which Southern Baptist women have influenced or inspired them, the majority responded, "Lottie Moon."

Rhonda Reeves, another WMU staffer, told me, "I felt very called, even as a kid, I think, to go into the mission field. I read the story of Lottie Moon and thought I was Lottie Moon! I would pretend, and I can remember telling my mom in fourth grade that I was going to go to China." Rhonda said, "I still haven't been to China, but one day I do hope to go." Lucy Elizalde remembered her mother giving her a book about Lottie Moon, and she was fascinated by Moon's willingness to sacrifice herself for the people in China.

For Linda McKinnish Bridges, now an associate dean at Wake Forest University, the impetus for missions was the desire to serve Jesus. When Linda was a child, her family would take vacations to whatever city the Southern Baptist Convention was holding its annual meeting in and then visit whatever denominational sites were nearby. "If we were in Georgia, we'd visit the Home Mission Board. And if there was trash on the ground, we'd go and pick up the trash; we'd go to Richmond, Virginia, to see the Foreign Mission Board, and we'd pick up the trash because we owned part of it." Despite her denominational heritage, however, she realized in the 1970s that she wouldn't be free to serve Jesus in the way she wanted in the United States. "But," she told me, "Lottie Moon had done it; and boy, did I link up to that story. I was Lottie: she was me. And she became the icon—and there was so much romanticism in that. She went over to China; I ended up going to Taiwan." With Lottie Moon in the back of her mind, Linda faced the Foreign Mission Board with her husband, Tilden, and asked for an appointment to do theological education. The board tried to appoint Linda to "church and home," but she refused, and at last the board relented. In the field, she spent two years in language school studying Mandarin Chinese and preaching on the weekends at a small Chinese chapel. A male missionary approached her and said, "You will not work in theological education by extension because the male missionaries will not be able to work with a woman." Linda remembered thinking, "Okay, I'm twenty-three years old, and I have given up my life to go be a career missionary in China because [of] Lottie Moon, a little story that I learned as a little GA, and I locked upon that as being the prime mover for my future, [and] now they're telling me that I cannot do that?" But Linda persisted and became the pastor of a Chinese congregation. "I kept it secret from the Southern Baptist missionaries in Taiwan," she said. "Of course, they knew, but they did not let me know they knew, and I just didn't talk about it. But I was preaching in Mandarin Chinese on Sunday mornings and working with that congregation until I came home in '81."

Shirley Powell, a laywoman at Travis Avenue Baptist Church in Fort Worth, Texas, also pointed to Lottie Moon's strength. "I think of Lottie Moon, going out when she did to China, in an era when most women in America would have been really terrified to do a thing like that. Go live in a foreign country and take God's love into that country and try to witness to those people. She spent her life for God in a foreign country, in a foreign land, away from her family. That to me just shows you the heroic side—she was a feminist before feminism ever really came about." Martha Gilmore, one of the first ordained Southern Baptist women, noted wryly, "Lottie Moon was so revered because she was in China. You know, the further away, the better." When asked which Southern Baptist women influenced or inspired her, Charlean Hayes Hughes answered, "For sure, Lottie Moon. I know that sounds extremely trite, but when you think of a woman who spent thirty-some years in a country where there were very different standards of everything, her love for the people—I don't know why she isn't an American hero!"

For generations of Southern Baptist women, Lottie Moon has been testimony to women's ability to do whatever God calls them to do. My mother worries that the declining emphasis on mission education for girls will have an adverse effect. She said, "If it hadn't been for Lottie Moon and Annie Armstrong, we wouldn't have missions, and I hate it that a lot of the churches are not teaching missions to the children now because we won't get it if we don't teach it. And that's where the women come in, because the women do the teaching of the children. So we need to learn ourselves about women and how God used them, because [God] said we are all the same."

My sister is almost five years younger than I am. When I left home, she was still a young adolescent. I asked Karen whether she grew up hearing about Annie Armstrong and Lottie Moon.

"I *was* Annie Armstrong and Lottie Moon!" she exclaimed. "For whatever reason, from seventh grade until I left West Rome Baptist [in college], every year during those two periods, Easter and Christmas, they dressed me up and I went from classroom to classroom in Sunday school and was Annie Armstrong and Lottie Moon, asking for people to give."

"Oh, the things I missed when I was away at seminary!" I replied.

"I could tell their stories in my sleep," she added, "and certainly was inspired by that, because they were way before their time."

Sarah Frances Anders also played Lottie Moon. At the time, she was five feet eight inches tall and could hardly pass for the petite missionary. Fortunately, she played Lottie over the radio, so it didn't matter.

When Southern Baptist women were considering organizing in the mid-1880s, Lottie Moon offered her support. She had heard that Methodist women had designated the week before Christmas as a time for prayer and support for missions, and in the December 1887 issue of the *Foreign Missions Journal,* she suggested that Southern Baptist women do the same. In one letter, she wrote:

> I wonder how many of us really believe that it is more blessed to give than to receive. A woman who accepts that statement of our Lord Jesus Christ as a fact, and not as "impracticable idealism" will make giving a principle of her life. She will lay aside sacredly not less than one-tenth of her income or her earnings as the Lord's money, which she would no more dare to touch for personal use than she would steal. How many there are among our women, alas, who imagine that because "Jesus paid it all," they need pay nothing, forgetting that the prime object of their salvation was that they should follow in the footsteps of Jesus Christ![5]

In 1888, when Moon heard that WMU had been formed and that it would be sponsoring the Christmas offering she had suggested, Moon encouraged them to set a goal of $2,000.

The other icon of Southern Baptist womanhood mentioned frequently by the participants—Annie Armstrong—was the first corresponding secretary of WMU, and she pleaded, cajoled, and nagged Southern Baptists to give their financial support to foreign mission work. For that first Christmas offering, she hand-wrote 1,000 letters to various mission societies and circulated thousands of programs, notices, and circulars, as well as 30,000 offering envelopes. That year, the women exceeded their goal, raising $3,315.26. Armstrong was also active in the cause of home missions, encouraging and supporting the work of women in the United States. In 1895, the head of the Home Mission Board asked the women of WMU to raise $5,000, and they began an annual week of prayer and offering for home missions. In 1918 Armstrong suggested that the Christmas offering be named for Lottie Moon, and in 1934 the Easter Offering for Home Missions was named for Annie Armstrong.

In many ways, Annie Armstrong opened doors for women, but like many of her peers, she insisted that women remain in their proper sphere. When Baptist women from Texas proposed a training school for women at Southern Seminary, Armstrong refused to put their proposal on the agenda for the 1895 annual meeting of WMU, stating, "It is not time yet to discuss the subject."[6] Nonetheless, the push continued, with E. Z. Simmons, a former missionary to China, enlisting support from the heads of the Foreign Mission Board and the Sunday School Board. Unfortunately, Simmons assumed that WMU's support would be forthcoming and did not solicit Armstrong's input. Although Armstrong had been open to the idea of a training school for women at some point in the future, Simmons's presumption so incensed her that she became an outspoken opponent and delayed the school's founding for several years. A significant number of Southern Baptists were concerned about the propriety of young women taking seminary courses, particularly if there were any suggestion that they would be allowed to preach, and a lively debate ensued.

Single women had been in classes at Southern Seminary since 1883, and married women had been allowed to attend with their husbands before that. The seminary, however, did not give the women grades, did not allow them to earn diplomas, and did not provide housing or financial support for them. The training school was intended to change all that. The motion for WMU to take on the school came before the annual meeting in 1905 and lost by three votes. Armstrong, sensing the growing support for the training school, announced her resignation. Finally, in 1907, WMU voted unanimously to found the Woman's Missionary Union Training School at Louisville, Kentucky.[7]

Girls' Auxiliary, Forward Steps, and Acteens

In many ways, the debate over the training school reflected Southern Baptists' ambivalence about the roles of women in the work of the church. They supported women's work, as long as it was performed within the confines of traditionally female roles. Each step of progress was circumscribed by the larger cultural (southern and Baptist) norms of femininity.[8] This paradox is highly evident in GA itself. GAs learned parliamentary procedure; they held office in the organization and ran meetings. They stood publicly during worship services and recited scripture verses they had memorized, and they did service in the community. The program that guided girls in these experiences, developed in 1928, was known as Forward Steps. Like the Girl Scouts, Forward Steps awarded badges for the completion of a variety of tasks related to the denomination, missions, and service. We began our Forward Steps as maidens. Following maiden, we could aspire to be a lady-in-waiting, princess, queen, queen in service, queen with a scepter, queen regent, and ultimately queen regent in service (service aide was added in the 1970s as a final step for truly exceptional participants). Every year, girls who had completed their Forward Steps received awards at a coronation service, complete with white gowns, crowns, capes, and scepters.

In my research, I've talked to many queen regents in service who are now renowned sociologists, theologians, missionaries, and pastors, and though they laugh about having been queens, they recall the great adolescent pride they felt when they achieved that status and the significant impact Forward Steps had on them. In GAs they not only learned about missionaries but also did missions themselves, to become queens. They took active leadership roles in their churches and communities, and they learned skills not easily accessible to girls in the 1950s and 1960s.

Sociologist Nancy Ammerman, a former queen regent in service who now teaches at Boston University, offered this perspective:

> I often laugh about the ironies of Girls' Auxiliary. On the one hand, it's "auxiliary"; it's on the margins. We're the helpmates, the Barbie dolls in white dresses. But on the other hand, this was a place that told me I was really important and that gave me opportunities to organize, to lead; it was the place where I studied about people from all over the world and had a really big view of the world. It was a place where I learned that women could do things, that women *had* done things that were really heroic and important; and in many ways, the church itself really depended on the leadership of women. And I learned about Lottie Moon and Annie Armstrong. And it was very clear that those were the women who made it possible for Southern Baptists to be who they are.

Karen Massey, who is now a professor of Christian education at McAfee School of Theology, was one of the first service aides and served on the first Acteens National Advisory Panel. Acteens was formed in 1970 in response to the changing needs of girls in grades seven through twelve. Karen traces her deep involvement in WMU organizations to an associational Acteens director who approached her and said, "I see some really neat gifts in you. I want to ask you and some other girls to help plan our associational meetings every year. Would you do that?" That initial step led Karen to other levels of leadership and eventually to national opportunities on the advisory panel. In that role, Karen spoke

My mother, JoAnn Shaw, epitomizes the strengths and contradictions of many Southern Baptist women. She may espouse submission, but she believes that God speaks directly to her.

My paternal grandmother, Dorothy Shaw, says that she's a Baptist "teeth and toe." She taught Sunday school in a Southern Baptist church well into her eighties. She's now ninety-eight.

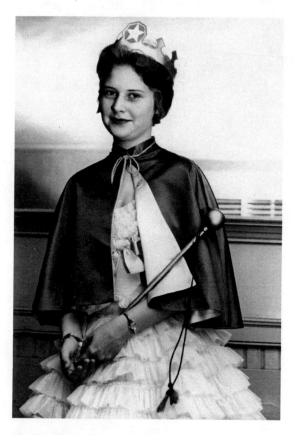

For Southern Baptist girls growing up from the
1930s to the 1970s, participation in Girls' Auxiliary was a highlight of denominational life. Here,
Dorothy Patterson poses as Queen Regent in Service, the highest level girls could attain through
scripture memorization, church leadership, and
service.

The Clique stands in front of West Rome Baptist Church.
They are (left to right) Nancy Moore, Shelby Christie,
Alicia Bennett, Lidia Abrams, Doris Bailey, Judy Masters,
Kayne Carter, and JoAnn Shaw.

Here, I'm performing a wedding for the daughter of my office manager. Even though the Southern Baptist Convention officially opposes the ordination of women, it is considered a local church matter, so women have been ordained as ministers for the last four decades.

Over peanut butter pie, these women of First Baptist Church in Batesburg, South Carolina, talked about their lives as Southern Baptists. In the back row are (left to right) Joan Lewis, Bettie Akins, Annie Mae Cockrell, and Nan Cook. In the front are (left to right) Paige Trotter, Earline Durst, Helen Winstead, Jean Gaston, Grace Geddes, and Sara Fox.

Like many women in my study, Zana Kizzee was close to her mother and grandmother, who taught her to be a strong woman and had a major influence on her spiritual development.

Despite the opposition of many men in the Southern Baptist Convention, women founded Woman's Missionary Union, Auxiliary to the Southern Baptist Convention, in 1888. Here are WMU's leaders from 1902.

If Southern Baptists had a saint, it would be Lottie Moon, who was a missionary to China at the end of the nineteenth century. The annual offering for international missions is now named for her.

April Baker and Amy Mears are breaking down barriers as co-pastors of Nashville's Glendale Baptist Church. This church has been on the forefront of social justice issues ever since its early support for the civil rights movement.

Karen Massey, now a professor at the moderate McAfee School of Theology, served as an associate pastor for Northside Drive Baptist Church in Atlanta before taking her current post.

Addie Davis was the first woman to be ordained by a Southern Baptist church (1964). She died in 2005 after four decades of ministry.

Fang-Lan Hsieh is a librarian at Southwestern Baptist Theological Seminary. Like many conservative women, she has found her place in service, despite changes in the Southern Baptist Convention over the past two decades.

before thousands of women at conference centers in Ridgecrest, North Carolina, and Glorieta, New Mexico, and wrote for *Accent* (the Acteens magazine). Karen said that the women at national WMU inspired her. "When I first met those women, I thought they were some of the most kick-ass women I have ever seen because I saw for the first time in my life it was women running an organization, and they did it and did it well. They were opinionated; they worked hard; they were committed to a cause." During Karen's seminary education, she spent a summer as an intern for WMU, at which time Carolyn Weatherford was its executive director. Karen noted the surprising turns of Baptist life: "Now I'm the national president of Baptist Women in Ministry, and [Carolyn]'s on my board!"

In many ways, GAs helped girls develop a sense of their own competence. Forward Steps allowed girls to exercise leadership, to achieve, and to be active in the church. In the 1950s, 1960s, and 1970s, girls had few places (other than Girl Scouts) where they could gain those skills. In those pre–Title IX days, few girls were afforded opportunities in athletics, and for most, the expectation was that their life trajectories would lead primarily to marriage and motherhood. Yet GAs reinforced a number of gender norms, even as it challenged others. The coronations, reminiscent of beauty pageants, supported notions of charm, gentility, and ladylikeness that were expected of girls and young women. Nonetheless, when I asked my participants to tell me about their journeys into ministry, many began with their experiences in GAs. Nancy Ammerman said, "I think probably the most formative influences really were those GA experiences of standing up in front of people and reciting scripture and telling missionary stories. That sense that I was a bearer of the story and could stand up publicly and speak the story just formed my sense of calling." Pam Boucher, who grew up with GAs, said, "In junior high, after all those years of mission study as well as Sunday school and all that, I just had a real strong sense that God wanted to do something special with me and had a very, very special plan for my life." April Baker still has her badges and her crown, scepter, and cape. GAs, she said, is "probably where I learned most of what it means to be a leader in the church and how to be a leader in the church. . . . I attribute an awful lot of leadership development to the time I spent in GAs and Acteens."

By the time I was in high school, GA and Acteen organizations were already declining in many Southern Baptist churches. Many fundamentalist churches opted for AWANA—a scripture memorization program not affiliated with Southern Baptists—for Wednesday night programming in place of GAs and Acteens. As a result of the women's movement, by the late 1970s, more opportunities were available to girls, providing competition for the time that previous generations had devoted to GAs. Changing social norms for girls and the explosion of technology also affected girls' participation rates. When I asked a group of young women at Baylor whether they had participated in GAs and Acteens, they said that they hadn't and referred to those organizations as "lame" and "hokey." Women's ministries have also begun to replace, rather than complement, WMU organizations in many Southern Baptist churches. Unfortunately, no other organization focuses primarily on mission education, so when WMU organizations are eliminated, so is mission education for many girls. Also, GAs is the place where we were told, "You can be anything God calls you to be." Now the denomination's official stance for women is essentially, "You can be anything God calls you to be, as long as God doesn't call you to the pastorate, ordination, or any position in which you might exercise authority over a man." All this leads me to wonder whether fewer Southern Baptist women will sense God's call to ministry, or whether more women will believe themselves limited in what they can be called to do. For now, however, WMU remains faithful to encouraging women to listen for God's call. While talking with current WMU executive director Wanda Lee, I said, "When I ask women, 'What made you think you could do ministry?' they all say, 'When I was a GA, they said to me. . . .'" Wanda interrupted, "God can call you. And we still say that today."

Serving Southern Baptists

Women's call to ministry was nothing new among girls who came of age in the 1960s and 1970s, but following the ordination of Addie Davis in 1964, there were significant changes. Up until that point, women who experienced a call to ministry understood it as a call to be a missionary, a religious educator, or a pastor's wife. But by the early 1970s, the women's movement began to create a new consciousness that permeated even the conservative, gendered atmosphere of the Bible Belt. I remember riding on the school bus with the radio blaring Helen Reddy singing "I Am Woman," and in my heart, my little fist was raised in solidarity and sisterhood. I had, after all, already experienced sexism when I was told I couldn't play football because I was a girl. And when Billie Jean King defeated Bobby Riggs in the Battle of the Sexes in

1973, I knew something much more important than a tennis match had occurred.

One of feminists' key concerns during this time was women in the workforce. More and more, women were entering traditionally male-dominated fields with the expectation that they could do the same work as men and should receive the same pay. So it's not surprising that in the 1970s the Southern Baptist seminaries suddenly experienced an influx of women who expressed a call to ordained ministry. If women could be CEOs and governors and university presidents, why couldn't they be pastors? The Convention's agencies responded surprisingly well, even hosting a consultation on women in church-related vocations in 1978 and addressing issues of women's equality in literature produced by the various publishing houses. Of course, not wanting to offend the conservative churches, the literature continued to affirm women's roles as wives, mothers, and homemakers.

During the research for this book, I talked to more than eighty women in ministry, representing a wide range of theological and ministerial diversity. Only a few are biblical inerrantists, but all hold a high view of scripture. Some are ordained; some are not. They are pastors, professors, social workers, counselors, chaplains, missionaries, and denominational workers; one is even a Missouri state representative. Many have left the Southern Baptist Convention, but many others continue to serve happily within the Convention. What they all have in common is a strong and certain sense of calling.

On the whole, the women who came of age before the 1980s first experienced their call as one to missions (mostly), education, or music. Women had role models in those areas, and they were the ones supported by the denomination. Nancy Sehested said, "When I was a high school student, I dedicated my life to full-time Christian service. At the time, I thought that probably that would mean being a home missionary or foreign missionary because that was the highest calling that I had ever seen among Southern Baptist women. I had seen some powerful Southern Baptist women missionaries—preaching and teaching all over the world. They would come through and tell their stories. It never was called preaching, but it was passionate, and it was a word from God."[9]

Many assumed that their call to ministry was actually a call to marry a minister and support his ministry. Pat Brown, a librarian at Lifeway, felt "a call to full-time Christian service—we didn't call it ministry as we do today. And it was understood in those days that that meant being a missionary. It would have been 1958." But Pat didn't feel a call to missions, so the best alternative she could come up with was to be a pastor's wife. She almost made the terrible mistake of marrying a young man she didn't love. "I woke up one morning with this ring on my finger, thinking, 'What am I doing?' God may want me to be a minister's wife, which obviously he did—later he sent one that was perfect—but I suddenly realized I was blindly following what I thought was his calling and not realizing God certainly wouldn't call you to marry somebody you don't love." Pat did marry a minister, but she also became a denominational employee. "You can always look back and see the steps," she said, "see where God had me here so I would learn this, because it would be needed here. So it's just like pieces of the puzzle. They fit perfectly. You can look back and see it in retrospect."

Diana Garland, dean of social work at Baylor University, felt her call to ministry at GA camp when she was twelve or thirteen. I asked her whether she understood it as a call to social ministry at that point. "Oh, no," she answered. "The only thing I knew was [to be] a pastor's wife or a missionary alone, and I really didn't want to go by myself. I liked boys. So I was really hoping for a pastor—and landed one." At the time, the Garlands thought they would end up on the mission field, because David's parents and grandparents had been missionaries. Instead, they both ended up on the faculty of Southern Seminary.

Jorene Swift felt called to ministry when she was at a conference at Glorieta, but she assumed that once she got married, she'd answer the call as a church volunteer. But when she was younger and played church, she "was always the preacher . . . and took up the offering, which was very important." At Glorieta, she heard WMU executive director Alma Hunt speak. "I remember her saying, 'Some of you young women are being called not to get married but to go be a missionary,' and I thought, 'That's what I'll be; I'll be a missionary.' I can remember praying, 'God, I don't want to go to Africa and never get married.' But I was ready to do that!! That's what I thought I would do. Then I got married, and I kind of thought, 'Well, okay, this is it. He never wanted to be a preacher, but he's got the seminary degree.'" Her husband ended up teaching at Golden Gate Seminary, and Jorene decided to use the opportunity to pursue her seminary education, although she still didn't think of herself as a full-time minister. When she and her husband had to leave the seminary because of the Controversy, Jorene was offered a position on the staff of Broadway Baptist Church in Fort Worth, where she is now the minister of congregational care.

Katrina Brooks told me, "I thought what I was supposed to do was be an extension of somebody else and live out my call through him, to serve in traditionally female positions within the church, and it just was so wrong. I tried to become the minister's spouse and do all those things, and it just was like acting out a part in a really, really bad B movie." Trying to live out her calling this way was hard on both her spiritual life and her marriage. Then she enrolled at the Baptist Theological Seminary in Richmond, a relatively new, moderate seminary founded after the Controversy. She mentioned a number of faculty members there, including Linda McKinnish Bridges, who reiterated the "truth" to her—"God calls whom God chooses and equips. And so this idea of my own call came out of that." As she and her husband, Tony, grappled with how they could fulfill both their callings if they were both called to pastor, they encountered the co-pastor paradigm. Katrina said, "It was as if it just all made sense at that time for both my husband and myself, because we knew that our family and our relationship was the most important thing. One of the things we struggled with was . . . who gets the kids? How do we do family together? Particularly if both of us are called as pastors, where's the time there? And trying to say, 'Well, Lord, how does that all fit together?' So we really stumbled onto this shared pastoral paradigm and . . . embraced it and really like it." Katrina and Tony are the co-pastors of North Broad Baptist Church in Rome, Georgia, my hometown (for more details of their story, see chapter 6).

When Karen Massey felt called into full-time Christian service, being a pastor never crossed her mind. What crossed everyone else's mind was missions, so Karen felt guided in that direction by the adults around her. "That kind of shaped my identity in my teen years and my early twenties," she explained. But then she went to Southern Seminary, where, Karen acknowledged, "for the first time in my life, I sort of found a voice that I never heard before. I felt empowered in a way that I never had before. I felt that it was okay to move outside the box I had grown up in, and so I began to see the world in a much bigger, more diverse way than I ever had growing up as a Southern Baptist girl." I asked Karen what exactly happened at the seminary that brought about this change, and she replied, "Though they didn't always practice what they preached at seminary, they did say this explicitly to me—these words were said to me—'if you feel called to be a pastor, you can do that.' No one had ever said that to me before. And it made me think about the church in a different way; it made me think about ministry in a different way." Following seminary, Karen became an associate pastor at Northside Drive Baptist Church in Atlanta and served as interim pastor there in 2005 after joining the faculty at McAfee School of Theology. In their study of women in evangelical seminaries, Nicola Hoggard Creegan and Christine D. Pohl likewise found that having supportive mentors was incredibly important for female students, even though, because of the composition of theological faculties, those mentors were almost always male.[10]

Sheri Klouda, who taught Hebrew at Southwestern Seminary, echoed Karen's sentiments about the importance of others' participation in identifying one's gifts. Sheri began to sense her call to teach when she was asked to fill in for the leader of a women's Bible study group. At first, she didn't like it at all. She was uncomfortable speaking in front of others and never felt prepared enough, so she was glad when the regular teacher returned. But when she was later put back in the same teaching position with the women's group, she felt differently. "I believe that a lot of our call to ministry and our place of service in the church is identified not by ourselves but by people who are around us," she explained. Her seminary professors further encouraged her to pursue a teaching career.

While she was in college, Becky Kennedy, who's now a campus minister at Baylor, met with a spiritual director who asked her, "Have you ever thought about music ministry?" Becky said, "It was like a light went on. I began taking on leadership roles in church, directing children's choir and those kinds of things, just to see if this is where God is leading me and calling me, and it just felt, I guess if I could use a quote from a movie—this is going to sound cheesy—[from] *Chariots of Fire,* when he said to his sister, 'When I run, I feel God's pleasure.' I could really feel God's pleasure when I would direct music and lead music and teach others."

Sarah Shelton, pastor of the Baptist Church of the Covenant in Birmingham, has found herself back in the association where she grew up. "These are the people who loved me and nurtured me and called out my gifts. They never told me I couldn't do it. So don't tell me at forty-eight I can't." Sarah felt her call to ministry the summer after she graduated from high school, during a youth choir tour in Florida. She had an unsettled feeling, so she prayed, "'I'll do anything if you'll get rid of this unsettled feeling in me.' And it just continued to escalate, and so I finally said, 'I'll even be a full-time minister if you'll take this away.' And it immediately disappeared, and it has never come back." She went to Southern Seminary intending to become a director of church kindergartens, but during her first semester in the fall of 1977, she visited one of her professors and told him, "'This isn't it.' And he said, 'What do you think it is?' and I said, 'I think I'm being called to preach.' He said, 'Why does that scare you?' and I said, 'Because I've never seen it done.' And he took both of my hands in his and put his knees right against my knees and got right up in my face, and he said, 'Wouldn't you rather be a part of something new and exciting than to be a part of something that has always been the same?' And I said, 'Yes.'"

A few years ago, Carolyn Hale Cubbedge was on a CBF panel when someone raised the question, "Why do you think women want to be preachers?" Someone chimed in and said, "Well, that's one of the places women haven't been able to serve, and women's liberation was saying everything should be open access." Carolyn interrupted and observed, "I don't think that's it at all. We're wanting to be pastors for the same reason you boys are wanting to be pastors; and that's because God called us."

Peggy Sanderford Ponder, a hospice chaplain, felt called to ministry during Youth Week at Ridgecrest Conference Center, during a performance of the song "The Touch of the Master's Hand." The song is about a violin that isn't worth anything until a master violinist begins to play it; then people suddenly want to buy the violin. The song made Peggy think that maybe she could make something of her life. As a conflicted adolescent, she thought about going into youth ministry, to help other teenagers feel connected to God. Then, during her first year at Samford University in Birmingham, she decided to talk to the youth minister of her church there—Sarah Shelton. "I want to be just like you," she told Sarah. "I want to be a youth minister." And Sarah replied, "I don't want to be a youth minister the rest of my life; I feel called to preach, and I want to pastor a church." Peggy remembered thinking, "Oh! I've not thought about that. That's kind of interesting."

Leah McCullough described her call to ministry by making reference to the story of Abraham. "It's 'Go to the land I will show you,'" she explained. She continued, "There aren't any maps and there's not a final destination, and so I feel like it's often been, 'Here's the call to the next step, to the next step, to the next step.'" She began with a call to teaching; then, after college graduation, she did an internship in campus ministry and found her calling there. During that internship, she felt a calling to attend seminary before entering campus ministry full time. "The call for me," she said, "has never been a 'once and for all' thing. It's kind of an ongoing, every day, wake-up-and-be-called-to-be-living-it-today, knowing that tomorrow it may change."

In her Baptist beliefs, Rosalie Beck found the very ideas that allowed her to defy gender restrictions. She said, "You know, interestingly enough, one of the basic teachings of the church that allowed me to rebel against the Baptists in the South, their position with regard to women, was the idea that God gives gifts individually. That God calls people individually." She continued, "When you take those [teachings] and you begin a pilgrimage toward a deeper understanding of what it means to be a person, . . . [you ask whether there is] anything good about limits placed upon a person by virtue of their gender, their race, their religious identity. . . . When you go back to the basics, the basics are: you are a child of God, and you are uniquely a child of God, and you are uniquely to fulfill God's will in a way that only you can. Then who has the right to put limits on anyone? So I saw that Baptist theology worked at that point."

Ironically, Karrie Oertli's first call to ministry took place in a fundamentalist church. "The funny thing is," she said, "when I surrendered to the ministry back at the first fundamentalist church, Jimmy Draper [one-time president of the SBC during the Controversy] preached the sermon in which I was called! And I sent him a note thanking him. He never responded to me, but, yeah, that's when I responded, during a revival that he preached." Her initial intention was to become a missionary. "That was always my dream, [but] I was divorced, and the pastor said, 'You can't be a missionary.'" Karrie went to Southwestern Seminary anyway, and one day her pastoral care professor invited her to participate in a year of clinical pastoral education (CPE). As she heard more about CPE, she said, "Like John Wesley said, 'My heart was strangely warmed.' I found my niche."

Not all women who express a call to ministry get a warm reception. Sandra Cisneros recognized her calling when she was only twelve years old and living in Guatemala. At age fifteen, she and her family (who were not Christian) immigrated to the United States. When she informed her family that she intended to leave home and pursue a higher education in preparation to do ministry, her mother told her not to expect any help. Sandra explained that in her culture, young women don't leave home until they marry, so for her to choose to attend college was controversial. Despite her family's lack of support, Sandra went to school, and since then, her entire family has become Christian.

Of course, some women who felt their call into missions actually went on to become missionaries or WMU staff members. I met Sheryl Churchill in the summer of 1983 when I was an intern at WMU. At the time, she was the consultant for Baptist Young Women; she's now WMU's ministry consultant. Although Sheryl cites her experiences in Sunday school and Church Training as being influential, she calls them "minor compared to the missions experiences. It was probably at one of those state Texas [WMU] meetings where . . . it was becoming clear to me . . . [that] I want[ed] to be like one of those women down there on the platform."

"And here you are!" I said.

"It wasn't as glamorous as it looked," she quipped. She explained, "It took a lot of hard work to get to that point. I discovered in being involved professionally in WMU that whether it was on the state level or national level, whatever gift or skill you had, it was a place where that could be used or could be developed into something that was even stronger."

Debra Owens-Hughes is a "church and home" missionary doing ministry with women and children in Colombia. When I asked her how she ended up in ministry, she replied, "Simply put, God called me out." She had grown up on a mission field, and her greatest struggle was to make sure that her desire to do missions was really God's call and not simply her own "homesickness" for international work. She said that not having the title of church planter, like her husband, doesn't bother her. "That's not a jewel I need to minister as God calls me. I'm as much a church planter as my husband, but I don't have to have a title to feel good about what I'm doing. It's actually more enjoyable doing something you are called to do, without being titled to do it."

Debra's comments reminded me of another theme among Southern Baptist women that seems to span the years. Women's concern is to do what they feel God has called them to do, even if they can't have the official title or office. Because they are typically polite and genteel, most Southern Baptist women try to work within denominational and church constraints, but when God's calling runs up against those constraints, they act in favor of God's call. That was true in 1888 when the women organized to support missions despite male opposition; it was true when Lottie Moon stood up to male missionaries who wanted to deny women equality in the missions; and it is true of the women who in the last four decades have answered the call to ordained ministry.

Rumblings

In 1979, when the fundamentalists began their movement to take over the Convention, their rallying cry was biblical inerrancy, but their intention to stop the progress of women in areas of ordained ministry quickly became evident. In 1984 the Convention passed a "Resolution on Ordination and the Role of Women in Ministry" that, though purporting to affirm the "equal dignity" of men and women, contended that women must be excluded from pastoral leadership "to preserve a submission God requires because the man was first in creation and the woman was first in the Edenic fall." According to the resolution, women's exclusion from pastoral leadership is necessary because "women are not in public worship to assume a role of authority over men lest confusion reign in the church."[11]

Dee Miller, a former Southern Baptist missionary to Africa, realized early on that women would be a central issue in the Controversy. "Back in 1982," she explained, "when we were on furlough, the pastors often would confide in me their concerns. I heard rumblings from some of them about how the 'women's issue' was going to be the downfall of the SBC. I began thinking, back then, that the inerrancy issues really had nothing to do with inerrancy. They were only raised because of the 'women's issue.' We were being perceived as such an awful threat to the establishment, of course."

The Mother Seminary

During the 1970s and 1980s, more and more Southern Baptist women were enrolling in Southern Baptist seminaries. Buoyed by the women's movement and the progress of women in society, increasing numbers of women claimed their call to ministry and their need for theological education. At first, women were tracked into traditionally feminine areas, such as religious education and music. When Linda McKinnish Bridges arrived at Southern Seminary in 1975, despite her desire to take courses for the master of divinity degree, she was told to do a master's in religious education. Then, when she took Greek as an elective, she was the only woman in the class.

Southern Seminary first admitted women to its classrooms in the 1880s—the wives of male students were allowed to audit classes. In 1902 the seminary admitted its first regularly enrolled female student. In 1949 the first woman enrolled in the bachelor of divinity degree program; until then, it had been limited to men preparing for a preaching ministry, but from that time onward, all degree programs were open to women.

In 1982 I went to the Southern Baptist Theological Seminary in Louisville, Kentucky—the mother seminary of Southern Baptists. It was founded in 1859, shortly after the founding of the Convention itself. Of the six Southern Baptist seminaries, Southern had a reputation as a place of openness, inquiry, and intellectual integrity. When Ferrol Sams described the "raised right" child in *The Whisper of the River*, he wrote, "A place called Nashville was the source of the Sunday school literature, but the more highly anointed preachers of the day came from a mystic place called Louisville. Elders may have thought that the seat of the Southern Baptist Convention was in Nashville, but to any Raised Right child, 'Seminary at Louisville' had exactly the same ring as 'Temple at Jerusalem.'"[12] Among Southern Baptists, Southern was considered the "liberal" seminary. By the time I got there, the entire faculty supported women in ministry—at least theoretically. Women made up about a third of the student body, and although we had to put up with a lot of the typical misogynistic treatment from some of the male students, on the whole, Southern was as welcoming to women as Southern Baptists could have managed. For all those reasons, Southern became the primary target for the fundamentalists.

Those first women called to ordained ministry in the 1970s finished seminary and then found that, in terms of Southern Baptist life, they had few places to go. Most ended up on the staffs of Methodist, Presbyterian, and Episcopal churches. In the 1980s, however, we thought that we would find a place in Southern Baptist life. Southern Seminary embraced us; it told us, as our GA leaders had, that we could be anything God called us to be. We had a sense that Southern Baptist churches were opening up and would welcome us, their daughters, into their pulpits and classrooms with open arms. Were we wrong!

I became a feminist at Southern Seminary. Two experiences in particular led me to my feminist convictions. The first was hearing a woman preach. The church I grew up in didn't allow women to preach—or even pray—in public worship. In fact, my pastor had been hesitant to send me off to Southern Seminary, and he warned me, "Those professors will try to tell you that the Bible isn't true" (which never happened, by the way). My first semester at Southern, I went to a chapel service to hear one of the winners of the Clyde Francisco preaching awards—Linda McKinnish Bridges. That day in chapel, she was fabulous. I sat there listening and thinking, "Wow! She's better than most of the men I've ever heard preach. Why wouldn't God want that?" Julie Pennington-

Russell's revelation about women in ministry was a little more personal and dramatic. During her first semester at Golden Gate Seminary, she used to get up extra early in the morning, go down the hall of her dormitory to the prayer room, and pray for all those "poor, misguided women who thought God was calling them to be pastors." A few years later, Julie became pastor of Nineteenth Avenue Baptist Church in San Francisco.

The second experience that led me to feminism was more complicated. My first term in seminary, I took a required course called Formation for Christian Ministry. This course was limited to twenty students, and it just so happened that my class had seventeen men and three women. The class also divided into small groups that met once a week, and I was the only woman in my group. Also in my group were three men straight out of the coal mines of eastern Kentucky. They were part of a program that allowed people without college degrees to take seminary courses. The thinking was that if they were going to preach anyway, better they preach with some seminary education than with none at all. All term, these men voiced very conservative views, especially about women. They said things like, "I don't *let* my wife wear pants." As you can imagine, I was not amused, even in my prefeminist state. One day the professor told us that we would be having a guest speaker at our next class—an ordained woman who was a hospital chaplain. I was thrilled. I was still trying to figure out what I thought about women in ministry, and I believed that listening to what this woman had to say would help. At the next class, as the professor began to introduce our speaker, one of these coal miners—who was about as big as a Kentucky mountain—threw his books in his briefcase, flipped the locks, stood up with great fanfare, and stormed out of class, slamming the door behind him. I was appalled. If he didn't want to listen, he could have stayed home. He had purposefully made a show of his disdain and, in so doing, broke a primary rule of southern culture—thou shalt not be rude. At our next small group meeting, the teaching assistant introduced the topic for the day—women in ministry—and the same coal miner started the same routine. Now, I had been very quiet all term. In fact, I don't think I'd spoken at all in class. But at that moment, I found my voice. I pounded my fist on the desk and said to him, "What are you doing? Do you think in ministry you can just walk out any time you disagree with someone?" I thought my life was about to end. He turned, told me that he could do anything he wanted, and went out the door in a huff, waving around his Bible and shouting about the inerrant, infallible word of God. But that's not the day I became a feminist. The next day his two buddies stopped me in the hall to tell me that he really wasn't a bad sort. Then one of them said to me, "Susan, I'll be praying for you that you don't get messed up with this women in ministry stuff." And I became a feminist on the spot. I suppose I should find that coal miner and thank him.

When I asked my sister how she became a feminist, she quipped, "You, girl!" As I was emerging into my feminist consciousness, Karen was finishing high school and starting college, and she was forced to listen to my feminist critiques of pretty much everything. Later, when Karen married, she followed her husband's career for many years, sacrificing her own. When she finally left him, she realized "that I had undermined my own capabilities by hiding behind him, and that I didn't have to do that; that I could certainly be successful in and of myself. And then, I had you preaching that to me as well!"

In the 1980s, Southern Seminary provided a contradictory environment for women. On the one hand, the rhetoric of the seminary faculty and administration was unambiguously supportive of women. In 1984 President Roy Honeycutt preached a rousing chapel sermon asserting his unequivocal support of women in ministry. On the other hand, the realities of seminary classrooms and extracurricular activities reinforced gender norms in subtle and often unrecognized ways. In the late 1990s, Tisa Lewis and I talked to most of the women who had earned PhDs at Southern Seminary from 1982 to 1992. They told us that Southern had been a place of liberation, yet for many of them, it had also been a place where sexism occurred on a daily basis. Much to our chagrin, certain fundamentalists used the article we wrote to suggest that the changes they made at Southern had been necessary, as evidenced by the reports of the women we interviewed.[13] Interestingly, some of the women I interviewed for this book had their own chilling stories about their experiences at Southern Seminary under its current administration.

One woman told me that, like so many others, she grew up believing that she could be anything God called her to be. But during her time at Southern, she "had to fight for that and prove that to more people than [she] ever thought she would." She said, "It wasn't just that doors were closed. It was just mean-spirited. It's not just, 'You're not right for this job'; it's 'There is something wrong with you.' I can remember walking down the halls of Southern, and people would shout out things to you, saying things like, 'Too bad this isn't Germany; we can't just kill y'all like the concentration camp.'"

"People said that?" I asked in disbelief.

"Oh, yeah. It was a daily thing. You'd get harassing phone calls. Groups of male students would follow you and back you into dark classrooms. People would write things about you. The administration tried to have private meetings with us, threatening to kick us out. Oh yeah. It was awful."

"That's a very different Southern than I went to," I said.

"It was just very outwardly and openly hostile. *Hostile.* Not just angry or tense; it was hostile. I remember one time in an Old Testament class, one of the guys in the class turned around and told me that I needed to go home and have a baby, because that's how I was going to be saved anyway."

Another woman told me that despite receiving all As and A+s in her seminary classes at Southern, "I did have some fellow students tell me that they didn't think I needed to be there." Faculty didn't come right out and say that, but they emphasized that the role of women in the church was to lead children. "And I said, 'I am not here to lead children. I do not feel called to lead children. I love children; I am not here to lead children.'" She got unsigned notes in her campus mailbox saying, "You don't belong here. As a woman, you don't belong in a Southern Baptist leadership role. You don't need a seminary degree. You need to find yourself a good husband and then be a good wife." She never reported these notes to the administration because she "didn't think it would make any difference. And I'm sure I'm not the only woman who got those kinds of notes." She also related the following incident:

> One student told me one day, he said, "It's too bad you'll never be able to pastor a church—you can't because you're a woman—but someday I'm going to be the pastor of a big church. I may have as many as a thousand people, and I'll be affecting their lives every week." And I looked at him and said, "Do you know that this very coming Sunday, I'm going to be affecting thousands and thousands of lives because the discipleship training materials that will be used in churches in the Southern Baptist Convention, I wrote." And the look on his face; he was astounded. And then, after he digested that, a couple of days later, he came back and said, "Your stuff's not touching men as well as women, is it?" I said, "Oh, yes! The stuff I wrote is going to be read by men." [He responded,] "Well, you can't do that—you're a woman!" He was very appalled at the idea that a woman would be writing something that a man would use as a study guide.

Despite these obstacles, she finished her seminary degree and took a position in the denomination. "I don't think these issues stopped me from doing what I feel God called me to do," she added. "But, I have to say, it's been with a lot of perseverance."

Roy Honeycutt retired, and Al Mohler became president of Southern Seminary in 1993. Mohler had been educated at Southern; in fact, while he was completing his PhD, he was Honeycutt's assistant. Following graduation, he became editor of the Georgia Baptist paper the *Christian Index,* and his views took a hard right. Having once led the fight to challenge the Convention's 1984 statement on women, Mohler began to impose a litmus test on prospective faculty members. When David Sherwood interviewed for a position in the Carver School of Social Work (which has since been dismantled), Mohler rejected his appointment because, despite Sherwood's agreement with every other point of fundamentalist ideology, he suggested that God could call women to any role in ministry.[14]

Heather King, former director of women's ministries at Southern Seminary, sees the changes at Southern in a positive light. She said, "My experiences teaching at a Southern Baptist institution have far exceeded what I could ever have hoped for. The administration is actively looking for ways to encourage and support women on campus. The faculty is encouraging and supportive." Heather describes herself as a complementarian, believing in the ontological equality of women and men but recognizing that God has given women and men different roles in the church and in the family. Thus, she is very comfortable in the environment of Southern Seminary, which reflects the values of the Convention's fundamentalist leaders.

When Women Preach

Despite the fact that Martha Stearns Marshall had preached in the Separate Baptist churches in the eighteenth century, no Southern Baptist church ordained a woman until 1964, when the Watts Street Baptist Church in Raleigh, North Carolina, ordained Addie Davis to the Gospel ministry. As a child, Addie played preacher. She told Eljee Bentley, "I have, as long as I can remember, had a very strong religious interest. As a child, I felt a call to preach, but women were not preachers, so I never expressed this openly."[15] After graduating from Meredith College, a Southern Baptist women's college in North Carolina, in 1942, she accepted her first church staff position as an education director. When her father died, rather than going to seminary, Addie returned home to help her mother with the family business and served for six months as interim pastor of a small Baptist church. Addie fell ill, and the doctors misdiagnosed her, resulting in a burst appendix during surgery. Afterward, during her recovery, Addie determined, "If I was permitted to live, I would do what I'd always felt in my heart I should do, which was to be a preacher."[16]

When her mother retired in 1960, Addie enrolled at Southeastern Baptist Theological Seminary, where she made her desire to preach known. She found support among the seminary faculty and its president, even though they all knew that her journey would be a difficult one. As Addie neared graduation, she began to look for a church to pastor, but no Southern Baptist church showed any interest in having a woman as its pastor. So Addie contacted a friend who had been a pastor in an American Baptist church in Vermont. The friend recommended Addie to the church, and in 1964 it called her to be its pastor. But first she needed to be ordained. She initially contacted the church she had grown up in but then withdrew the request, knowing that the pastor didn't support women in ministry. Then she contacted the church where she had served as interim pastor, Watts Street Baptist Church. Pam and Keith Durso tell this story of Addie's ordination committee:

> All of the committee members promised to evaluate [Addie] based on her calling and confession. On the day of the examination, Addie was one of two candidates for ordination. The committee voted to recommend the other candidate, a chaplain to Baptist students at Duke University, despite the young man's unorthodox belief concerning the Virgin Birth. Addie's conservative theology, however, posed no problems for the committee, but two members confessed that despite their previous assurances, they could not recommend a woman for ordination. After a heated discussion [pastor Warren] Carr recalled, one member who supported Addie's ordination asked the two holdouts to explain their apprehension: "Brethren, you leave me confused. In the case of our first candidate, you were quite insistent that he believe that a Virgin bore the word. How is it that you are now so adamant that a virgin should not preach the word?" The committee then voted unanimously to ordain the "virgin," though one member abstained.[17]

Addie's ordination didn't exactly open a floodgate of women seeking ordination in Southern Baptist churches. In fact, not until the early 1970s were the next Southern Baptist women ordained. In 1970 the Antioch Baptist Church in Wadley, Alabama, ordained Ruby Welsh Wilkins. Priscilla Denham was ordained in 1977, and the church asked her to preach. The thing she remembered most vividly was that the pulpit had been built for men like her father, who was six foot two. She was only five feet four, so she had to stand on an upside-down Coca-Cola crate to be seen behind the pulpit.

Even after thirty years on the mission field, Carolyn Goodman Plampin hadn't given the issue of women's ordination much thought, until she taught a course on the ministry of Christian women. She taught the course from 1980 to 1986 but didn't include information on ordination until that last year.

"Why do you think it took you that long?" I asked.

"Honey," she said, her southern drawl still pronounced despite living all over the world, "we had never been taught that. Men are the gatekeepers of our information, and therefore they had never said, 'This is an important issue to study.' It is not taught in the seminary; you do not know how to find it; and therefore I had to learn how to find out this information. So when I learned to find out this information, then that changed me."

In Southern Baptist polity, ordination is a local church issue. That's why women have been ordained at all. Despite the pronouncements of the SBC, any local Baptist church can ordain anyone it wants. It may mean being kicked out of the local association, but the local church is autonomous, and if its membership decides to ordain a woman, the church is free to do so. Among the women I talked to, their ordination is a precious thing. Unlike their male counterparts, for whom ordination has always been a given, these women realize that they are outsiders who can be denied ordination simply on the basis of their gender—regardless of any other qualifications or preparation. When they talked of their ordination, they often cried and spoke with great awe and tenderness about the experience.

Not all the churches that ordained these women were leaders in supporting women's ordination. As several women explained, their ordinations were more about their relationships with the congregations. The congregations saw the gifts of ministry and calling in these women, so they ordained them—not as a statement about women in general but as an affirmation of the ministries of these women in particular. Nancy Hollomon-Peede said of the church that ordained her, "In theory, they weren't for women being ordained, but they were for me."

Kandy Queen-Sutherland actually resisted ordination for a while. She and her husband, Dixon, were working on master's of divinity degrees at Southern Seminary in the mid-1970s when he became pastor of a small church. In the meantime, Kandy was fielding a lot of offers to preach in area churches, and when she was gone, Dixon would say to the congregation, "Let's remember Kandy as she preaches at so-and-so to-day." During a Sunday evening business meeting at Dixon's church, one woman stood up and said, "I think we should ask Kandy to preach. If she can preach everywhere, she can preach here." So she did, and after a bit of time had gone by, Dixon came home from a church business meeting one night and told her that the deacons wanted Kandy to share the pas-toral duties of the church with him. The church they pastored offered to ordain them many times over the next four years, but they always said no because they saw ordination as something used "to separate and discrim-inate." Finally, when they finished their PhDs and took jobs at Stetson University, the congregation said, "Please let us ordain you. We want to be part of your future ministry, and this is our gift to you." At that point, Kandy and Dixon agreed, and they were ordained in 1982.

I was not ordained when I finished seminary. I took a teaching posi-tion in the Religion Division at California Baptist College (now Uni-versity) and probably would have been fired if I had been ordained. My first day on campus, a young male student approached me and said that he'd never take one of my classes because women shouldn't teach men the Bible. Many of the pastors in the state also seemed terribly uncom-fortable with a young woman teaching religion. They often launched attacks against me, and when the president or the dean called me into his office to answer the most recent accusation, I was rarely provided with the name of the pastor leveling the charges. And in practically every case, the accusation was based on misinformation about what had or hadn't happened in my classroom. For example, one time a pastor complained that I had told students that the book of Esther doesn't belong in the Bible. What I actually said was that the book of Esther doesn't mention God, so it is a disputed book in the canonical process. Then I made the case for why it does indeed belong in the Bible.

Another time, I had a denominational employee come and speak to my class. During the break, she and I were talking about the difficulties of teaching religion in a Southern Baptist setting. She asked me, "Well, what do you do when you get to those verses in Paul about women." I laughed and said, "I just tell them Paul was wrong." Of course, I was kidding. But apparently, a student overheard me and told his pastor, who promptly called the president of the college. When I explained to the president that I had been joking around with someone in a private conversation, he told me not to make jokes anymore.

I never found out who perpetrated the most upsetting attack on me. The outside of my office door had a bulletin board (as did my colleagues'), and I occasionally posted cartoons on it. I came to work one morning to find that the cartoons had been shredded into tiny pieces and a note had been tacked to the bulletin board that read, "Dr. Shaw is a feminist, socialist, Marxist, communist, bitch." I still had copies of the cartoons, so I replaced them. I gave the note to campus security, and I stopped going to my office at night to work. The next morning, and each morning for the rest of the week, I found the cartoons shredded. Then, just as suddenly, the harassment stopped.

The great irony of my time at Cal Baptist is that it was also wildly successful. At the end of my first year, I won the Faculty Member of the Year Award, which gave me the opportunity to deliver the convocation address the following fall term. I won other teaching awards over my four years there and worked with amazing students who went on to become successful professionals themselves.

After four years, however, I felt battered and vulnerable, so I took a teaching position in the Religion Department at George Fox College (now University), an evangelical Quaker institution. Quakers don't practice ordination, but they do record ministers—those people whom the meeting identifies as being gifted for ministry. I was the only woman in the Religion Department, and all my male colleagues were recorded Quaker ministers. I was worried about what that example might say to my female students, so I started to consider ordination. When I lived in California, the pastor of the church I attended in Riverside tried to have the congregation there license me, but opposition had arisen, and we dropped the idea. I attended a wonderful moderate Southern Baptist church in Oregon, but I knew that it couldn't ordain me without a high likelihood of being kicked out of the local association and the state convention. So I asked my seminary church, Shalom Baptist Church in Louisville, Kentucky, to ordain me. Without hesitation, the congregation agreed.

I had been on the West Coast for six years when I returned to Louisville in the summer of 1993 to teach a course at Southern Seminary. And while I was there, Shalom Baptist Church ordained me. Friends from my seminary days came to the service. One group gave me a white satin stole embroidered with gold Celtic crosses, and the congregation presented me with a leather-bound New Revised Standard Version of the Bible. We sang "Be Thou My Vision":

Be thou my vision, O Lord of my heart;
Naught be all else to me, save that thou art:
Thou my best thought, by day or by night,
Waking or sleeping, thy presence my light.[18]

Co-pastor Jane Lites preached the charge to the candidate. Then the entire congregation came forward to lay hands on me as I knelt at the front of the church.

The laying on of hands is a biblical practice that confers a blessing, and it is performed in many Christian denominations as part of the ordination to ministry. Traditionally, although Baptists believe that the entire church is doing the ordaining, only ordained ministers are allowed to lay on hands. However, a common theme in the ordination stories of my participants was the involvement of the entire congregation in the ritual. For many of the women I interviewed, the symbolism of the entire congregation's participation was important, perhaps because of the significance they attach to community and their egalitarian impulses. Having been excluded from ordination for so long, they don't want to exclude others.

When Priscilla Denham was being ordained, she told the pastor that although she had seen only ordained people participate in the laying on of hands, she "believe[d] in the priesthood of all believers." Therefore, she said, "I would like [there] to be an option that anyone who's a member of the church can lay hands on me." The pastor agreed, and the women in the church were allowed to participate. Priscilla added, "Women who had never been able to do anything except observe ordination participated. And it was very important to me; it felt like my ordination was really an affirmation of all of us in the church who had gifts and a commitment to God." Likewise, Beth Crawford called the laying on of hands an "incredibly moving kind of experience. Folks came down, and just one at a time laid their hands on my head; sometimes prayed over me, sometimes just whispered some word of encouragement to me; sometimes they were just silent. That was an incredible gift." Amy Mears said that when the women came down to lay hands on her, they didn't really know what to do, because they'd never done it before. Her grandmother came down and whispered in her ear, "Amy, this is Lou." Mothers brought their young daughters, Amy explained, because now that women could participate in ordination, they wanted their little girls to learn what to do.

I don't remember what most people said to me as I knelt there, but I do recall the words Maryanna Bernard spoke. Maryanna was an African American woman in her late seventies at the time. She had been a great inspiration to me while I was attending seminary and taught me much about graciousness, determination, and strength. Maryanna bent over, put her hands on my shoulders, and whispered in my ear, "If I was as young as you, if I'd been born in times like these, I'd be a preacher too."

Ordination is a church's affirmation of a person's call to ministry. Traditionally, in Baptist theology, ordination conveys no hierarchical power or authority. It's really about recognizing someone's gifts. In fact, the Baptist idea is that the members of the local church are the ministers, and the pastors equip the members of the church to do ministry. But with fundamentalist thinking, ordination began to carry a connotation of ecclesiastical authority. And for women to receive that authority was a threat.

For the fundamentalists, the pastor is an authority to whom church members must submit, and because men should never have to submit to the authority of a woman, a woman cannot be a pastor and command authority over men. As a Southern Seminary administrator explained:

> Paul uses Genesis 2 to support his contention that women need to display, in the church, their submission to male leadership. The woman ought to have a symbol of authority on her head because she is the glory of man, because she originated from man and because she was created for man's sake. Because Paul links the woman's submissive role in the church to God's created design, it is evident that these instructions to the church at Corinth are not applicable only there, but instead are applicable universally in the church. . . . Women are to submit to male leadership and teaching because Adam was created first, and because Eve was deceived and sinned first.[19]

Of course, not all ministry requires ordination, and many women in ministry have eschewed it, either because they feel no real need for it or because it may cause more trouble than it's worth. As Debra Owens-Hughes explained, "The scripture does not call for ordination to be serving. Ordination is simply the sending and approval of your church. That I have. They are behind me." Pam Boucher pointed out that although she has thought about ordination, she doesn't have a strong desire for it, nor does she need it for the ministry she does. Rather than causing conflict by pushing the issue, she simply does the ministry to which she feels called. She explained, "I know I'm a minister and called to ministry, and the people I work with recognize that and respond to that, and that's really what's been important to me through the years."

Some women in ministry, however, oppose women's ordination, as do most of the women currently on the faculty of the six Southern Baptist seminaries. They do not believe that God calls women to ordained ministry, nor do they believe that ordination is necessary for the kinds of ministry to which women are called. That was not true two decades ago when I was in seminary, but it is a result of the Controversy that has so engulfed our lives.

Backlash

As women began to claim a place in ministry, particularly ordained ministry, a backlash ensued against the progress made in the 1970s and early 1980s. Many of the churches that did ordain or call women were promptly expelled from their local Baptist associations. Mission boards refused to send a married woman as the primary missionary in a missionary couple. In 2002 the North American Mission Board decided that it would no longer endorse ordained women as chaplains, and in 2004 the board announced that it would no longer endorse women to chaplain positions "where the role and function of the chaplain would be seen the same as that of a pastor."[20] Primarily, this affects women seeking employment as military chaplains, because they "administer the Lord's Supper and baptism, preach, counsel and perform weddings and funerals." In June 2004 the Convention voted that Southern Baptists should disaffiliate themselves from the Baptist World Alliance, citing as one reason the "continued emphasis on women as pastors."[21]

The North Broad Baptist Church in Rome, Georgia, called Tony and Katrina Brooks as co-pastors because the congregation felt that they were the best fit for the church. The Floyd County Baptist Association dealt with this in a unique way. Rather than voting the church out of the association (an option chosen by many other associations), it decided to adopt the revised *Baptist Faith and Message,* with its statement excluding women from the pastorate, as its official statement of faith. A number of congregations in the association opposed this move, but the majority approved it. I was in Rome doing interviews shortly before the vote, and my mother was very upset. Although she didn't necessarily think that women ought to be pastors, she still believed in the Baptist notion of local church autonomy. For her, this meant if

North Broad wanted to call a woman as pastor, it was well within its rights to do so, and the association shouldn't interfere. Mom was slated to go to that meeting as a messenger from her church. Messengers aren't supposed to be instructed how to vote by the church; because Baptists believe that God speaks directly to each individual, the messenger is supposed to vote her or his conscience. But her church ignored this custom and suggested that she vote according to the will of the congregation. Mom refused to go to the meeting. She also challenged her pastor to rethink his position and to honor the autonomy of the local church. After the association adopted the revised *Baptist Faith and Message*, the members of North Broad decided as a matter of integrity to disaffiliate from the association rather than wait for the association to vote to disfellowship them.

The first Southern Baptist church disfellowshipped by its local association for calling a woman as pastor was Prescott Memorial Baptist Church in Memphis, which had called Nancy Sehested in 1987. According to Nancy, the Credentials Committee of the Shelby County Baptist Association recommended at the annual meeting that no action be taken against the church, but another pastor got up and made a motion to disfellowship the church. Following Robert's Rules of Order, other messengers began to speak for and against the motion. Just as Nancy got to the microphone, someone called the question. Nancy was stunned that democratically principled Baptists would deny her an opportunity to speak. Adrian Rogers, president of the Southern Baptist Convention at the time and a Memphis pastor who supported disfellowshipping the church, interceded, and Nancy was allowed to speak. Despite her eloquent plea, about 75 percent of the messengers voted in favor of the motion and disfellowshipped the church.

Perhaps the most high-profile backlash came against Molly Marshall, a professor of theology at Southern Seminary. Molly was a lifelong Southern Baptist, a queen regent in GAs, who heard the call to ministry at church camp when she was fourteen years old. "One of the regular camp hymns was 'Wherever He Leads I'll Go,'" Molly explained in an essay in the Dursos' collection. "It never occurred to me that I was disqualified from following simply because I was a girl."[22] In 1973 Molly enrolled in the master of divinity program at Southern Seminary, and upon graduation she joined a church staff in Arkansas as a minister of youth and single adults. Soon thereafter, she felt a call to theological education, so she returned to Southern to pursue her PhD. At that time, there were no women on the theology faculty at Southern, although the Christian education and music faculties included some women. As she neared the completion of her degree, Molly began to apply for teaching positions, but Baptist schools were afraid to hire a woman to teach religion. About that time, she decided to accept a position as interim pastor of Jordan Baptist Church, a small, rural church in Eagle Station, Kentucky; St. Matthews Baptist Church in Louisville ordained her; and shortly after Molly's arrival at Jordan, the church called her as its regular pastor. Six months into her tenure as pastor, Southern Seminary invited her to become the first woman on the faculty of the School of Theology. Her appointment upset many fundamentalists, who began a campaign of letters and scrutiny to undermine her. The seminary granted her tenure in 1988, but that provided no protection from her detractors. When fundamentalist Al Mohler became president of the seminary in 1993, the Board of Trustees, by now dominated by fundamentalists, enjoined Mohler to get rid of Molly, which he did. By threatening a heresy trial, and pointing out that he already had the votes on the board to convict her, Mohler forced Molly to resign. The events leading to her resignation have been documented in the film *Battle for the Minds* (Lipscomb, 1996). Molly left Southern and joined the faculty of Central Baptist Theological Seminary, an American Baptist institution. She was named president in 2005, making her the first female president of a Baptist seminary in North America.

For many Southern Baptist women, the issue of women in ministry is related more to exposure than to doctrine. When I asked about women as pastors and preachers, many participants told me that they couldn't really say how they felt about it: they had never seen a woman do those things. Some stated outright that women shouldn't preach or pastor because the Bible teaches that they shouldn't. Many more said that although they couldn't envision it, they weren't willing to write off the possibility completely.

My mother had never heard a woman preach until just a few years ago. At the time, she and my father were attending a Southern Methodist church whose pastor had a Pentecostal background. Southern Methodists generally don't allow women to preach, but because this pastor had grown up with women preachers, he really didn't have a problem with it. He heard that I was coming home and invited me to preach in their church. I did—with some apprehension, knowing that my parents believed (at the time) that women shouldn't preach. My mother has never been one to heap on praise, but after the service she came up to me and said (and to this day, I consider this a high compliment), "Well, there was nothing wrong with that."

Because so much of our identity is constructed from what we experience, women's lack of exposure to women preachers and pastors prevents them from even seeing the possibility. Carolyn Hale Cubbedge's story of her own calling points to the importance of mentors and role models. Carolyn said, "I do remember when I was about seven years old saying to myself, and never voicing this to anyone else, 'If I were a boy, when I got older, I'd be a preacher.' I'd never seen a woman preacher. So I just said to myself, 'No.'" Only much later after spending more than a decade working in higher education did Carolyn finally answer the call to prepare for the pastorate.

Molly Marshall's story from her pastorate in rural Kentucky shows that the perception of limitations can go both ways. One day during children's church, a problem arose because the little girls wouldn't let the little boys be preachers. After all, their only experience was seeing a woman in the pulpit. One of the church workers had to explain to them, "Now girls, little boys can be preachers too."[23]

The women of First Baptist Church in Batesburg, South Carolina, had an interesting discussion about women in ministry. Although their church doesn't ordain women as deacons, it has been supportive of its female members who have felt called to ministry. In fact, Tisa Lewis has preached in her home church on occasion. I asked these women, who are in their sixties and seventies, whether any of their ideas about women in church, home, or society have changed over the years.

ANNIE COCKRELL: I worked all my life and retired. So I was a working mother. And I think I raised my children to the best of my knowledge to go to church and be Christians; and if I hadn't worked, we couldn't have provided for them to have the education that they got. And my mother stayed at home. So it was a big step.

PAIGE TROTTER: I believe that it's getting to the point where the spiritual heads of the house are women. I wish it weren't true.

JOAN LEWIS: It's that way at church, too.

SUSAN SHAW: Why do y'all think that's true? Why do you think women are leading more?

JEAN GASTON: I do think that women ought to be allowed to participate more as far as serving as deacons and serving in places of worship, and a lot of the Southern Baptist churches they will not allow women to be pastors or assistant pastors. I have a sister-in-law, by marriage, her second marriage, and her granddaughter by her first marriage was an assistant pastor at a Baptist church in Florida. They just kind of had an uprising practically because she was serving as assistant pastor. She's no longer doing that. Fine girl. And could preach as well as anybody. And I just think it's too bad that we don't allow women to serve in that capacity.

JOAN: I know for a fact that when my daughter got up one Sunday morning and taught, we had somebody leave from our church because they did not believe in that.

ANNIE: I think women should be allowed, but you know it all goes back to our ancestors when the man was the head of the house. You know what I'm saying? And the woman was at home. But it's all changed now. Sure, I think women like my aunt, she was a Methodist and she was a—they didn't call them deacons, but was a stewardess in the church. I think that's what it was. And as far as education and all, I think the minds work the same. So I don't see why women can't do it either.

JOAN: I think the women really and truly would make good deacons.

BETTIE AKINS: I really can't understand why women are not allowed to be—I know in the past they were not allowed to be leaders in the church. But things have changed; women are leaders. We studied in the Bible; there were several women had leadership roles in the Bible. So I don't think it's unscriptural.

For these women, the changes they've seen in society and experienced in their own lives have led them to question why women can't serve in any capacity in the church. They recognize that women are as capable and as gifted as men in terms of providing pastoral leadership, and they question the barriers to women in ministry. Most significantly, they recognize that the barriers are the result of social structures and antiquated beliefs that support women's subordination rather than the result of responsible biblical exegesis and theology.

Survival Strategies

For many women who answered the call to ministry in the 1970s, 1980s, and early 1990s, the Controversy has been a central theme. For most of us, it has meant an identity crisis. We went into ministry intending to spend our lives serving Southern Baptists, but then we discovered that Southern Baptists, the very ones who had nurtured and affirmed us, no longer wanted us. This forced us to rethink both our identities and our callings. Nancy Hollomon-Peede said that the Controversy called her identity into question: "If I don't work in a Baptist setting, who will I be? I'm an ordained Baptist minister, and that's who I feel called to be."

The women who attended seminary during the Controversy have adopted several different strategies for dealing with this identity crisis. Some have chosen to stay in the SBC. For a small group of women, the Controversy has not generated an identity crisis; they are comfortable with the Convention's stance on women in ministry. They themselves do not feel called to ordained ministry. They do the work they have been called to do, and they feel supported by their churches and the Convention. Another group that has stayed in the SBC disagrees with its position on women in ministry, but these women continue to feel called to work among Southern Baptists. They have distanced themselves from denominational politics and focus instead on their ministry in local churches, on the mission field, or in denominational agencies.

A larger group of seminary-educated women has chosen to affiliate with one of the moderate splinter groups—either the Cooperative Baptist Fellowship or the Alliance of Baptists. The CBF is the more conservative of the two and has been described by many women as "same song, second verse" or, as one woman put it, "The CBF—patriarchy all over again. They wear better ties." Although the CBF affirms the idea of women in ministry in its rhetoric, in reality, the organization has rebuilt patriarchal structures in which women still lack equal representation or voice. Some of the women I interviewed, however, related only positive experiences with the CBF. The Alliance is much smaller and more liberal, even taking a stand on affirming gay and lesbian people. Sarah Shelton was called before the local association to answer for her church's affiliation with the Alliance because of its stance on homosexuality.

A small group of women left ministry altogether; some even left the church. Other women have chosen to change denominations. Many have become American Baptists, Methodists, Episcopalians, Presbyterians, and United Church of Christ (UCC). Priscilla Denham used the image of Lot's wife to explain the pain of leaving the Southern Baptists. "Who could grieve, leaving a place like Sodom? But [Lot's wife] did. She turned around; and her grief immobilized her. That's what I feel like leaving the Southern Baptists. How can I leave, and, at the same

time, how can I be grieving that? And yet I did. But I said, thank goodness, I have something I'm moving toward, a denomination that fits me
better; the denomination as a whole fits my values better than the
Southern Baptists as they are becoming. But that was the image that
was very powerful for me. You've gotta leave, but, gosh, you want to
turn around and look back. You want to somehow take it with you."

Paula Sheridan attended an SBC meeting in New Orleans at the
height of the Controversy, when moderates were losing vote after vote
after vote. While sitting in the Café du Monde, she and some moderate
friends saw a group of fundamentalist leaders come in and order donuts
and coffee, and while standing there, they started singing "Victory in
Jesus." Paula said, "I knew that my family had changed the locks on the
door, and my key no longer worked." She continued, "It's like that line
from *Fiddler on the Roof,* when they're all packing up to leave, and someone comes to the rabbi and says, 'Where will we look for the messiah?'
And the rabbi says, 'We'll look for the messiah someplace else.'" She
recalled turning to her friends and saying, "We'll look for the messiah
someplace else."

For the majority of these women, their experience with Southern
Baptists in the last twenty-five years has been characterized by pain.
One denominational employee told me that the Controversy caused her
to question who she was in God's eyes. "Who am I in God's creation?
What did he create me to be? So sometimes [the Controversy] would
cause me to ask those questions of myself personally, as a Christian, as
a believer in God. Who am I in the eyes of God? Well, I'm his child;
I'm created in his image. Even now I have to go back to that. I'm created in his image, and he loves me for who I am because I reflect him.
So I think I began to look for things that would help legitimize my
creation as a woman." Karen Massey recounted how the Controversy
affected her seminary experience. After the 1984 convention, where the
resolution excluding women from the pastorate was passed, she cried all
the way home. "That was the first time it truly hit home," she explained.
"After that it just became this snowball effect at seminary. We ate, slept,
breathed, you know; you know, every day the Controversy just hung
over my entire seminary education like a cloud." A former seminary
professor told me that during the Controversy she ended up on antide-
pressants. She said, "I felt abused. I felt rejected by what I thought was
my place in ministry. I felt alienated, like I didn't belong anymore—and
I didn't."

Over and over, women in ministry have told me stories of being excluded, marginalized, attacked, berated, threatened, harassed, and fired. But the other thing that characterizes them is a sense of calling that withstands these attacks. None of these women denies her calling. None says, "Gee, maybe the fundamentalists are right, and I misheard the call of God." They are all quick to point to patriarchy and the abuse of power as the real culprits. Similarly, Creegan and Pohl found that a strong sense of calling, particularly in the face of resistance, characterized the responses of almost all the women who participated in their study of evangelical women in seminary.[24] Likewise, a study of Protestant clergywomen found that a sense of calling is essential: "It sustains them in the face of difficulties and discrimination. It informs their understanding of ministry and the world."[25]

In his master's thesis, Howell Williams argues that Southern Baptist women in ministry continue to engage with the denomination and its offshoots because of what he calls the "myth of progress."[26] These women believe that change will come slowly, that they can work from the inside to create a more open denomination for women, and that if they just play by the rules, eventually everyone will see that women really can be ministers. But in his recent book *Southern Baptist Sisters*, historian David Morgan contends that the status of Southern Baptist women in the Convention today is pretty much the same as it was in 1845.[27] Nonetheless, for southerners in particular, denominational allegiance is a key part of Southern Baptist identity, and many women are loath to let go of it. It's as much a part of who they are as their family identity. In fact, in many ways, Southern Baptists are one gigantic dysfunctional family. Julie Ingersoll notes how difficult it is for women raised in conservative Protestant traditions to leave those traditions. She writes, "Women in conservative Protestantism who face gender-related conflict over their leadership roles, which is ultimately gender-related conflict about their very identities, show remarkable perseverance within those subcultures; they stay despite tremendous turmoil. . . . The women least likely to leave are the women who grew up in the tradition."[28]

The majority of Southern Baptist women in ministry with whom I spoke grew up in the denomination. Their sense of calling is profound—and it is a calling that was nurtured by Southern Baptists. They were taught, "You can be anything God calls you to be," and that's why their rejection by the denomination is so confusing and painful. Even in the moderate offshoots, women in ministry still contend with sexism, the old boys' network, and a vast majority of congregations that are not yet ready to call a woman as pastor. Katrina Brooks said, "It's really hard not to have an identity crisis when a lot of people are saying you can't do it. . . . There are times in all of our lives when we're more susceptible to hearing other voices and the comments that they make, and so I really have to work hard not to embrace those and allow them to become who I am. I have to really rely on the basics. I'm called by God. I'm called by this church. That is enough."

Although the fundamentalists took control of the denomination more than a decade ago, when these women talk about their lives and their ministries, that event still plays a major role in how they understand themselves. In many ways, they are survivors of trauma, but they have also found ways to thrive, within Baptist life and without. They are pastors, professors, seminary deans and presidents, social workers, and counselors. They have persisted in claiming and carrying out their vocations, and they have forged the way for new generations of young women, providing role models that these women didn't have.

New Generations

The experiences of women who answered a call to ministry after the early 1990s have been very different from those of women who attended seminary in the 1970s through early 1990s. One group of women continues to identify with Southern Baptists. They attended Southern Baptist seminaries, and they are comfortable with the roles offered to them in the SBC. They agree that women should not pastor churches and that wives should be submissive to their husbands. They are also quick to point out that they believe that women and men are of equal worth before God. They believe that God has given women and men different but equally valuable roles, and they are able to carry out the ministries to which they feel called within those parameters. Another group of women came of age in CBF or Alliance churches and attended moderate Baptist or other denominational seminaries. They believe that women and men are equal in church and home and that both women and men can fulfill any role to which they feel called. They may have grown up in Southern Baptist churches that were in the SBC initially but became CBF or Alliance during the Controversy; they tend to have very little sense of themselves as Southern Baptist. They see themselves as fully part of the CBF or Alliance. For both groups of women, the Controversy is history, and it has had very little effect on them that they can identify. Both express a strong sense of agency—they are doing exactly what they feel called to do.

Under Scripture

Again and again, conservative Southern Baptist women expressed the opinion that they have not been prevented from doing the ministries to which they feel called. They emphasize the belief that God can use women in many ways other than the pastorate, and that those other forms of ministry are just as valuable. As Heather King pointed out, the need is so great that she "could work tirelessly every day and still not minister to all the needs." She feels encouraged by the administration and her faculty colleagues at Southern Seminary in the ministry she does there. She said, "My worth and value before God is equal to that of the opposite gender. When I understand that God has designed a different role or function for me to carry out that does not denigrate my value or worth before him, then I am better able to carry out God's plan for me as a woman."

In particular, these women reiterate that their beliefs about women's roles are shaped by the Bible, which they understand as excluding women from the pastorate. In a 2004 *Baptist Press* editorial, Dorothy Patterson responded to a statement by WMU of Virginia that affirmed the "diverse and unlimited" vocational possibilities for women. Dorothy disagreed with the Virginia WMU's assumption that gender doesn't limit women's roles in ministry. Instead, she argued that the Bible clearly articulates certain gender-based requirements for some leadership positions. Nonetheless, she continued, other than pastoral leadership, women are afforded innumerable opportunities for ministry.[29] In an earlier unpublished manuscript, Dorothy offered an exegesis of pertinent passages and concluded, "Nothing in Scripture infers that godly women assumed positions of authority over men in either the church or the home. My position, then, is that Scripture does not permit a woman to be ordained as a ruling or teaching elder. Concerning the diaconate, I do not think the Scripture supports ordination, but neither do I see a clear prohibition to the woman's serving in the diaconate following the New Testament pattern of this office. Subordination in the home, church, school, or marketplace has never abolished equality any more than equality has abolished subordination."[30]

For conservative Southern Baptist women in ministry, the limitations that exclude them from the pastorate are a direct reflection of biblical teachings. As Faith Wu put it, "I'm either underneath scripture, or I'm not." For these women, however, exclusion from pastoral leadership hardly seems to limit what they can do in ministry. Rather than focusing on the one role women can't have, they focus on the myriad ways women can serve in other ministry positions. Faith explained, however, that she believes that women shouldn't teach men in seminary classes that include doctrinal content. She cited 1 Timothy, which states, "Women should not teach or have authority over men." So when Faith teaches courses with any theological content, only women are allowed in those classes, but if she teaches a language class, men can enroll.

Sheri Klouda, a professor of Hebrew at Southwestern Seminary at the time of her interview, said, "I do feel that an academic setting is not a local church; so it's legitimate for females to teach theology and biblical studies. . . . I don't look at the church and an academic institution as the same thing." But Sheri was worried that she would be denied tenure at Southwestern because of her gender. The seminary president had openly declared that he wanted the theology faculty to model the local church, and in his view, of course, women were excluded from pastoral ministry. Nevertheless, he initially assured Sheri that she had nothing to worry about as long as she didn't make gender an issue. In 2004, however, Sheri was told that the president would not recommend her for tenure, which meant that her case would not even come up for review, despite her good record of scholarship and her excellent teaching evaluations (from men as well as women). Sheri tried to work out a compromise that would allow her to stay on, perhaps outside the School of Theology. After all, she had a mortgage, a daughter trying to finish high school, and a seriously ill husband who needed her health insurance to cover his costly medications. Nonetheless, in 2006, seminary administrators told Sheri that her contract would not be renewed after the spring semester. In early 2007, Sheri filed a lawsuit in U.S. District Court in Fort Worth, accusing the seminary and its president of breach of contract, fraud, and defamation.[31] As of this writing, the outcome of the case is pending.

In contrast, Candi Finch, a PhD student in theology, described her seminary experiences at both Southeastern and Southwestern with great enthusiasm. She has felt supported as a woman in seminary and has been encouraged to read from a wide variety of theological thinkers in order to form her own opinions. "They've challenged my thinking," she explained, "and told me not to settle, not to believe something just because a person says it. They've encouraged me—all of my professors have—encouraged me to base my belief on the Word of God."

Doing What God Called Me to Do

The women currently attending CBF- and Alliance-supported seminaries represent the other end of the theological and ministerial spectrum. They believe that women can be called to the pastorate, and some
of them have actually experienced women in ministry. Some have had
to overcome resistance from more conservative family members and
pastors; for instance, Leah Grundset's pastor's wife encouraged her to
think about working with children, because the role of pastor was reserved for men. Others have felt support for their calling from the beginning. Eva Buford, a Truett Seminary student, grew up seeing
women as leaders. She laughed, "It wasn't until I arrived at Baylor that
I realized that women aren't supposed to go into ministry. I never knew
that [limitation] existed before I came here." For the women attending
Truett, its openness to women in ministry was a key factor in their
choosing it over Southwestern. Eva visited Southwestern but felt that it
limited women's roles too much. Jennifer Wagley went to a Baptist college in Louisiana and was accepted at both Southwestern and New Orleans Baptist Theological Seminary, but she chose Truett instead. I
asked her why.

"Because I didn't want to fight the battles that I knew I'd have to
fight there."

"Which you considered to be . . . ?"

"In college I fought the preacher boys the whole time, and so I felt
like I'd rather fight a more moderate preacher boy."

Many of these young women attending moderate seminaries came
from traditional churches where they never saw a woman preach, pray,
or even take up the offering. For a number of them, studying Baptist
history in college had a profound effect on their understanding of wom-
en in ministry. Amy Bigbee, for example, realized how oppressive it was
"that women did not have prominent roles in the churches; all the committees, all the deacons, all the ushers, everything was men." Likewise,
Kathryn Seay had never really thought about women as pastors until she
learned how Baptist women have been involved in ministry throughout
Baptist history.

Nonetheless, for many of these women—like the first women who
answered the call to ministry—an overpowering sense of calling drives
them to challenge the gender constraints imposed by their home
churches. When Charla Milligan told her pastor that she had been
called to ministry (she was sixteen at the time), he informed her that she

was going to be a pastor's wife, and she and her husband would become missionaries. In college, however, she realized that mission work was not her calling, and she began to search for the right area. She went to Truett to become a counselor, and during her first semester there, she met another woman who professed a call to the pastorate. "I totally said to her, 'You cannot be a pastor!' I was like, 'That is *wrong*!' I said, 'You cannot do that; it is against the Bible.'" Then Charla took a preaching class, and she began to struggle with the issue of women in ministry and her own calling. The professor told her, "I normally do not let people write their papers on women pastors and women ministers, but you need to." Charla called that semester "mind-blowing," as she came to terms with her own calling.

When I spoke to a group of Truett students, Katie McKown recalled how she reacted to the contention of W. A. Criswell, who said that if a woman heard a call to the pastorate, she had heard wrong. Katie couldn't believe it; she felt perfectly capable of interpreting her own call, whatever that call was. She said, "And if it's not my call to be a pastor, there's some other sister out there!" The group responded with raucous laughter. Lisa Williams pointed out that one of the advantages of being a woman at seminary is that, because of their small numbers, they all know and support one another. "I think that's one of the fun things about women in ministry," she added.

Many of these young women pointed out the inconsistency between moderates' supportive rhetoric about women and the reality of placing women in churches. LeAnn Gardner noted that Truett may pat women on the back and offer affirmation, but the school doesn't actively encourage churches to call these women as pastors. "So," she concluded, "it's like there's one step missing; there's a lot of lip service, and it's not taken one step further." Melissa Browning recalled getting her name on the school's pulpit supply list, but in four years she was never called. She asked about it, and a staff member told her, "Well, a lot of churches don't want women to preach." Melissa responded, "Well, do you try to persuade them? Is there some persuasion going on?" And, she concluded, "I don't think there is." Charla added that when she worked in the office responsible for the pulpit supply list, churches would call and say, "Do not send women's résumés." But, she laughed, "I wanted to send them anyway." Again, the group roared with laughter.

Many of the women who attend Truett also go to Calvary Baptist Church in Waco, where Julie Pennington-Russell is pastor. Some chose the church specifically because Julie is there; some weren't aware that the church had a woman pastor until the first time they visited; others went just to check out the novelty of a woman pastor. Now, they all see Julie as a role model. Leigh Jackson explained, "I think it's much easier if you have at least one mentor that's a woman, and we are so lucky to have Julie. . . . It's the presence of seeing a woman in the pulpit." Several young women also mentioned Julie's pastoral care abilities. Charla pointed out, "I have to really fight the point of view that *all* pastors should be women. What pastors send encouraging cards when they know you're having a difficult time in your life? What pastors send cards that congratulate you on the birth of your child? I've never had that happen to me, *ever*, until Julie. She sends birthday cards. I mean, please!" Meghan Becker believes that Julie is a role model for all pastors, not just women. She said, "I think Julie . . . does what God calls her to do, and . . . if she's a great role model, great; but it's not like this is her banner . . . she doesn't think 'I'm such a great woman.' She just does what God calls her to do."

The women at McAfee School of Theology point to Karen Massey as an important influence on their lives and ministries. Karen teaches at McAfee but is ordained and has served in pastoral positions at local churches. They credit Karen with both opening their eyes to the possibilities for women in ministry and showing them that women can be successful in ministry among Baptists. These women recognize that the generation of women in seminary before them paved the way. Nikki Hardeman said, "I don't feel like I'm going to have to fight my way into a position in a church. I don't think I'm going to have to convince every person I come into contact with that I am valid as a minister. I think I will find places of employment in a local church where people who reject me as a minister will be the minority rather than the majority."

April Baker loves to preach at churches and have all the little girls sitting in the front rows see "Reverend April Baker" in the pulpit. That allows them to recognize at an early age all the possibilities available "when you say 'you can be anything God created you to be.'" April said, "I never heard a woman preach, didn't know such a thing happened, until I was in college and had that door opened up for me."

The changes that came as a result of the Controversy have created markedly different experiences for women who now attend seminaries. The six Southern Baptist seminaries that, to varying degrees, supported women in pastoral leadership throughout the 1980s and early 1990s no longer do so. Their faculties reflect the view of the more conservative leadership of the Convention, which believes that God calls women to a multitude of ministries, but not to the pastorate. The newer moderate seminaries that cropped up as conservatives took control of the SBC seminaries are decidedly supportive of women in the pastorate, although in many ways, sexism is still pervasive, even among moderate men. The experiences of young women at these moderate seminaries are more similar to those of my generation of seminary women (because, in many cases, we shared the same professors), but there are differences: they have more female role models on the faculty; they are more likely to have seen women doing ministry in local churches before coming to seminary; they are more optimistic about their chances of being employed as pastors; and they are not consumed by the doubts and fears we faced during the years of the Controversy.

When I went to seminary, ordination had never crossed my mind. After all, I had grown up in a church that didn't allow women to preach or teach men the Bible. By the time I got to seminary, I thought that women probably could preach, but I didn't think they should be pastors. My seminary studies opened my mind to other possibilities. Without that exposure to biblical studies, theology, and church history, I'm not sure that I would have arrived at the place I am today, and I'm not so sure that I would have been ordained. My openness to a calling different from the one I first heard was made possible by what I learned from my professors and peers at Southern Seminary.

Some might point to me as a good example of why seminary education needed to change. But for me, discovering that I really could be anything God called me to be—and that God just might call me to preach—was profound and life-changing in inestimably positive ways. Because Southern Seminary didn't limit me, I discovered gifts I didn't know I had, and I found a deep gladness that could speak to the world's deep hunger.[32] Certainly, I could have found many other ways to carry out my ministry, but the ways I discovered at Southern are right for me; they are a proper fit. That is what my more progressive participants told me, too. Their calling to ministry is all about what they feel God has called them to do and the gifts God has given them. That is why they must do those things, despite other options in ministry and despite pressures not to challenge gender norms. Even most of those who don't feel called to preach or to be ordained themselves support the women who do. All these women hold the Bible in high regard, but whereas conservatives read the Bible to exclude women from pastoral leadership, progressives read it to support women in all forms of ministry. Katrina Brooks told me, "I believe that God can call whomever God chooses to call and God can equip whomever God chooses to equip for whatever it is, the task." That's the message women at the moderate seminaries hear. For women at the SBC seminaries, where the prevailing attitude is that God limits roles for women, they don't seem to experience it as a problem. Somehow, those who hear a call find a way to answer it.

6

Gracious Submission

Southern Baptist Women and the Family

Have thine own way, Lord! Have thine own way!
Thou art the potter, I am the clay!
Mold me and make me after thy will,
While I am waiting, yielded and still.
—Adelaide A. Pollard, "Have Thine Own Way, Lord"

During World War II, white women entered into the paid labor force, so when the soldiers returned from the battlefields, an ideological shift was required to force women back into their traditional roles in the home. Thus the 1950s emphasis on domesticity emerged, idealized in the pop-culture image of television's Cleaver family. Beginning in the 1960s, however, the women's movement challenged these idealized notions of family and demanded equality for women in the home and in the workplace. Women's growing consciousness of sexism and inequality affected even conservative Protestant women, including Southern Baptists. In fact, Southern Baptist publications in the 1970s were quite supportive of women's equality and advocated for women's rights in the workplace, while continuing to affirm women's choices to be homemakers. The important shift in the literature was the emphasis on choice— the publications framed homemaking as one of the choices available to women, but they no longer singled it out as the "godly" or only option.[1] The Controversy that began in 1979 quickly refocused the emphasis on returning women to more traditional roles, culminating with this 1998 addition to *The Baptist Faith and Message*:

God has ordained the family as the foundational institution of human society. It is composed of persons related to one another by marriage, blood, or adoption.

Marriage is the uniting of one man and one woman in covenant commitment for a lifetime. It is God's unique gift to reveal the union between Christ and His church and to provide for the man and the woman in marriage the framework for intimate companionship, the channel of sexual expression according to biblical standards, and the means for procreation of the human race.

The husband and wife are of equal worth before God, since both are created in God's image. The marriage relationship models the way God relates to His people. A husband is to love his wife as Christ loved the church. He has the God-given responsibility to provide for, to protect, and to lead his family. A wife is to submit herself graciously to the servant leadership of her husband even as the church willingly submits to the headship of Christ. She, being in the image of God as is her husband and thus equal to him, has the God-given responsibility to respect her husband and to serve as his helper in managing the household and nurturing the next generation.

Children, from the moment of conception, are a blessing and heritage from the Lord. Parents are to demonstrate to their children God's pattern for marriage. Parents are to teach their children spiritual and moral values and to lead them, through consistent lifestyle example and loving discipline, to make choices based on biblical truth. Children are to honor and obey their parents.[2]

The Convention may have made its official position clear, but nowhere are the complexities and contradictions of Southern Baptist women's identities more clearly revealed than in their family relationships.

The Centrality of Family

For almost all the participants in my study, regardless of age, race, region, or theology, family is a central theme in their construction of identity. Second only to seeing themselves as Christian, they identify themselves as wives, mothers, daughters, sisters, and grandmothers. Many answered that the most important thing they've done in their lives is to raise their children, particularly to raise their children to be Christian. When I asked Clique member Judy Masters to name the most significant experiences of her life, she replied, "My marriage, the birth of my children, the grandchildren, my son going on the mission field." Despite this common valuing of family, the participants also represent a variety of family structures and hold widely divergent views on family roles. Interestingly, however, the actual practices of family life are quite similar.

To a great degree, the women's different beliefs about family parallel the larger divisions in Southern Baptist life that gave rise to the Controversy. Not surprisingly, the more conservative women tend to hold more traditional beliefs, while the more progressive women hold more liberal beliefs. In many ways, the more conservative women are very much like the women described in Sally Gallagher's excellent work on evangelical families, *Evangelical Identity and Gendered Family Life*. As suggested in an earlier chapter, contemporary conservatives in the Southern Baptist Convention have more in common with Christians in evangelical churches than with many of their Baptist forebears or with contemporary Baptist sisters and brothers who are evangelistic but whose emphasis on voluntarism distinguishes them from the evangelical movement. In contrast to evangelical women, however, the women in my study tend to be much less traditional in their beliefs about family life, shunning notions of submission and headship and embracing egalitarianism.

Gender and Hierarchy

Although conservative Southern Baptists and evangelicals may share a common belief in notions of hierarchy, the former's emphasis on and interpretation of the Bible are the primary forces behind their recent embrace of gendered hierarchy and their understanding of complementarianism. Complementarianism rests on the parallel ideas of the full equality of women and men and the God-ordained roles assigned to them so that they complement each other. Or, as Dorothy Patterson put it, "Complementarianism is a position that espouses equality and difference." In the view of complementarians, submission of wives to husbands does not make them any less equal; rather, it allows them to fulfill the roles God has set out for them as women—roles that are of equal value to the leadership roles of husbands. Heather King explained, "Both genders have the same value and worth as bearers of God's image. Within the creation account God designs that each gender fulfills a different role or function. Complementarians believe ontological equality is not related to function; egalitarians or feminists believe otherwise. For example, let's take the issue of submission. A feminist would assert that if a woman is submissive to her husband, it makes her of less value or worth. Complementarians assert that if a woman is submissive to her husband it speaks of a function, not to her value or worth." Likewise, Candi Finch noted, "I believe that the Bible teaches that men and women are equal in essence before the Lord, but God has designed us with different functions within the church [and home]."

Dorothy Patterson said that when she was helping to write the *Baptist Faith and Message*'s statement on the family, which expresses her understanding of complementarianism, she encouraged the committee to begin with the Bible to determine what the statement would say. She pointed out that the present statement, which evolved from this process, is replete with scriptural references to support each point it makes.

Within this framework, submission is an act of agency. It is something a woman freely chooses as a matter of obedience to God; it is not coerced. As Dorothy explained, it is voluntary: "No one can force submission."[3] And it is not a matter of women's inferiority. Judy Masters explained this paradox: "I think that the Lord made women as special, in our place. Because Adam needed somebody special; and [the Lord] took the woman from Adam's rib, right under his heart. And I think that our sons should all be taught that women, whether it's their girlfriend, their mother, their wife, their sister, should be respected and kept under their heart. And I think that is the way we should teach our sons. And we should also teach our daughters to be submissive, to also have a mind of their own." In this idealized version of submission, women can both be submissive and have minds of their own because husbands are under God and love their wives as Christ loved the church. Submission, then, really involves mutual respect, discussion, and joint decision making, although the man is ultimately the head. Dorothy explains it this way:

> There is in the [biblical] text, number one, definitely a mutual submission. My first point is that if you are going to be a servant leader, if you're going to be willing even to die for the person there, are you submitting? I mean, to me, if you're going to wash someone's feet, if you're going to die for them, that's pretty much submission. I think there's definitely reciprocity in the submission process. But on the other hand, when you take the metaphor used between Christ and the church, you cannot say that Christ submits Himself to the church in the same way the church submits herself to Christ. There's just no way. Otherwise He's not God, and you lose your whole line of comparison there.

She then draws a distinction between complementarianism and egalitarianism:

Yes, there is equality of personhood. Yes, we are both created in the image of God. Yes, we both come to God in the same way. Yes, God has a plan and a purpose for the both of us. Yes, we both have responsibilities for ruling with him. But we have also a responsibility of how we relate to one another and that's submission and headship. That's where one person has the ultimate responsibility. Another fact that's missed so often is that when you see *submission,* and you're trying to think, "Well, my goodness. That would just be terrible to have to submit to someone all the time." If you're really one-minded, if you're both committed to the Lord, you're both committed to Scripture, and you have a warm intimate relationship as God describes it in Scripture, there are not going to be that many times when you're at an impasse. At least that is true in our marriage.[4]

Using her own marriage as an example, Dorothy notes that although she submits to her husband, Paige, they rarely reach a point where he makes a final decision that she disagrees with. When they have a disagreement, Paige doesn't immediately demand that she submit. Instead, she explains, "We have an interchange of ideas about it, and he will share his feelings and he wants to hear my feelings and many times we finish that and we've already come to a meeting of the minds. We've already made a decision and there is not really the necessity for submission to come into play in the sense of my giving into his wishes against my own preferences because we have decided together." When she does disagree, she's honest with him and then says, "I just can't see it. You've got to make the call."[5]

Cari Garrett talked about a time when she and her husband had to make a decision about a career change. They both prayed about it separately and then prayed about it together. They went back and forth asking each other, "Are you sure that's what [God] told you?" But they were getting the same answers, and in the end, they felt "total peace" about going in a new direction. "So it was interesting," she concluded, "how we did things separately but also together, and it all came together in the same answer." Similarly, Jamie Cline and her husband pray and communicate to make decisions together. "I think communication is such a key in marriage," she explained. "I share all my random thoughts with him because I just want him to know what I'm thinking because that helps us as we make decisions and as we walk in our life with Christ." To Cari, submission requires trust that her husband is listening closely to God's leading. "Just to trust him as he is trusting God . . . makes it easy to submit." But, she noted wryly, "if we had come to different decisions, I'm sure I wouldn't be saying all this."

Dorcas Pérez feels comfortable having a man in charge at church so that all the responsibility isn't on her shoulders. "In a way it is good," she explained, "even though it is a submissive role." She admitted, however, "I have some problem with that at home, yes, because my husband and I are very strong-willed."

When I asked members of my mother's Sunday school class what it means for a man to be the head of the house, LaDonna Burton explained, "I don't think it means that he rules over his wife, or she has to do what he tells her to do. I think if a husband and wife are both Christians, and they're submissive to God, I don't think there'll ever be a problem with, 'You need to do this' or 'You need to do that.' But I do think it's the man's ultimate responsibility to lead his family in a Christian life and teach his children to love God." Nancy Moore concurred that women and men are created to fulfill different roles and that the husband should be the head of the family. But, she quickly added, if the husband is wrong, "the woman has every right in the world to speak up and make her desire and her feeling known. So if . . . 'submission' [means] accepting any- and everything from the man, I would be totally against it. But if in the organization of the home, if he should be the head of it, then she should look to him as the head of it. And a lot of times, men are the ones who are contributing the support of the family, and a lot of the decisions have to do with how that's used, but I have never known many women who were totally in submission to their husbands. I really have not."

Beginning in 1975, the Southern Baptist Convention began to pass resolutions on the family that focused on the need for churches (and occasionally the government) to enact strategies to strengthen families. Often these resolutions contained statements about modern society's attacks on the family—presumably referring to those arising from the women's movement and the gay and lesbian liberation movement. For example, the 1980 "Resolution on the White House Conference on the Family" commended the national conference for supporting aid to combat alcohol and drug abuse and criticized it for supporting "abortion, homosexual rights, and a general undermining of the biblical concept of the family."[6] The 1987 "Resolution on Honor for Full-Time Homemakers" suggested that publicity had focused on wives and mothers pursuing employment outside the home "for personal fulfillment, financial reward, and independence" and had ignored the benefits to families, churches, and the nation provided by full-time homemakers. In 1988 the Convention affirmed that "the family and biblical values are under constant attack from materialism, secular humanism, substance abuse, and rebellion against authority" and that "traditional Christian values of home and family are often attacked and ignored in the media and secular education."[7] By 2003, the Convention defined the threats to the biblical model of family as "a divorce culture that sees marriage as a temporary social arrangement," as well as "marital infidelity, abandonment, and divorce within our own churches" and "current attempts to redefine the family itself and to marginalize the importance of the nuclear family."[8] Perceiving that the traditional family was under attack from a larger culture that was redefining women's roles and becoming more open to alternative models of family, the Convention reacted by heightening its emphasis on the nuclear family and clearly defining roles within that family.

Yet, as part of the larger culture, the Convention was not unmarked by the progress of women's rights. Even as it espoused traditional roles for women, it reshaped its rhetoric to emphasize women's full equality. Of course, we had always been taught that we were all equal at the foot of the cross, but for women, that sense of full human equality had not extended much further before the 1970s and 1980s. Although women's inferiority was rarely stated explicitly, the prevailing sense in Southern Baptist churches was that women were somehow less than men. Linda McKinnish Bridges recounted this story: When she was twelve years old, she and her father were driving on a meandering road through the mountains of North Carolina, on their way to a revival where her father was going to preach. She asked, "Dad, why are girls not as good as boys?" Her father replied, "Well, Adam was created first, Eve was created second, and that means that God has ordained his created order. And your place, in order to find a comfortable, happy place in God's created order, is to accept the fact that you were created second."

As the Controversy gained force in the late 1970s and early 1980s, moderate Southern Baptist men began to speak more directly to women's issues, although few moderate churches ever called women as senior pastors. In response to moderates' criticism of their views on women, conservatives began to emphasize both gender equality and gender roles, and their reading of the biblical passages dealing with women, men, and families included both.

The most extreme rhetoric about gender roles in the family seems to come from Southern Seminary. While this rhetoric espouses complementarianism, it also exposes a thinly veiled assertion of male power and domination that doesn't accord with the descriptions of equal worth and difference in function delineated by other complementarians. In an article on headship in the winter 2003 issue of Southern Seminary's alumni magazine (the topic for the issue was "The Beauty of Biblical Womanhood"), one administrator describes the husband's role as that of "ruler." He reads Genesis 3:16 to mean that "sin would bring about in Eve a wrongful desire to rule over her husband. . . . Eve's desire will be to rule illegitimately over Adam, and in response Adam will have to assert his rightful rulership over her." He concludes that "sin produced a disruption in God's order of male headship and female submission, in which, a) the woman would be inclined now to usurp the man's rightful place of authority over her, and man may be required in response, to re-establish his God-given rulership over the woman, and b) the man would be inclined to misuse his rights of rulership, either by sinful abdication of his God-given authority, acquiescing to the woman's desire to rule over him (and so fail to lead as he should), or by abusing his rights to rule through harsh, cruel, and exploitative domination of the woman."[9] Another article in the same issue forcefully reasserts the notion that woman's place is in the home:

> [The young woman] is "busy at home" (NIV), a home worker. Her home is her primary base of operation and the main focus of her attention. Proverbs 31:10–31 teaches us that a diligent homemaker may be involved in a wide range of activities and interests. She is not lazy or a busybody, nor is she distracted by outside pursuits and responsibilities that eat up her precious time and attention. This woman is not seduced by the sirens of modernity who tell her she is wasting her time and talent as a homemaker, and that it is the career woman who has purpose and is truly satisfied.
>
> The recent turn in women leaving the workplace and returning home has become too noticeable to be ignored. It is a reflection of what God planted in the heart of a wife and mother when He made her a female in His image. The blessings and joy she will discover as a wife, mother, and homemaker can never be matched by a career that in the end cannot make good on its promises. Being a homemaker is not an institutionalized form of bondage and slavery. It is the greatest context for a woman to experience liberation and liberty as she is set free by the plan of God to be the woman God created and saved her to be.[10]

This rhetoric harks back to an idealized past in which (white, middle-class) men were the breadwinners and rulers of their homes and their subservient wives dealt with the responsibilities of child rearing and household work. Although the women in my study valued homemaking, even those who espoused male headship did not argue that women's true (and only God-ordained) place was in the home. And certainly none of them used the terms *ruler* or *rulership* to describe their husbands' roles in the family.

The theme of the winter 2005 issue of the magazine was "Show Yourself a Man." Several articles focus on the need for men to reign as patriarchs over their families, embodying Christian masculinity and rejecting "the feminized version of manhood espoused by our culture."[11] In his preface to the issue, the seminary's president draws on the work of Terrence O. Moore to argue that the breakdown of family values and discipline has created a generation of boys who are either barbarians or wimps. "A regime of passive parenting," he contends (citing Moore), "has led to soft discipline that produces soft boys who grow to become soft men. Parents are now afraid to discipline and seem to be more concerned with the development of an artificial 'self-esteem' in their boys."[12] Emphasizing gender distinctions rooted in biology and God's divinely ordained order, articles in this issue advocate male headship in the home as "leader, provider, and protector."[13] Conflating femaleness and femininity and maleness and masculinity, another article titled "The Marks of a Godly Husband" reifies gender:

> God's Word clearly states that men are to be the providers and the protectors. Women love being provided for and protected. It is the man's responsibility to provide for the family. There may be seasons where creative help is needed. One quick read of the Proverbs 31 woman and you are reminded that women can help and work—and this may be needed at times—but it should not be the way it is all the time. Seasons come and go but men are to be the providers for the family.
>
> I'm not sure exactly when it all started but somewhere along the way, we lost what it means to be male and female. We have masculine women and feminine men, and we have to put an end to it. Give me a man's man any day of the week. Look for a man to lead who looks like a man, thinks like a man, leads like a man and is proud to be a man. Christian women need to be feminine and men need to be men—no apologies. Marry a man who is stronger than you are—physically, mentally, and spiritually. Marry a man who will be a patriarch for the family and will model what biblical manhood is all about. This will be a man that you can respect and the kind of man that will make it easy to follow him.[14]

These articles express an essentialist understanding of gender rooted in biology and a divinely ordained created order. They argue that traditional notions of masculinity and femininity correlate with biological maleness and femaleness and that to challenge the roles associated with biologically and divinely defined gender is to upend God's intentions for creation. For these writers, the only acceptable and theologically correct form of family is that of feminine wives working only in the home who submit to their masculine husbands who are the breadwinners, protectors, and patriarchs of the family.

Although many of the women in my study espouse male headship and argue for the merits of femininity and masculinity, few are as rigid in their interpretation of gender as the leaders of Southern Seminary are. This suggests a disconnect between many of the Convention's leaders and the average Baptist woman's continued exercise of soul competency. Despite leaders' frenzied reaction to feminist gains, women in churches still tend to interpret scripture and live out their faith in practical ways that make sense to them. They draw from both feminist thought and conservative theology to shape Christian lives that work for them and their families.

One denominational employee in particular exemplified these tensions. She herself is an inerrantist and is very traditional in many ways. Because of her husband's illness, she is the family's breadwinner, but because he is very traditional in his views of housework, she also has primary responsibility for the household. She admits that she is more advanced in her faith development than her husband is, so she is also the spiritual leader in their home. She struggles with the vision of denominational leaders who insist that the chief role of women is to raise children. She explained, "While I think that that is a very important and significant role, it leaves out so many other women; it doesn't address the exceptions, and, given this life, there are more exceptions than there are necessarily the norm. So I resent being made to feel guilty, that in some way I'm not doing all the motherly or wifely things I should be doing because I'm working. They don't see that this is the way we support our family, and this is the way that we live, that our circumstances dictate that I do this."

Most of the conservative women I spoke with believe that the husband should be the head of the house. They read literally the passage in Ephesians that commands, "Wives, submit yourselves to your husbands." But when I asked them how things really work in their families, most of them described something that resembled a partnership rather than headship. I began to wonder whether they espouse headship (at least in their words) because they truly believe that's what the Bible teaches and, therefore, as Bible-believing Christians, they are bound to believe and profess it, even though they practice partnership in their daily decisions and interactions and, in fact, sometimes exercise leadership in their homes.

Doris Bailey is an excellent example. When I asked her what the Bible teaches about women, she responded as follows:

> I think the Bible teaches that women are on the same level ground as men, as all people; according to the cross, according to the Bible, we are all equal. I feel the Bible teaches that the man is to be the head of the house, that God is to be the head of the house really; but the man's leadership under God is to be respected. I don't think that women feel that they are usurped in any way by the man being the head of the house when he is a Christian person in a leadership position. I think the Bible teaches that women can do so many things, and they are gifted to do some things men are not gifted to do, and I think that's just through gifting.

Then I asked her to clarify what she meant when she said the man is the head of the house. She explained, "As long as the man is under the leadership of God, . . . if he decides the family goes to this church or that church, then I think it's the woman's decision to go with him, to be supportive in those roles." But like many of Gallagher's evangelical women,[15] Doris has assumed spiritual leadership in the home by default, despite her belief that it is men's responsibility. Doris added, "Now in my situation, my husband does not attend church, but he does not hinder me in any way. He is respectful of the decisions I make as far as churchgoing and things like that."

My mother understands headship to apply in the spiritual realm, not the material one. She explained, "God says he's no respecter of persons. So that means in God's sight all people are equal and the same. [Submission] means, in my opinion, that, . . . as God intended it, the man is responsible for the spiritual training in the home . . . but to submit doesn't mean that he is better than you are, that he walks over you or that he rules over you; the decision-making should be shared." When I asked her about mutual submission, she agreed. "[My husband's] supposed to love me as Christ loves the church, and if he loves me as Christ loves the church, he's not going to rule over me." I asked her why she thought people held on to the headship language. She responded, "I still think that all God was talking about was the spiritual aspect of it. That

God's going to ultimately hold that man responsible if those children are not trained spiritually to learn the will of God."

"Yes," I prodded, "but in the Clique, the women did it all."

"Well, that doesn't make it right," she retorted. "Just like in the church, the women do most of the work too. That's not how God intended for it to be."

I noticed an interesting pattern in conservative women's responses to questions about male headship in the home and in the church. Although these women love and respect the men in their lives and believe that the men should lead, they often see themselves as the real driving forces behind men's leadership. Many conservative participants told me that they essentially push their husbands into leadership in the home. They have learned, they told me, that men's egos require them to be in leadership positions for them to feel like real men and to do what God calls men to do. Candice Christian explained, "I've learned so much more about the dynamics of a man and what his needs are. And his need is truly to be the head of the house; this is the way God has ordained it. And, in order for us to truly have him be comfortable in that role, our job is to support them. Sometimes to even guide them, although you never let that be known. It's always like this—this is our job, this is what we're good at. As women, this is what we do well."

Several conservative participants explained that men need to be leaders in the church for much the same reason. They pointed out that if men can't lead, they may not serve at all. That's why some of the participants oppose women becoming deacons or pastors. They fear that if those roles aren't exclusively male, men won't do anything at all in the church, since women are already doing most of the rest of the work. Jennifer Adamson put a positive spin on this phenomenon. She said, "Men are given more of a position of power . . . women are given a place of influence, and influence is many times a much greater place to be than a place of power."

The Neck that Turns the Head

Despite the influence of patriarchy, southern culture is largely matriarchal. Southerners know that Mama is the one who holds the family together, and the family's happiness depends on Mama's happiness. Southern culture is also genteel, so resistance to patriarchal norms is often very subtle—some might even say manipulative. When I asked

Lidia Abrams whether the husband is the head of the house, she replied, "Well, the Bible says he's supposed to be. And I respect mine." Then she quipped, "Man is the head, but woman is the neck that turns him." She gave me this illustration: "If he comes home, and I say, 'Honey, I have to have some money. I saw a dress, and I want it.' He might say, 'I'm not gonna do it,' or whatever. But if you go, 'Oh, I saw a dress, but I know I can't have it. I know there's no way, but I sure love it,' he'll say, 'Well, why not? Why don't you go get it?' You see? You have a way."

Conservative participants affirmed their belief in male headship, but they also described relationships that were much more reflective of partnerships, with family decisions being made together. Lidia said that she and Ralph make all their big decisions together. For example, when he wanted to buy a car, he took her to see it first.

In many of these relationships, wives remain responsible for the bulk of child rearing and housework, even if they also work outside the home. The (white, middle-class) women of my mother's generation expected to be homemakers. When they talked about male headship, it was mostly in terms of economics: since the husband earned the money, he should have a greater say in major decisions, such as buying a home. Shelby Christie explained, "We talk about things and we make decisions together, but ultimately, he usually knows better. And he makes the bigger decisions when it comes to a lot of things that I may not understand or that he knows. But I think the Bible teaches that a woman is a helpmate and is equal to a man in that way, but I think that the man should be under God too, you know, have God's influence on him . . . ; otherwise, if it's not of God, I think the woman sometimes has to make a decision, especially as far as the home or the children is concerned."

Betty Sue Drury explained that in her marriage, "We always talked about things together, but he was the one who led out in things. He was the one who made the money. I was at home. I stayed at home until my boys were [grown] up; then I went out to work, but he made the money, and he could go out and make decisions and do some things for our home without my being there, and it was fine." She offered this example: "He bought a lot of the furniture when we moved into our new home, and it was beautiful! I didn't have to be there and get the last word in and do all that, but he felt comfortable in that because if I didn't like it I would tell him, and we could change that."

For many of the older women, their husbands' retirement has brought a subtle shift in the relationship. The husbands may take on more responsibility in the household, while the wives exercise more independence, often traveling with friends and leaving their husbands at home to fend for themselves. Several times a year, the Clique takes off on one- or two-day junkets to craft fairs, festivals, or historic places. Alicia Bennett's husband, Don, has learned a lot about what it takes to maintain the home, now that he's retired. "Well, I tell you what," she exclaimed, "it has opened his eyes to what goes on at home, and he did *not* have any understanding." I asked whether he helps more around the house now. "Yes, he does," she replied. "I couldn't believe it; he fixes his own breakfast every morning! He gets up when he wants to, and I get up when I want to. And he does his own thing, and I do my own thing. Yeah, he pitches in now and helps, and he just had no idea that it was as difficult to get everything done."

Kayne Carter told a similar story. She and her husband, Bill, have had a very traditional relationship: he was the breadwinner and she was primarily responsible for raising the children. She believes that the Lord set the order of the home for the husband to be the head, but, she added, Bill has put her first in everything. "He doesn't try to control me, and I don't try to control him." When they make decisions, they make them together. And now that he's retired, he's more involved in the home. Kayne laughed, "Like I said before, his main job was working and coming home. And now—the kids was just shocked, because he didn't do much around the house at all, and when we ate, when he got up from the table, he just pushed his chair back, and now he pushes his chair back and if I've done a lot of cooking, he says he'll do dishes. Theresa says, 'I can't believe that's my daddy.' So he's changed a lot. But he says, 'I'm home now; I don't mind doing those things.' So he's changed a lot."

Middle-aged women who grew up with the women's movement and its challenge to traditional gender roles expect to have input into family decisions and to divide household responsibilities along practical, rather than gender, lines, especially if they also work outside the home. Debra Hochgraber, who is a women's ministry specialist and consultant for the Baptist General Convention of Texas, exemplifies the attitude of many younger and middle-aged conservative women: "The [husband and wife] are to submit to one another out of reverence for Christ. As the husband loves her as Christ loved the church, she submits to his leadership. She then has the unique opportunity of an umbrella of spiritual protection. Both have the responsibility for their own spiritual growth and of their children. They mutually determine financial and household responsibilities."

Many of the younger conservative women described relationships in which they are primarily responsible for work inside the home, but their husbands take on more responsibility than did men in earlier generations. Among the married women in my focus group from First Baptist Church in Hendersonville, Tennessee—all in their twenties and thirties—the women mostly maintain the home. Missy Loper explained that while her husband provides financially for the family, she has responsibility for the home. Nonetheless, she added, her husband "helps out" in any way he can and cares equally for the children. Jamie Cline, who works full-time outside the home and is a graduate student, still retains responsibility for most of the housework, but her husband gladly helps out, especially when she reminds him what needs to be done. When Melissa Ashley's husband lost his job, she went back to work and her husband stayed home and cared for their six-week-old and three-year-old children—successfully, she noted. "My friends even say, 'Melissa, Paul packed a better diaper bag than you did,'" she laughed. Now their roles are reversed again, but the experience taught them that, if need be, they are both capable of filling either role.

The reality for conservative women is a balance between submission and independence. As Nancy Moore noted, women don't really submit. They have their own minds, and unless they're in situations of abuse, they usually feel free to challenge their husbands. The rhetoric of submission gets idealized to posit a husband who loves his wife as Christ loves the church, and who wouldn't be able to submit to a man who loved her that way? Missionary Debra Owens-Hughes explained it this way:

> I have learned that there is a wonderful peace in a family when the man is the head, if that man is a true believer and follower of Christ. It takes the stress off women who seem to be more emotional about life and therefore more easily exhausted. With a husband led by God, I can trust him to make the right decisions. Now God uses me and my intellect to have an enormous amount of input, but his is the final decision. When he is wrong, he finds out from the conviction of the Holy Spirit, and we talk about it, and we work it out. He listens to me. And if he makes a wrong decision and doesn't see it that way, hey, it's life. God is sufficient to take care of me.

Of course, most marriages rarely live up to this ideal. Both men and women are shaped by patriarchal notions of power and gender that enter into the best of relationships, and often the social construction of gender in the family produces people whose needs and approaches to life are so different that they may not communicate well or meet one another's needs, despite the best of intentions. In response to the realities of gendered relationships, these women make compromises and adjust their choices and expectations to create the best situations they can for their families. Mostly, they make decisions together with their husbands, and, when necessary, they assume leadership in the home, even if it's not their first (or idealized) choice. Even as they espouse the rhetoric of headship and practice a modified version of submission, these women continue to enact agency and autonomy. Frankly, they choose when to submit, and they choose when to do what seems right to them, with or without their husbands' approval. These are practical women. They know when going along will make things better for the family, and they know that sometimes the best decision is the one that causes some conflict.

The Dark Side of Male Dominance and Female Submission

The idealized version of family and gender touted by conservative Southern Baptists assumes good, faithful men behaving righteously in relation to the women in their lives. But the truth of the matter is that not all men are good and righteous and that domestic violence, sexual abuse, and incest are as prevalent in conservative Christian families as in the larger society. Many participants told stories of sexual abuse and domestic violence at the hands of Southern Baptist men.[16]

Thaeda Franz lists six typical beliefs that allow predators (and churches) to justify their behavior: (1) "God intends for men to dominate and for women and children to submit," (2) "because of her role in the Fall, woman is morally inferior to man," (3) "children are inherently evil and must have their wills broken," (4) "marriage is to be preserved at all costs," (5) "suffering is a Christian virtue," and (6) "Christians must promptly forgive those who sin against them."[17] Franz suggests that these beliefs often make churches unwilling or unable to assist victims of sexual abuse. In particular, in conservative Protestant subcultures, issues of power and patriarchy put women at risk for abuse and often limit their ability to report abuse or leave violent relationships.[18] Nancy Nason-Clark points out that although abuse may not be more prevalent or more severe in families of faith, religious women "are more *vulnerable* when abused." She adds, "They are less likely to leave, are more likely to believe the abuser's promise to change his violent ways, frequently espouse reservations about seeking community-based resources or shelters for battered women, and commonly express guilt—that they have failed their families and God in not being able to make the marriage work."[19]

Although religious beliefs may trap some women in abusive and violent situations, they also provide a sense of empowerment that allows women to survive and leave violent relationships.[20] For these women, their spirituality becomes a source of comfort and sustenance. Yet, conservative Protestant churches in particular may not be best equipped to help. Research indicates that conservative male Protestant ministers are more likely to adhere to narrow definitions of domestic abuse, male headship, and myths about domestic abuse than are their more liberal colleagues. These assumptions, then, may limit the assistance some ministers can provide to abused women.[21]

And, as has become painfully obvious in recent years, male clergy members may themselves abuse the women entrusted to their pastoral care. When women report such abuse, it is often covered up, or the women are blamed for "seducing" the minister.[22] Christa Brown has been bringing this issue to light among Southern Baptists. Christa was sexually abused by the Southern Baptist youth pastor of her Texas church when she was an adolescent. Another pastor knew what was happening but did nothing about it. The abuser took a job with another congregation, and Christa was told to keep quiet. As an adult, Christa reported the abuse to a number of Southern Baptist leaders but found no help. Eventually she filed a lawsuit when she discovered that the man was doing children's ministry in Florida. Only after the *Orlando Sentinel* did a story on the lawsuit did the church remove the man from ministry. Because Southern Baptist churches are autonomous, no mechanism exists to censure or remove abusive ministers. In fact, Southern Baptists have no means of reporting abusive clergy so that unsuspecting congregations don't hire them. Frustrated by Baptist leaders' lack of responsiveness, Christa founded Voices to Stop Baptist Predators and joined forces with the Survivors Network of Those Abused by Priests (SNAP) to push Southern Baptists to develop a system for reporting clergy abuse.

Dee Miller, a former Southern Baptist missionary in Africa, experienced sexual assault at the hands of a fellow missionary. Fully expecting the denomination's mission board to support her, Dee was shocked by the level of collusion among Baptist leaders. Her anger at the situation eventually led her to write an autobiographical account of her abuse and her quest to have her abuser removed from the mission field.[23] Both Dee and Christa still marvel at the extent to which churches and denominational leaders conspire with abusers to protect both the perpetrators and the image of the church and the Convention.

For many women, experiences of abuse and violence and the collusion of Southern Baptist church members and leaders have fundamentally altered their faith. Neither Christa Brown nor Dee Miller participates in Southern Baptist life any longer. They have found other groups with which to express their faith. Other abused women have remained Southern Baptist but struggle against the constraints of churches that stigmatize divorce, even on the grounds of domestic violence. Many women, however, have used their hurt and rage to construct new understandings of God that take into account women's suffering and to demand justice for abused women.

For Southern Baptists in particular, the issue of abuse is a direct assault on fundamental notions of agency and autonomy. In response to the clergy abuse scandal in the Catholic Church, the Southern Baptist Convention approved a resolution, "The Sexual Integrity of Ministers," in 2002. The resolution calls for ministers to have integrity in their dealings with church members, and it asks churches to discipline abusers and cooperate with civil authorities in prosecuting offenders. Interestingly, but not surprisingly, the resolution focuses on the morality of individual ministers without examining the structures that inherently foster abuse. In fact, nowhere does the resolution take gender into account as an essential feature of clergy abuse. The resolution mentions the "tragic consequences" of abuse, but it never clarifies the direct affront to cherished notions of Baptist identity inherent in abuse, nor does it examine how Baptist constructions of manhood and womanhood may play a significant role in the shape of abuse in Southern Baptist life. Research suggests that beliefs about female submission can be used to justify abuse. These beliefs, coupled with the reality of sexual assault and domestic violence, certainly assail the integrity of women's agency and autonomy.[24] Abuse is a mechanism of power and control, an attempt to prevent women from exercising agency and defining an independent identity for themselves. On the one hand, the Convention may decry abuse and call for sexual integrity, but on the other, it promotes beliefs and systems that undergird abuse. Christa Brown has offered a public challenge to the Convention, but so far, the Convention has not responded.

Egalitarian Relationships

Moderate women are much more likely than conservative ones to disavow male headship and focus on family roles as a matter of mutuality and practicality. These women agree with conservative women that the Bible teaches the concept of full equality of women and men, but they disagree that gender hierarchy is part of that vision. They point to the passage in Ephesians that commands, "Submit yourselves to one another," and suggest that family roles are better decided by giftedness than by gender. Kristy Carr explained, "I see marriage as equal. There are things I do better than he does. I pay all our bills; I deal with all the finances. Not that he's not capable; he's very capable. But I do a better job of it. And he knows that. And we're fine with that. There are things that he does, and I can certainly do, but I don't want to deal with it, and he does." Jean Cullen pointed explicitly to the idea of the priesthood of believers to explain that different people within the family lead at different times:

> I believe that as a Christian and as a woman who God speaks to and can speak to, that within the family you lead at different times. . . . There are times when my son leads, and there are times when my daughter leads, even at age three and six, and there are times when I lead. And . . . as my kids get older, the areas in which they lead will grow in responsibility and number. But I see the family unit being a place where the priesthood of believers is lived out almost more so than at any other time, and the respecting of God's ability to work in everybody.

Beth Cox noted, "I feel like [marriage] is an equal partnership, and you each have different talents, you each have different things you can contribute to the marriage, but one is not better than the other."

Nancy Ammerman told me, "I was pretty much taught that submissive wife thing, but again, by the time I got to be twenty-two and married, it didn't take long for me to say, 'Huh?' Somehow the explicit teachings, to the extent they were there, were shed very easily as I actually reached my own adulthood." Joyce Reed said in no uncertain terms, "My husband and I do not have the type of relationship where he's the head of the home. Uh-huh. No way. We share the role of the head of the household, I guess you might say."

"No 'gracious submission' there, huh?" I asked.

"No, in fact, I'm probably not very gracious," she laughed. "I hope we're mutually submissive, and I think we are, but, no, he's known from the very start that that was not me."

Likewise, Jean Cullen explained, "I think in a marriage, both are to submit equally. I think in a marriage God brings two people together—in any relationship—God brings two people together, with skills and abilities and strengths and weaknesses, and God brings you together to complement one another. And so then it is a constant give-and-take of submitting. There are times when one submits, and times when the other submits, based on where your strengths and weaknesses are and your current situations." Jean's comments highlight the profound difference between complementarians and egalitarians. Although both advocate mutual submission and complementary roles, complementarians define those roles by gender, and egalitarians define them by gifts and abilities. For egalitarians, leadership roles, housework, and breadwinning have more to do with individuals' specific personalities and situations than with their gender.[25] So, for example, women like Mary Key and Kryn Freehling-Burton who stay at home and raise their children (and even home-school them) do so not because it is their role as women but because they want to, based on their own abilities and needs. Mary also started a Moms and Tots Sunday school class so that mothers and children can be in the same classroom, which makes both the kids and the moms happier.

Nancy Hollomon-Peede, who is the minister for community involvement at a Baptist church in Virginia, said that her title should be "I Do Everything." Her husband works in downtown Washington, D.C., and has a long commute by train, so he's gone most of the day. That leaves her in charge, because she's the one who's around. She's also the spiritual leader in the home because they both recognize that that is her area of giftedness and training. "I would say as far as the home, I would be the centering force, the centering presence."

Kate Campbell has been married for twenty years and considers her husband "a very liberated man." Their marriage has always been egalitarian. "There has never been any kind of assignment of roles in our marriage," she explained. But not every man in her life is so evolved. She once hung up on her father when he tried to convince her that her role was to have children.

Pat Brown learned from her grandmothers that girls were supposed to do certain things and boys were supposed to do other things and wives were supposed to certain things for their husbands. When she married Robert, he was thirty years old and was used to doing most household chores for himself, but because of her family's implicit and explicit teaching, Pat started to do all those things for him. Then, about two years into the marriage, she realized that she had taken over duties that he was perfectly capable of doing for himself. After their first child was born, they went to visit her family, and the two of them took turns changing the baby's diaper. She told me, "He heard this little whispering going on: 'He's changing the diaper.' And he came back, and he said to me privately, 'Is this something I'm not supposed to do?' I said, 'Why do you think so?' And he said, 'Well, I heard your grandmothers talking about it.' And I said, 'It's not that you're not supposed to do it; they are amazed that you're doing it. Please don't stop.'"

Diana Garland, who is now dean of the School of Social Work at Baylor University, said, "I grew up in an era where you first got your man, and then you figured out—let me back up. My parents wanted me to go to college, so that if my husband ever left me, I could support myself. That was their thinking. My mother required me to take typing in high school so I could always support myself. Who would have thought I'd be writing books instead of typing as a secretary?" Her mother's concern that she be able to support herself is a common theme among my middle-aged participants. Their mothers, having come of age at a time of limited employment options for women, recognized their own dependence on male economic support and encouraged their daughters to be more independent, even though they still expected them to marry and have children. This generation of women anticipated a wider range of life options for their daughters than they had experienced themselves.

Nancy Hollomon-Peede said, "I think part of my sense of gender came from my family. First and foremost my mom and dad giving us equal opportunity. I think this sense of your gender was no hindrance of what you could do and attain. That was pretty much strong in our family. So I already had that when I hit up against it in seminary, you know, 'Oh, you came for the MRS degree,' and things like that. It didn't cause me to question anything; it caused me to challenge it, to have a better sense of what gender meant in a religious setting." Lucy Elizalde also developed her sense of egalitarianism through her family. As part of a Latino family, she saw strong women who didn't put limitations on what women were capable of doing.

A few participants are the primary breadwinners in their families, and their husbands follow their wives' careers. Wanda Lee, executive director of WMU, has lived on both sides of the breadwinning fence. She described her relationship with her husband as "partners in ministry." She married him while he was in seminary studying to be a pastor.

She became a nurse, and they juggled child-rearing responsibilities. He was the primary breadwinner, but he pitched in to get the housework done. "He can cook as good as or better than me," Wanda noted. "His mother died before I was able to meet her, but I love her; she taught him everything. He was an only child, so he came into the marriage being able to cook, do his own laundry, clean the house. And he has always done just that. Whatever needed to be done, he did it. And I can cut the grass with the best of them!" Wanda and her husband were appointed as missionaries to St. Vincent, where he was a church planter and she was a nurse. They eventually returned to the United States, and he became a hospital chaplain while she continued nursing. She had been active in WMU in Georgia, and when Dellanna O'Brien retired as executive director of the national agency, the nominating committee invited Wanda to take the position. Thus began a deep personal struggle. She continued the story: "My husband said to me one day, after I'd said 'No' three times to the committee, he asked me one of those questions you hope your husband never asks you—'Did you pray about this?' I said, 'No, and I don't intend to.' He just looked at me, and I'll never forget what he said: 'If you're not doing this because of me and my role and what I do in ministry, we're both in trouble. If God is leading you, he has something for me. We need to listen and together make that decision. And so I would suggest you pray about this, because we're both going to be in real trouble, spiritual and every other way.' And so he was the one who really challenged me to really discern God's will." Now, they're in a "major role reversal." Her husband has taken on primary responsibility for the home, although he continues to do interim supply work in churches—and, she said, he's loving it. She also sees the repercussions of his modeling in their children. "My daughter is an attorney, and she is who she is because of him. . . . [She] has married a man who can wash and cook and clean. She said, 'I can't go into a relationship where I'm not treated as an equal and respected.' So she's married to this wonderful guy who works, and they have a brand-new baby, and he's doing feedings and diapers."

"How do you like being a grandmother?" I asked.

"It's wonderful," she replied. "I think I could get used to this."

Family and Ministry

For Southern Baptist women in ministry, the place of family is especially tricky and complicated. The wives of pastors are in many ways

expected to be über-wives and mothers, embodying all the congregations' ideals (both theological and cultural) about what wives are supposed to be and do and even look like. Women who are themselves
ministers face the dilemma of being women in a traditionally male field
and being wives and mothers; their congregations and religious organizations have expectations for ministers and expectations for women that
may well be at odds.

The Pastor's Wife

A number of the women in my study are or have been pastors' wives.
That role in Southern Baptist life brings unique challenges. Southern
Baptist churches tend to have particular expectations of pastors' wives;
some of these expectations grow from the sense that calling a pastor and
his wife is a two-for-one deal, and some come from southern culture
itself. The pastor's wife is usually not a church staff member, yet most
congregations expect an extraordinary level of involvement in church
activities. When I was in seminary, many of my single female class-
mates lamented that their male colleagues were only looking to date
women who could play the piano.

Carolyn Weatherford Crumpler is hardly the typical pastor's wife.
She spent thirty-one years as a single woman engaged in WMU work,
including fifteen years as the national organization's executive director.
Carolyn never intended to get married. In fact, because so many people
associated WMU workers with singleness, she purposefully set out to
make sure that married women were added to the WMU staff. In as-
sessing her time at WMU, she acknowledged that she couldn't have
been as productive if she had been married: "I could not possibly have
done the things I did; I could not have traveled the miles and miles I
went; I couldn't have been available at the snap of a finger to do the
things I did if I had been married."

Carolyn met Joe Crumpler when she was in her mid-fifties. She was
in Ohio to speak at the state Baptist convention, and the state WMU
executive asked Carolyn if she'd mind if a pastor joined them for dinner.
His wife had died a year and a half earlier, but Carolyn didn't think the
dinner was intended as a setup. "I think she was really surprised when
it really worked out that way. We didn't get married until six years later,
but we were sort of 'the item' for six years." When they got married, Joe
offered to take early retirement and move to Birmingham, where WMU
is headquartered. "Huh-uh," Carolyn told him. "I'm not going to add a
husband to what I'm doing already. I just can't do it." So she left her

position with WMU and moved to Ohio. She notes that as a pastor's wife, she has learned a lot about the behind-the-scenes work. "I spent a lot of time cooking, serving, and entertaining," she writes.[26] The pressure on pastors' wives is tremendous, and defying the expectation that they will be involved in every program offered by the church requires an amazing amount of strength and fortitude.

Amy Corbin has witnessed the way wives support pastors in her own home. She explained, "My dad is a Southern Baptist minister, and I've been able to watch my mom, growing up. And the way that she supports my dad, to me, is just as much a ministry as what my dad is doing up in front of the church all the time. Even if you don't see that, her support of him is a ministry to the church in lots of different ways, and I think that everyone can support the church in lots of ways that are usually not seen—they're behind the scenes—but the church could not function without those things being done."

Wife, Mother, and Minister

With the movement of some Southern Baptist women into ordained ministry, a new kind of minister's family has emerged; some men are now the pastor's husband. Martha Gilmore's husband has always been supportive of her ministry. As a dual-career couple, they had to learn to navigate family life. Early on, her children learned to do their own laundry and cook. "The wash came pretty early," she explained, "but the kitchen was a little harder to conquer. Jerry would just throw them all in the car and take them out." In recent years, Martha has battled cancer, and Jerry remains supportive. She gave this example: She was about to leave for a doctor's appointment when Jerry stopped her. "Wait a minute," he said. Then he combed the back of her hair. "And I was telling the nurse," she recounted, "boy, when you say 'for better or worse,' you never know what worse is."

Nikki Hardeman, a student at McAfee School of Theology, wonders how she will balance the demands of family life and ministry. She and her husband are talking about having children, and she isn't sure how she will manage the change in her role. She would like to be a stay-at-home mom, but she realizes that her ministry will probably preclude this. It feels, she laments, "like I'm supposed to be able to do both," and she admits that she'll probably try. But, she points out, "If my husband's role doesn't change where he has to do both too, then I'm stuck holding two huge positions, where he's still only holding one."

Julie Pennington-Russell and her husband, Tim, have managed to balance career and family. They moved from Nineteenth Avenue Baptist Church in San Francisco, where Julie was pastor in the 1980s and early 1990s, to Waco, Texas, where she now pastors Calvary Baptist Church. "It's funny," she laughed, "Tim and I have joked before—harking back to that old awful Bill Gothard thing—about poking each other in the eye with our umbrellas, me under his umbrella of authority in the home, him under my umbrella [in the church]. I think that being a wife and mother is all part of my trying to be a disciple of Christ. Because God led me to Tim, because God gave us these children, and it's a huge part of our lives; and my calling is also a huge part of my life, and I think that what I do mostly is try to be faithful to all of them in a healthy proportion on any given day. . . . I just juggle it and try to be faithful."

Charla Milligan, who is in her last semester of seminary, is always shocked when people assume that she's going to stay home with her two children once she graduates. She's looking for a full-time ministry position and plans to put the children in day care, but the responses she gets are pretty critical. "It's like [they think] I must not be a nurturer," she lamented, as if being "a woman called to ministry means I'm not nurturing my children. It's offensive." Jennifer Fuller added, "I've been at home with my children, and I am working now for my children. Each and every one has the right to choose and do whatever the heck is right for you to do. The woman who stays at home and breast-feeds is a feminist [too]; you know, we empower each other."

Gladys Peterson, a retired missionary to Japan, tried to instill in her two sons the idea that all people are equal before God. When she was ordained later in life, she asked her son to speak at her ordination service. "I was moved by what he said," she explained. "He said, 'I know that God ordained you a long time ago.'"

Co-Pastors

What happens when both wife and husband feel called to pastoral ministry? Many Southern Baptist clergy couples have found places where one serves on a church staff while the other is a hospital chaplain or a campus minister; some couples serve together on a church staff, with one as senior pastor and the other as associate pastor. But a small group of ordained couples has forged a new model for ministry—the co-pastorate. In this model, both the wife and the husband share the title of pastor, and though they may differentiate tasks based on gifts and abilities, neither is primary or senior; their positions are equal.

Lynda Weaver-Williams was a student at Southern Seminary in the mid-1970s when her professors suggested that she consider preaching. Lynda's husband was a pastor in a Presbyterian church at the time, and she started to preach at his church. When they left the Presbyterian church, they became co-pastors of a Southern Baptist church in Kentucky. At the time, Lynda and her husband faced little opposition as co-pastors.

That was not the case in 2003 when North Broad Baptist Church in Rome, Georgia, called Katrina and Tony Brooks as co-pastors. Despite opposition from the local association, the church stood firmly behind its pastors and eventually left the Floyd County Baptist Association in 2004. Katrina initially thought that her calling was "to be an extension of somebody else and live out my call through him, to serve in traditionally female positions within the church." But, she pointed out, "It was just so wrong." She tried to become the pastor's wife and do all the things expected of her, but the role was not fulfilling and she didn't feel that she was carrying out her own calling. The struggle was hard on both her and her family. Eventually she understood that her calling was to the pastorate, but she worried about the potential conflict with her husband's calling. Eventually, they came across the shared pastorate model.

In both church and home, Katrina and Tony share responsibilities based on their abilities rather than gender roles. As co-pastors, Tony has primary responsibility for administration, while Katrina works with missions, discipleship, and outreach. Tony supervises the youth ministry; Katrina, the children's ministry. They split pastoral care responsibilities and take turns preaching. Although Katrina and Tony excel at their pastoral duties, they both see their relationship and their family as their most important responsibilities. At home, they both take care of their teenage children and manage household tasks.

For Katrina, being a co-pastor hasn't always been easy, given the opposition from the local association. Nonetheless, the church has stood firmly behind both Katrina and Tony. Katrina has had to work hard not to allow the critical voices to shape who she is. Instead, she focuses on her calling and her church's confidence in her as she works to minister alongside her husband.

All Mothers Are Working Mothers

All the mothers I spoke with consider mothering one of their most important roles—whether they are stay-at-home moms or moms in the workforce. Across the board, they recognize the difficulties and tensions that come with either option. The stay-at-home mothers believe that they are fulfilling a divinely ordained role, although they are well aware that this role is greatly devalued in society, despite rhetoric about the importance of families. The mothers in the workforce are no less concerned about their children and no less involved in their lives, even as they juggle the demands of the double shift. For both sets of mothers, raising their children to be Christian is a top priority, and they intentionally strive to inculcate Christian values in their offspring. Clique member Nancy Moore made this clear when I asked what she had tried to pass on to her daughters:

> I just wanted them, first of all, to have a life that included the Lord, because there is no successful life apart from that. After that, we encouraged them that they could do whatever they set their minds to do. We wanted them to be independent and happy in their work and find their niche in life and [feel that] the world would be a better place because they were here. I feel like we all owe that. We just encouraged independence, and they all were; they're very independent. And [they] have all been active in their churches and raising their children in the Christian mind-set too, which is good.

Stay-at-Home Moms

Mom told me, "I was a homemaker, and I think that's the job God intended for women to do, was to raise and nurture their children. I feel that's the most important job any woman can do." Over and over again, the women who stayed at home to raise their children emphasized, like my mother, that this is women's highest calling, their most important job. When I asked these women about their relationship to the women's movement and feminism, they tended to distance themselves; they felt that the movement had devalued them because they were homemakers (I return to this topic in chapter 7). For them, the focus on women in the workforce suggested that women's work in the home was less important and less valuable, even to the women who purported to be advocating for women's rights. This sense of devaluation may explain why these women have not embraced feminism and don't see feminist struggles as their own. Instead, they have reacted against feminism and refocused their sense of self on their role as homemakers in the context of the divinely ordained order in which homemaking is God's highest calling for women.

When Dorcas Pérez came to the United States from the Dominican

Republic, she saw women entering the workforce and decided that she needed to be educated in case she had to provide for her family. After she married, she worked outside the home for many years, but, she asserted, "My main job, the most important job in the world, was raising my family." During the years she stayed home with her children, she felt "accused of not doing much because we didn't go out and do it," despite the long hours of child care and housework that were her responsibility.

Elaine Richards finds being a wife and mother a very fulfilling role. "Five years ago, if you had told me that, I would've laughed," she explained. "I thought running a company was what you were supposed to be doing. I look back on that now, and that was the most boring thing in the world. What I do now is a hundred times more fulfilling than running a company. So I think women need to know that being a wife and a mom and being involved in the community and the school and raising children is very fulfilling and very rewarding."

When I asked about women's roles in the home, many conservative participants referenced Proverbs 31 (King James Version):

Who can find a virtuous woman? for her price is far above rubies.
The heart of her husband doth safely trust in her, so that he shall have no need of spoil.
She will do him good and not evil all the days of her life.
She seeketh wool, and flax, and worketh willingly with her hands.
She is like the merchants' ships; she bringeth her food from afar.
She riseth also while it is yet night, and giveth meat to her household, and a portion to her maidens.
She considereth a field, and buyeth it: with the fruit of her hands she planteth a vineyard.
She girdeth her loins with strength, and strengtheneth her arms.
She perceiveth that her merchandise is good: her candle goeth not out by night.
She layeth her hands to the spindle, and her hands hold the distaff.
She stretcheth out her hand to the poor; yea, she reacheth forth her hands to the needy.
She is not afraid of the snow for her household: for all her household are clothed with scarlet.
She maketh herself coverings of tapestry; her clothing is silk and purple.
Her husband is known in the gates, when he sitteth among the elders of the land.
She maketh fine linen, and selleth it; and delivereth girdles unto the merchant.

> Strength and honour are her clothing; and she shall rejoice in time to come.
> She openeth her mouth with wisdom; and in her tongue is the law of kindness.
> She looketh well to the ways of her household, and eateth not the bread of idleness.
> Her children arise up, and call her blessed; her husband also, and he praiseth her.

By constructing an identity around this passage, these women create a powerful sense of value for themselves as traditional homemakers. In these verses, they find both a justification for their choice and an elevation of their status as they fulfill a sacred duty. Though they are certainly not expected to spin their own yarn or plant their own vineyards, in this passage, women find a valuing of homemaking tasks and a sense of pride in creating a comfortable and nurturing home for their husbands and children.

Kryn Freehling-Burton said that her "journey into mothering is what made me question gender roles." Kryn chose to stay home after her children were born, even though that meant a reduction in family income. Then, when she did reenter the workforce, she discovered that men doing the same job were making more money than she was. Because she was working at a Southern Baptist institution, she found herself wondering how people who professed to be Christian could practice such inequity.

Moms in the Workforce

Mothers who work outside the home also face cultural pressures, particularly if their churches believe that mothers should be home with their children. The reality, of course, is that some women need to work for financial reasons; others choose to work for reasons of self-fulfillment and believe that doing so makes them better parents. Kristy Carr and her husband realized that they couldn't afford for her to be a stay-at-home mom, so when she was offered a staff position at WMU, Kristy was elated, although she had mixed feelings. "I knew financially I needed to go back to work [but] I didn't want to leave my child. . . . There's no winning. You'll be criticized if you go to work, and you're criticized if you don't." Nonetheless, she took the job with WMU and has "felt good about it ever since." I asked how she and her husband are raising their daughters in relation to gender. "What we've told our daughters," she replied, "is, 'You do whatever God's called you to do. And he will show you what that is.' . . . Are you limited in any way of serving in any kind of capacity? No! You look in the Bible: spiritual gifts are not gender-specific. They never have been. So you're not limited."

Although many of their mothers encouraged them to go to college or develop job skills in case they needed to support themselves, the women I interviewed have given much more overt messages to their own daughters. Diana Garland taught her daughter "that God has gifted her as a person, not just to be a spouse." And apparently, her daughter has taken that message to heart: she has earned a graduate degree, lived in Mexico, and worked with members of international gangs. "I'm very proud of her," Diana said, although that was already obvious. "She is not married, and I hope she will be someday. I've been so happy married for thirty-five years now and want her to have that kind of happiness in her life. And I want her to be happy in her life, whatever that might include." She and her husband, David, have also raised their son to be egalitarian, and they modeled that kind of relationship as both of them taught at Southern Seminary and parented their children equally. Her son, who was engaged to be married at the time of our interview, was also an Americorps volunteer.

"The social ministry gene must run in your family," I observed.

"Yeah," she replied, "I think so. As David says, 'We've failed miserably to inculcate materialistic values into our kids.'"

When I asked the very conservative Sheri Klouda how she's raising her daughter, she responded, "[I tell her] that she can do anything she puts her mind to, and that the whole world is her goal; she just needs to figure out what she wants to do. She's going to be fourteen, and deep inside I think she still has a few traditional ideas but, well, we'll see where she goes. But I want to encourage her that she shouldn't feel that she's limited simply because of her gender."

Carolyn Matthews, as a single mother in ministry, gave a clear message to her children. "Because I was the breadwinner, and because I was at seminary, because they saw me preaching, they came to understand, my daughter and my sons, that there are no roles that women can't fulfill if they are able and willing." Likewise, Joanne Parker consciously tried to raise her daughter "with the idea that she could do whatever it was that God gave her to do, no matter what any person—man, woman, relative, schoolteacher, person in the church—no matter what that person told her." Joanne prayed and studied the Bible with her daughter and told her repeatedly, "It's what God wants you to do that's important." Now, she's a strong woman, Joanne said, a physical therapist with a good marriage.

Being a Grandmother Is Even Better

The grandmothers I interviewed were effusive when they talked about their grandchildren. For them, having grandchildren seemed to be an indicator of their own success as parents and provided them with a strong sense of contributing to the future. Grandmothering, even more than mothering, affirms the importance and centrality of family and the ability to pour one's life into something larger and longer lasting than oneself.

Martha Gilmore's involvement in ministry may have been hard on her children (as preacher's kids), but her experience with her grandchildren has been very different. They, she explained, have little awareness that she was a pioneer. Martha told this story: She was working in a church that televised its worship services, and one Sunday, her daughter and one of her grandsons had the television tuned to Martha's church service. Her grandson was playing, but when he heard her voice on the television, he stopped what he was doing, crawled over to the television, pulled himself up, and started patting her face on the screen. "That's just the dearest!" she exclaimed. "I'm just basically their grandmother, which has been the way I wanted it, because I only have seven shots at that, and I have a lot of shots at being a pastor."

Carolyn Weatherford Crumpler became an instant grandmother when she married later in life, a role she truly relishes. After leaving WMU to become a pastor's wife, Carolyn continued to be active in the Cooperative Baptist Fellowship, speaking all over the country and even serving as a moderator. "Being a grandma is my all-time favorite ministry," she writes. "Once our granddaughter Abby was studying about itinerant preachers, and she said, 'Isn't that what Grandma was?'"[27]

Women on Their Own

Southern Baptists have a long history of valuing the work of single women, all the way back to Lottie Moon, whose single status allowed her to be especially effective on the mission field in China. Recognizing the increasing number of people who delay marriage or never marry at all, Southern Baptist churches have developed extensive single ministries and have invited single adults to find family within the church. Divorced singles are more problematic, because many Southern Baptists believe that divorce is a sin. However, in recent years, many churches have challenged the stigma that once prevented divorced people from serving in positions of leadership or having the option of remarrying in the church. Still, many churches remain uncomfortable with the idea of divorce, and few would be willing to call a divorced person as pastor.

Single Women and Missions

Among Southern Baptists, single women have a long and valued tradition in mission work. Beginning with Lottie Moon, single women have served as missionaries in the United States and around the globe. In a related form of service, many single women have held positions on state and national WMU staffs. Others have been church staff members, denominational employees, and Baptist college and seminary professors.

In the nineteenth century, missions provided single women with an opportunity for professional fulfillment.[28] Many of them enjoyed great freedom that was usually unavailable to married women, yet people often pitied them, as if the lack of a husband was a terrible thing.[29] Although some of these young women did want to marry (Lottie Moon was engaged briefly to seminary professor Crawford Toy), most saw their singleness as beneficial to their ministries.[30]

Annie Jenkins Sallee, a missionary to China in the early twentieth century, writes poignantly in her journal about not wanting to marry. She believes that the constraints of marriage will undermine her effectiveness as a missionary. In 1905 she writes:

> I didn't want to marry for many reasons, I had decided on so much work I was going to do. I feel a single woman can do so much more work than a married one with household cares. I feel I could have more influence with the young unmarried. I never did feel called upon to keep house for a man. I want to be in the work myself. As yet I have not been able to find the great importance and "privilege" as some term it of being a "wife"! It seems to me I'd be cut off from everything and shut up to house-hold cares.[31]

Then she meets William Eugene Sallee, also a missionary in China, and he asks her to marry him. She struggles with her decision, for at the time, marrying meant giving up one's own work and identity and assuming the role of wife and helpmate. She writes:

I've told him how it seemed to me my education and all the years of training I had put on myself would be useless. He wouldn't need it, and I couldn't use it. It hurts him when I talk that way. He says he knows it is asking me to give up everything for nothing; but he loves me. . . . I have learned such things and had such high ambitions for myself as a single woman that I can't give these all up just now. I know that Papa says a woman's highest possible attainment in this world is to be a wife and mother but oh! I have seen the other side. . . . The taste I had of public work, of meetings with the women, of moving whole audiences, and of helping people make decisions for God, of counciling [*sic*] with people about their work, and helping the discouraged—has taken a bigger hold on me than I thought and I flinch when I think of merging my own self, identity and all, literally losing right of self and all for him.[32]

Despite her love for Sallee, Annie agonizes over marrying him. She decidedly sees the choice as one between her own identity and work and his. She writes, "My how it hurts my pride. I don't want to be 'Mrs.' anybody. I don't like married women as a general rule." She goes on to say that married women are too wrapped up in their husbands to be of any use. When she finally does marry Sallee, she has the officiant take the word *obey* out of the vows and replace it with the word *help*. Later that year, she writes, "I don't feel I can get used to being Mrs. S. and really don't want to. I hate to think I gave up my name."[33]

Clearly, Annie saw marriage as severely limiting and as an eradication of her own individual identity. As a single woman missionary, she was free to develop a sense of self and do her work as she saw fit, finding purpose and fulfillment in doing so. Despite her love for her husband, marriage took those things away from her. As a married woman, Annie's identity was forced to undergo acute reconstruction, whereas Sallee's essentially remained the same, even though he took on the role of husband.

Lottie Moon made a very different choice. While in China, Lottie corresponded regularly with Southern Seminary professor Crawford Toy. Toy became the focus of controversy because of his progressive biblical interpretation, and he eventually left Southern Seminary for Harvard University. Lottie announced that she was leaving China to marry Toy, but what happened next is unclear because of a gap in the correspondence covering that period. Some suggest that Lottie broke off the engagement because of Toy's liberal views, but as Catherine Allen points out, she would have known about his progressive ideas before she agreed to marry him.[34] Instead, Allen suggests, Lottie chose to stay in China and continue her work. She cites a quotation attributed to Lottie when asked by a young relative whether she had ever been in love: "'Yes, but God had first claim on my life, and since the two conflicted, there could be no question about the result.'"[35]

Living Single in a Partnered World

Among contemporary Southern Baptists, many women still find the freedom to serve by remaining single. For many, this is not a conscious choice. Because marriage simply isn't their primary objective, they focus their energies on their careers. Their independence and strong sense of vocation may not be appealing to young men who expect their wives' careers to take a backseat to their own. Or these women may be unwilling to compromise their own goals in order to enter into marriage.

On the whole, young women in the United States are choosing to delay marriage (the median age is twenty-five—the highest ever), but most young women still expect to marry and have children someday.[36] Twenty-nine-year-old Raquel Ellis told me about a friend of hers who is in her fifties and "still patiently waiting for the Lord to bless her with a companion. This is really inspiring to me, given that I too am trying to wait patiently for the Lord to bless me with a companion." Pam Boucher's primary consideration in life has been being where God wants her to be and doing what God wants her to do. "For me," she said, "that has been in ministry; it's not been to marry and have children," although Pam is open to marriage if she should meet the right man. For Candi Finch, her singleness gives her a "wide open area to minister to other women in the church. You know, I believe that to be my calling right now."

Some of the unmarried middle-aged women I spoke with now consciously choose to remain single, having found other ways to build community and family that allow them to remain independent. Some participants, however, got married for the first time in midlife—much to their surprise.

Dealing with Divorce

When I was growing up, divorce was highly stigmatized in my church, and in some places, it still is. One denominational worker told me that despite her calling, she knew that her divorce would probably prevent her from working in a church. She went to seminary anyway, where she had to defend her divorce, and she had to do so again when she applied for her first ministry position. "Divorced people are not second-class citizens," she emphasized. "Jesus never said that. Divorced people can be used in the church just as clearly as other people." She has persevered because of her strong sense of calling.

Although her experiences are not uncommon, the pervasiveness of divorce in American society has forced Southern Baptist churches to become more welcoming of divorced singles. Many of the women in my mother's Sunday school class are divorced single moms. When Jennifer Wofford went through her divorce, she felt that the church members supported her. She felt like she had let people down, but no one in the church ever made her feel that way. "This church," she added, "was a big part of helping me get through such a bad time." LaDonna Burton concurred: "People in the church have never ever treated me any different than they would anybody, couples, married, or whatever." These women are also realistic about their responsibilities as single mothers. LaDonna explained, "In my situation, [I] had to be everything—spiritual leader, the breadwinner, everything."

Carolyn Matthews's experiences were similar. I asked her how being a single mother affected her identity as a minister. "It was just another part of who I was," she replied, "and what I had to do. I didn't think about, what does this make me or who I am. I had my family to take care of, and they came first. Then there was school, and there was work. You just finagle your way around everything that needed to be done."

Becca Gurney's marriage fell apart while she was in seminary, and she ended up the single mother of a toddler. Still, she felt that she had to follow her calling, so she continued her theological studies. When the time came for her ordination, she had a huge disagreement with the pastor of the church because she wanted to have all the people in the congregation lay hands on her; the pastor refused, stating that only ordained deacons and clergy could lay on hands. During the ordination service, Becca's parents and son were seated in the front row of the sanctuary. When the time came for the laying on of hands, her parents stood and came forward anyway, despite the pastor's pronouncement. To Becca's surprise, her son joined his grandparents. She told me, "He came forward with them, and he put his little hand on my head, and he was so tearful, because we're both just really emotional people that way. And he just broke up crying. So I scooped him up next to me, and then, after that, everyone who came forward put their hands on my head *and* his head. And you know, here is this little child who has been with me on this entire journey, who is being blessed, and it just was phenomenal to me to be able to have him there at my side when all of this happened."

Certainly, Southern Baptists' changing views on divorce became apparent in 2000 when Charles Stanley, a fundamentalist leader and pastor of the First Baptist Church of Atlanta, and his wife of more than forty years divorced. During their separation, Stanley had stated that he would resign if he and his wife divorced, but when reconciliation became impossible, church leaders asked Stanley to stay on as pastor, and he did. Most Southern Baptists still believe that divorce is wrong, and although some still condemn those who divorce, many others are more realistic, more tolerant, and more accepting of those who do.

Invisible and Unspeakable

Perhaps the most divisive issue among Baptists today, as in many other Protestant denominations, is the issue of same-sex relationships. Not surprisingly, the overwhelming majority of Southern Baptists are opposed. This issue is also the primary dividing line between the Cooperative Baptist Fellowship and the Alliance of Baptists (which openly supports same-sex relationships). Since 1976, the Southern Baptist Convention has approved fourteen resolutions on the topic and even amended its constitution to define membership this way: "Among churches not in cooperation with the Convention are churches which act to affirm, approve, or endorse homosexual behavior."[37] This amendment, enacted in 1992, was significant because it was the first time in the Convention's history that any theological criterion for membership had been expressed. The impetus for the amendment included the ordination of a gay person and the blessing of a gay couple's union in local Southern Baptist churches. The most recent resolution, passed in 2006, chastised U.S. senators who did not support the federal "marriage protection amendment" (which would define marriage as a union between a man and a woman), encouraged the House of Representatives to pass the amendment, and encouraged states that had not enacted laws prohibiting gay marriage to do so before judges imposed it on them.[38]

Of course, despite the sentiments of the Convention and Southern Baptists, many gay and lesbian people are part of Baptist life. Many leave Southern Baptist churches as part of their coming-out process; others are forced out. Some, however, choose to stay and work for change from within. Perhaps one of the most visible of the latter is April Baker, co-pastor of Nashville's Glendale Baptist Church. April joined the church's staff as an associate pastor in 2002; when the pastor retired in 2003, April stepped in as interim pastor until 2004, when the church called her and Amy Mears as co-pastors. During the interview process for the associate pastor position, April was an acknowledged lesbian. When the church's search committee asked for guidance on the issue, the church told the committee to choose the best person for the job, so April got the call. "I just nearly fainted," she said. "Because this is the phone call I never expected in my whole life to get but always hoped would happen." Of course, the church's decision raised the ire of the Nashville Baptist Association, the Tennessee Baptist Convention, and the Southern Baptist Convention. A band of sign-waving hatemongers even showed up to protest. But April and the church also received a lot of support. The upside, she said, was that "an awful lot of people heard that there's a Baptist church that they really might be able to go to and find a word of love and grace and acceptance."

April's colleague, Amy Mears, is a straight woman with a husband and four children. She realized that accepting the call to co-pastor with a lesbian was a "terminal maneuver," because once she went to Glendale, she could never go back to a less open place. She said, "I was never up-rooting and going somewhere else that I was going to have to compromise again. There is no going backwards." She explained, "I am just so tired of under-living, under-speaking: I can't appear too intelligent, might intimidate somebody; I can't be controversial, people will gasp. Worried about what my kids were saying in Sunday school. Didn't matter that they're two and three and four years old; they were offending their Sunday school teachers. They were singing about 'our mother' when everybody else was singing about 'our father.'"

April and Amy agree that their work relationship has been beneficial both for them and for the church. They share duties, including preaching, and the church has embraced their ministry. Amy noted, "We've had so much fun. Part of it is that my husband Dave and April's partner Deborah are good friends; they . . . talk frequently about their temptation to RSVP to the pastors' wives conference and go together." We laughed, and April added, "We're pretty sure they're gonna create trouble somewhere."

Glendale Baptist Church is now a member of the Association of Welcoming and Affirming Baptists, a group begun by American Baptists in 1993 to offer support to lesbian, gay, bisexual, and transgender people and advocate for their inclusion in Baptist communities of faith.[39] A number of other former Southern Baptist churches that now affiliate with the Alliance of Baptists are also members of this association. In contrast to the SBC, the Alliance offers this statement on same-sex marriage:

> Affirming that our federal and state constitutions exist to protect the rights of minorities from the tyranny of the majority and in the context of the current debate over same-sex marriage, we of the Alliance of Baptists decry the politicization of same-sex marriage in the current presidential contest and other races for public office. We specifically reject the proposed amendments to the Constitution of the United States and state constitutions that would enshrine discrimination against sexual minorities and define marriage in such a way as to deny same-sex couples a legal framework in which to provide for one another and those entrusted to their care.
>
> As Christians and as Baptists, we particularly lament the denigration of our gay, lesbian, bisexual, and transgender sisters and brothers in this debate by those who claim to speak for God. We affirm that the Alliance of Baptists supports the rights of all citizens to full marriage equality, and we affirm anew that the Alliance will "create places of refuge and renewal for those who are ignored by the church."[40]

Undoubtedly, the controversy over the place of gay, lesbian, and bisexual people in the church will continue among Baptists, even as it does in the larger society. For conservative Southern Baptists, the issue of homosexuality goes straight to the heart of their understanding of the nature of scripture. They believe that the Bible, as the inerrant and infallible Word of God, clearly prohibits same-sex relationships. Even many moderate Baptists agree that the Bible teaches that homosexuality is a sin. More progressive Baptists, in keeping with their more contextual interpretation of scripture, read the Bible as prohibiting exploitative sexual relationships of any kind, but they do not understand it to condemn loving and ethical relationships between two people of the same sex.

The significance of these positions becomes evident in the actual lives of lesbian, gay, and bisexual people in Southern Baptist, CBF, and Alliance churches. Many feel guilt-ridden and pray desperately for God to change them. Others feel compelled to leave the churches that nurtured them but no longer welcome them once they come out. Some find places of acceptance and inclusion in churches such as Glendale Baptist in Tennessee, Olin T. Binkley Memorial and Pullen Memorial Baptist in North Carolina, and Oakhurst Baptist in Georgia. One participant, obviously pained by the experience, told me that she had left her Southern Baptist church because she didn't want to attend a church where she couldn't be with her partner. Another told me that she no longer maintains contact with the church she grew up in for fear that the congregation would reject her if they knew the truth about her. One researcher has found that evangelical women in particular experience a great deal of dissonance and struggle during the coming-out process.[41]

Allies of gays and lesbians also face difficulties in Southern Baptist life. Professor Paula Sheridan was called in to the college president's office and instructed to present homosexuality as sinful behavior. She told him, "That is one Southern Baptist view, but there are many Southern Baptist views on homosexuality, and, if we're talking about representing Southern Baptists, let's be inclusive." When he persisted, she finally said, "I'm not the maitre d' at God's table; I'm a welcome guest. I don't decide who gets seated and who gets turned away."

For many Southern Baptists, homosexuality is the dividing-line issue—even for those who are supportive of other progressive causes, such as women's ordination. Listening to my participants talk about the issue from all sides, I find myself less than optimistic about the possibility of finding common ground in the near future. Passions still run too high, and meanwhile, real people are caught in the crossfire.

7

I Am Woman

Southern Baptist Women and Feminism

Sisters, will you join and help us? Moses' sister aided him;
Will you help the trembling mourners who are struggling hard with sin?
Tell them all about the Savior, Tell them that he will be found;
Sisters, pray, and holy manna will be showered all around.
—George Atkins, "Brethren, We Have Met to Worship"

Contemporary Baptist women are conflicted about feminism. Some are proudly feminist; they wear the label and support the movement's goals. Others are adamant that they are not feminist, even though they acknowledge the benefits brought about by the women's movement. Most of these women, however, see feminists as extremists and so distance themselves from the label. But all the women I spoke with believe in women's equality, and when I defined feminism as a belief in and willingness to work for equality between women and men, almost every one admitted that she might well be a feminist based on that definition.

The Generational Divide

Interestingly, I found that women's attitudes about feminism are generational and depend on their proximity to the women's movement. The women of my mother's generation, who are now in their late sixties and older, are of the same generation as the feminist activists of the women's movement, but most of these women were stay-at-home mothers who had only a passing awareness of the movement gleaned from television and newspapers. They do not necessarily see themselves as feminist, nor do they feel that they specifically benefited from the women's movement. In fact, some believe that the movement devalued them as home-makers. They do, however, admit that the women's movement brought about many positive changes for women, and they are especially grateful that their daughters and granddaughters have benefited from those changes. Many mentioned how important it is that their daughters can choose to work and receive equal pay for that work. They also noted that because of the women's movement, they have been able to raise their daughters to be independent and self-sufficient. Of course, they believe that, ideally, their daughters should marry and have families, but they're realistic enough to know that the prevalence of domestic violence and divorce means that their daughters may have to provide for themselves and their children. Many still distance themselves from feminists whom they consider extreme, although they might grudgingly admit that these extreme feminists brought about necessary changes.

More surprising are older women's attitudes about women's role in the church. Many of them, even those in very conservative churches, believe that women should be deacons. The more progressive ones also believe that women should be pastors, but even most of those who don't are able to create a space in their theological thinking for the possibility that God might call a woman to pastor. And, as Baptists, most of them feel very strongly that, although they wouldn't attend a church with a female pastor, local churches have the right to call anyone they wish as their pastor. A small group of older participants was much more aware of the women's movement and supported its goals. These include the pioneering women who went to seminary in the 1970s to pursue pastoral ministry, although even some of those women weren't especially aware of the movement at the time.

Middle-aged women seem to be the most comfortable with feminism. The younger of these women (now in their early to mid-forties) were the first generation to benefit from Title IX, which mandated equal participation in educational programs and activities receiving federal funds. Although most of the middle-aged participants were only vaguely aware of the women's movement in the 1970s as they watched bits and pieces of it on television, they were able to see firsthand how the movement benefited women. California Baptist University professor Beverly Howard "started seeing opportunities, mostly in, say, a generation younger than me, possibilities that they had." When Gwen Dellinger went to work, she was the first professional woman in her workplace; all the other women were secretaries. When she discovered that a newly hired male employee was doing the same job but making more money, she asked her boss, "Why is he making more than me?" And her boss replied, "He has a family to support." "Evidently," Gwen surmised, "I was working for the fun of it."

These women were most likely to volunteer to me that they were feminists. But when I broached the subject, many were astute enough to ask what I meant by the term *feminist*, recognizing that there are a variety of feminisms. When I gave my generic definition, most were able to say that they are in agreement with it. These women are decidedly raising their daughters to believe that they can do anything God leads them to do (although many of them don't think that God will be calling their daughters to pastor). They are also raising their daughters to expect equal and respectful treatment in the home, and they are raising their sons to see women as equal to men, even if they believe that wives should be submissive to their husbands. Having watched the momentous changes in society across the 1970s and 1980s, these women recognize that equal pay, sexual harassment policies, domestic violence laws, equality in educational opportunities, and a host of other structural changes that benefit women are the direct result of feminist activism.

Some of the women of North Broad Baptist Church in Rome, Georgia, which recently called a woman as co-pastor, observed that the history of their church reflects the movements of society. They see this as a good thing. Patty Carter explained, "I think men in the church had to learn how to give and take, just like they have in society. And I really feel like, as women, we feel more free and liberated, because we feel like we've come farther. Men were always deacons and were always pastors and were always expected to do that; but now that women are taking on some of those roles, it's a different sort of thing. So I think the church reflects society in general in that way."

Middle-aged women may still distance themselves from what they perceive as feminist extremes, but on the whole, they are comfortable with liberal feminists whose primary goal is the proverbial level playing field. However, in no way do they themselves want to be considered feminists of the more radical ilk. Some middle-aged participants refuse to claim feminism of any variety, although they may grudgingly recognize the much-needed gains it has brought.

Younger women's attitudes about feminism are especially interesting. Some are emphatically feminist. They don't know a world without feminism and its attendant benefits, and they see themselves as part of an ongoing feminist effort. For Suzanne Whisler's mother, the only options were to be a secretary, a nurse, or a teacher. She told Suzanne, who is an intern at Baylor Student Ministries, "If I were your age, and I could do it all over again, I'd have been an architect or something completely different." Suzanne said, "It never occurred to me that my options were limited. To hear Mom say that—I was thirteen or fourteen at the time—just really changed me, because at the time I was considering being a vet or a statistician or a lawyer; and for her, those doors weren't open. So, yeah, definitely [the women's movement] has benefited me in a way that I don't even think I can comprehend."

Lucy Elizalde recognizes how gender and race intersect in defining feminism. She sees feminism as a movement for white women and prefers the term *mujerista* for her Latina feminism. *Mujerista* theologian Ada Maria Isasi-Diaz explains that the goals of *mujerista* theology are "to provide a platform for the voices of Latina grassroots women; to develop a theological method that takes seriously the religious understandings and practices of Latinas as a source for theology; to challenge theological understandings, church teachings, and religious practices that oppress Latina women, that are not life-giving, and therefore, cannot be theologically correct." She adds that *mujerista* theology is not exclusively for Latinas but is "a theology *from* the perspective of Latinas."[1]

Other young women identify with feminist issues but don't necessarily want to label themselves feminist. Leah Grundset, an intern at Baylor Student Ministries and a first-year student at Truett Seminary, said, "If you look at the way [feminism] is defined, I think that's just something we all agree with and wouldn't even have to say we're a feminist. I mean, for me personally, I wouldn't have to say I'm a feminist. Though there are things that have been instilled in me that I believe."

Many of the young Southern Baptist women I spoke with are actually more conservative than older generations on women's issues and more distant from the term *feminist*. These young women often assume the benefits of feminism without knowing or understanding the history that led to them. They don't make the connection between the women's movement of the 1970s and their own access to equal pay or higher education. In many ways, they assume that sexism was an issue "back in the day," but no more. Because many of them intend to be homemakers (and thus don't believe they need to worry about workplace issues) and are opposed to abortion and gay rights, they don't really see the need for feminist work anymore. In fact, they perceive feminists as taking on issues with which they profoundly disagree, so they see no connection between feminist agendas and their own.

The generational divide was starkly evident in my conversation with a group of women from First Baptist Church of Hendersonville, a very large, very conservative church just outside of Nashville. Tammy Hayes, who is in her mid-forties, arranged the focus group. At that point in my research, I didn't have much representation from younger women, so I asked Tammy to pull together a group of women in their twenties and thirties. Ten of us sat around Tammy's comfortable living room, where she and I were the oldest people present by at least a decade. When I asked these young women whether they had benefited from the women's movement, they nodded, but then they clarified, "yes and no." Mitzi Sayler noted that the women's movement has allowed women to enter practically every career, but she still believes there are certain things women shouldn't do, such as go into battle. Cari Garrett, too, acknowledged the benefits but worried that feminism's challenge to gender roles has created confusion, especially for men who are no longer sure how to be leaders. When I asked whether they considered themselves feminists, there was dead silence.

"Anyone?" I probed.

At that point, Tammy spoke up: "You got one." Then she added, "Jesus Christ was the greatest feminist that ever walked the face of this earth. He raised the woman's status. . . . And women followed Jesus; they gave their monies to the ministry of Jesus and the disciples. Jesus did more for women. That to me is a feminist, who raised that status and standard for woman; [who told her] she is valued."

Like many women of all ages, young Southern Baptist women, both conservatives and progressives, have a lot of misconceptions about feminism, and I was amazed at the persistence of stereotypes across the decades, apart from any connection to reality. Many of them see feminists as bra-burning extremists, even though they weren't old enough to witness the movement of the 1970s. Of course, they are probably greatly influenced by the rhetoric they've heard from their pastors and other church leaders and the power of southern culture to construct femininity as soft, quiet, and demure. Whether the young women I interviewed embraced feminism or rejected it, they did not want to be identified with what they considered feminist extremes.

Of Course I'm a Feminist

For the Southern Baptist women who answered with a resounding, "Well, yeah!" when I asked whether they were feminist, their feminism arises from their faith. They understand Christian faith to be about equality and social justice for all people. Priscilla Denham, one of the first Southern Baptist women ordained in Texas, told me, "I felt like I was a feminist because I was a Christian. Jesus related to women with immense respect, and all persons had value. All persons are the children of God. Therefore, no person should be denied the right to earn the same amount of money or go into the same places. To me, civil rights, obviously, were something that I was very sharply aware of. Feminism was the logical and natural expression, just as to be against racism was a logical and natural expression, of Christianity." Carolyn Goodman Plampin explained, "If you call a feminist a Christian woman who believes in Christian women and believes that they have a biblical ministry, yes, I am a Christian feminist." In an essay in a volume on Southern Baptist women in ministry, Molly Marshall points out that women in ministry may be accused of following a "secular feminist" agenda. Her response to that accusation is this: "I am a feminist because I am a Christian. I became a feminist reading the apostle Paul, not Betty Friedan and Gloria Steinem."[2]

Counselor Kathy Manis Findley defined feminism this way: "It means that in every way, women need to be empowered to live their lives. They need to be empowered for employment, they need to be empowered for keeping themselves safe from violence, they need to be empowered from abusive situations they find themselves in; every day, every single day, either in the workplace or in their homes, in their churches. That's what it means to me. It just means empowerment in every aspect of life, over their own bodies; just the whole nine yards."

Although Pam Boucher doesn't see herself as an activist, she does claim the title feminist because she believes in equal opportunity. She's not aggressive and overbearing about it, but "people know where I stand." Sarah Frances Anders grew up in the feminist movement, although she never considered herself a "flaming feminist." Nonetheless, through her long teaching career, Sarah has managed to stand up for herself, but not without a "sense of manners and courtesy" befitting a southern woman. As a professor of social work, Sarah has caused her share of "trouble" on campus, standing up for the disenfranchised and the marginalized and advocating equality for all people. Zana Kizzee and her family were so wrapped up in their own African American experience of poverty that she wasn't aware of the women's movement. But, she added, "We always had the example of our mother, who was a social worker. She was a single mother of five kids. We lived with our grandmother a lot, just to help out. We always saw our mother, she was the breadwinner; she went out to work. So I guess we saw the feminist movement in our house, out of necessity."

Carla Moldavan wouldn't say one way or the other whether she's a feminist, but she offered to tell me a couple of stories and let me decide for myself. When she was in junior high in the early 1960s, she wrote to the manager of the New York Yankees and proposed that she and a friend be bat girls. He wrote back complimenting her on a "revolutionary" idea but told her that they already had their bat boys lined up. I decided that she is indeed a feminist.

For many participants, feminism is specifically connected to their Baptist understanding of equality and soul competency. Professor Carolyn Blevins explained, "[Feminism] means that a woman has choices . . . in Baptist life, it means all of that fullness of priesthood and authority in terms of interpreting scripture. So feminism for me is a lot about choice and unlimited opportunity." Beth Duke noted that she considers herself a Christian feminist. For her, that means, "God gives individuals gifts, and he wants them to use them, and gender doesn't matter to him. . . . It's not about playing a part or having a role; it's [about] being an individual [who] does what God wants her or him to do." Missionary Debra Owen-Hughes concurred: "In its best form, [feminism is] doing what God calls you as a woman to do, in spite of the 'rules' society or organizations want to limit you to." Even though these women may not embrace feminism in all its expressions, most agree that feminism is about choice; in particular, in the Baptist way of thinking, it's about women's ability to do what God has called them to do.

Nashville pastor April Baker said that her feminism took a while to wake up because she hadn't been raised with a feminist consciousness. "But," she added, "when it woke up, it made perfect sense because it feels so much like what Jesus was about." To Mary Zimmer, feminism means to be "equal before God, and thus equal in all other kinds of things. If God doesn't make the distinction, then there's no point in humans doing it." Phyllis Rodgerson Pleasants said, "God really gave me no other choice but to be a feminist." To her, feminism means owning one's own perspective and resisting the categories into which society tries to place women and men based on gender. "It means standing clear," she added, "knowing who you are, warts and all. Stand firm. Be clear. It's about mutual respect." For her, feminism is about being true to the person God created each of us to be and not becoming what society expects us to be. Similarly, sociologist Nancy Ammerman explained that feminism is connected with her Baptist faith because of "the notion of being part of a religious tradition that says all of us come equally before God; all of us hear God's voice equally—gender is a part of that. It means that women come before God as equals; it means that women hear God's voice equally."

Two students from McAfee School of Theology readily embrace a feminist identity. Mary Beth Byram said that she could "talk about feminism all day long!" She explained that she's a feminist because feminism "means working toward freedom and toward equality." She's not bothered by feminism's negative connotations because she believes they just provide an opportunity for her to educate people about what feminism really is. Feminism, she added, "has given so many women freedom. If there weren't feminists, I'd still be wearing a long skirt and be barefoot and pregnant. I think that's the reason I am such a big supporter, because I want this to keep going." Her colleague Nikki Hardeman also mentioned the inclusiveness of feminism. "Feminism is not only about making a way for women," she pointed out. "It's about making a way for all people. I think feminism is a different way to live, a different way to relate to one another, a different way to relate in society. That's why I'm a feminist; I think it blazes the trail for the underprivileged, for underdeveloped countries, for women, for any oppressed people."

Many of the women I interviewed came to feminist consciousness because of their exclusion or marginalization on the basis of their gender. Nashville pastor Amy Mears explained, "I had two older brothers and never understood why it was that they could go out and cut the grass and I had to unload the dishwasher. [My feminism] started there." Jorene Swift used to believe that there was no prejudice against women and that if she worked hard and did a good job she'd be accepted and rewarded. Then she ran into the reality of working in churches. The sexism she experienced wasn't intentional; in fact, she contends that most people are completely unaware of the subtle ways they practice discrimination. "You think you'll be judged for who you are rather than if you have the right body parts," she lamented. When Dixie Petrey went to Southern Seminary, she began to feel that she was somehow less because of her gender. All the controversy over women caused her to degrade her own image of women, but her studies in feminist theology helped her reclaim the positive value of women.

For Tisa Lewis, the treatment of women in her church influenced her feminism. "Ephesians 5 wasn't stressed that much in my church," she explained, "women being subject to your husbands, but people believed it, and I hated to watch that and was determined that I would never be a part of it." After watching what happened to women during the SBC Controversy, she became even more committed to helping students understand that subordinating other people is immoral. When I asked her to define feminism, she quoted Rebecca West, who, at the turn of the twentieth century, said "that whenever she tries to differentiate herself from a prostitute or a doormat, people call her a feminist. She's saying that a hundred years ago. I think there's some truth to that. I think a feminist is a person, male or female, who believes that men and women should be treated equally in all ways. I think that's a feminist."

A few years ago, Peggy Sanderford Ponder wouldn't have called herself a feminist, but she does now.

"What made you change your mind?" I asked.

"I got smarter," she replied, generating raucous laughter around the dinner table. "I think it's more just coming to realize how women are treated as second-class citizens," she explained. "I don't think we deserve to be treated like second-class citizens; likewise I don't think men ought to be treated like second-class citizens, or African Americans, or whoever else. My understanding of feminism is empowering the person. I think that's what I want to do, is empower people, whoever they are and whatever they do."

Laywomen in the workforce were reminded of the need for feminism by their experiences of workplace discrimination. Patty Lamb explained, "In the workplace . . . there is a lot of the 'good old boy' network, where women are doing a lot of work and not necessarily being rewarded for it." Likewise, Angelyn Turner ran into that good old boy network when one of her three supervisors balked at increasing her salary. Patty added, "It's that kind of thing that you run across, and you think, 'This can't still be happening in the real world.'" Debbie Williams responded, "Feminism means gender-blind opportunity such that women are not eliminated from certain jobs or professions based on gender alone. Therefore, because I believe that women can be qualified for any profession or business, I guess I am a feminist." Although Nancy Ammerman grew up with an innate sense of feminism, she became a "conscious feminist" the year she worked as a secretary for a Baptist state convention and had to deal with men who exploited her.

For many of these women, their feminism counters hegemonic notions of women. Music professor Beverly Howard said that her feminism helps her "take off the male lens" and look at the world through a female lens. She noted, "I certainly am supportive of women in their aspirations, and I kick butt with students when I see them wanting to settle for 'barefoot, pregnant, and married to a preacher.'" For others, their feminism provides hope for their children's futures. Amy Mears worries about her three daughters and her son. She felt a strong need to get them into a church where they could see gender equality modeled.

When I asked my sister about the intersection of feminism and Southern Baptists, she had this to say about our own family:

> In spite of all the things that Southern Baptists do to beat women down, we actually come from a long line of strong Southern Baptist women. And so I think . . . , whether they want to admit it or not, they made us feminists. And you know [our paternal grandmother] taught Sunday school from sixteen to eighty-eight. That's unheard of. Mother stood up to [the pastor]. So there are things like that, that make me chuckle. . . . They don't want us to be feminists, and yet they, in their own right, have been feminists and taught us to do that. And to me, our first feminist was Aunt Nellie because she told her drunk husband to go take a hike, and she was self-sufficient and . . . used to preach to me, "You don't need a man to be anything."

Many Southern Baptist women, especially (and not surprisingly) women in ministry, have fully embraced a feminist identity. For them, feminism is about equal opportunity and choice. And they see equality and choice as aspects of humanity given to women by God. Therefore, for them, a comfortable compatibility exists between their identity as Christians and their identity as feminists. They may not agree with everything the larger women's movement seeks to accomplish (and, of course, feminists frequently disagree among themselves), but they are earnestly committed to the goals of equality, respect, dignity, and choice affirmed by the larger feminist movement.

I'm Not a Feminist, But . . .

Even though many participants responded immediately, "Oh no, I'm not a feminist" (usually followed by an explanation involving bra-burning and man-hating—more about that later), Southern Baptist women actually support many feminist positions. They believe in equal pay and equal job opportunities; they denounce violence against women and sex abuse. Lisa Vang is a good example. When I asked whether she considers herself a feminist, she responded, "I support equality for women in the workplace and in the church, but I am not a strong feminist." Pat Brown doesn't consider herself a feminist either, because feminists seem to be pushing women's roles in one direction. Yet, when I asked whether she believes in the equality of women and men, she said, "Yes, yes, oh certainly!" Nan Cook of Batesburg, South Carolina, summed it up: "We believe in women's rights, that we have the right to do things as well as a man; but is any of us considering ourselves feminists? No."

When nudged a little, many of the women who initially claimed not to be feminists admitted that—if feminism is defined as a commitment to equality between women and men—they probably are feminists after all. In fact, in 2006 *Ms.* magazine noted that 53 percent of American women and 35 percent of American men considered themselves feminist, including first lady Laura Bush.[3]

When I asked one of my former seminary professors, Doris Borchert, whether she considers herself a feminist, she said, "I never named myself that."

"Why is that?" I asked.

"My actions and behavior I think would say I am, but I have not called myself that."

"How do you think you became this unnamed feminist?" I laughed.

"I guess I had never thought of myself as other than equal with men," Doris responded. She added that her first experience of being treated as less than equal came with the fundamentalist takeover of Southern Seminary.

"So, in some ways, your connections with being Southern Baptist probably increased your feminist commitments?" I probed.

"Oh, yes. Yes. It forced, it brought it on, encouraged, whatever words you want to use."

Occasionally, participants started off denying any feminist leanings and then talked themselves into identifying as feminist. Initially, Rhonda Reeves said she wasn't a feminist and pointed to the 1970s and Gloria Steinem as her first negative reaction to the term. Then she continued:

I am not a man hater by any means; I love men. My husband's one and my son. No, I think there are some issues there in the rights of women. Certainly women have rights. But I wouldn't say that I'm a feminist to the degree . . . to say you are a feminist is way over here. I'm kind of middle of the road, but I would fight for the right of a woman to do what she needs to do, to vote, to have freedoms that she needs; oh my goodness, yes, we're equal.

And in pay, and that sort of thing. I can get off on that one too, because I know. But I still don't see myself as a feminist, but absolutely women deserve just pay, equal pay, to make what a man makes. . . . I *am* a feminist, and I don't realize it.

She even rethought her comment about Gloria Steinem. "I go back to the Gloria days, and I see her, and I think, 'Oh my gosh, what she was doing back then!' But had we not had her back in those days, maybe we wouldn't be where we are today."

"There is a range of feminisms, really," I explained helpfully.

"And maybe I am on that scale somewhere," Rhonda responded.

Then I gave her my best thirty-second introduction to feminism lesson, explaining how the media have distorted feminism when most women really do agree with its goals, even though they may differ about how to get there.

"That's right," she affirmed. "Okay, I change my answer: Yes!"

I was often struck by the irony of these strong, successful women distancing themselves from feminism. My favorite example comes from the conversation I had with my longtime friend and WMU staff member Sheryl Churchill. When I asked Sheryl what feminism means to her, she laughed and said, "I ain't no flamin' liberal!"

"That would be me," I replied.

"There's the difference!" she responded. "The word *feminist* is a hot word; it's one of those red-flag words. It's not a word I necessarily like. You can take anything to the extreme, and if it doesn't accomplish anything and it's only extreme, then maybe you need to back off a little bit here. I do think there have been advancements in society in general, because women, if you want to call them feminists—they won us the right to vote! And it was within my mother's lifetime that that happened. So that always helps me put a perspective on it, even though it's been many, many years ago. But had those women not stepped to the forefront, women today would not have the right to vote, and women today oftentimes don't care. Because they don't know their history; they don't know the price that was paid in order for them to have that privilege."

"Now, do you consider yourself a feminist?" I asked.

"No, I don't. Because I see feminism as being extreme, and I'm not extreme."

When I asked her why she sees feminism as extreme, she pointed to the suffragists. If she had lived then, she might have been part of the crowd demanding the right to vote, but she wouldn't have been a leader.

"Now here you are at WMU," I said, pointing out the obvious, "having spent a lifetime leading women."

For many Southern Baptist women, the word *feminism* carries too many connotations of extremism and militancy. For raised-right women who have been taught to get along well with others and always be nice, the idea of being an extremist is terribly disconcerting. In many ways, these women have accepted the popular misconceptions of feminism and fail to recognize that feminism is about empowerment, choice, and equality in all sorts of ways. These same women are often leaders in their churches and homes; they are involved in their communities, effecting social change through their involvement in local politics or by volunteering at the county women's prison. They are less opposed to feminism than to the connotations associated with it. These women share a number of common understandings with other conservative and evangelical women who support women's rights and women's equality but decry what they see as extremism and man-hating.[4]

Some oppose what they see as feminists' anger. They perceive feminists as complainers who could "use a few sessions of anger management." One participant commented, "And you can't just huddle up in the universities and complain and write policies; that is a self-destructive posture. It doesn't benefit women; it certainly doesn't benefit the people studying all that; surely they've got to be depressed, having just complained for eight hours."

Other participants truly are philosophically and theologically opposed to feminism and see it as contradictory to their Christian beliefs. Heather King said:

> In its most basic definition, feminism as defined by feminists themselves means putting self over God. The self's identity, desires, needs are exalted over God's identity, purpose for humanity, and desires for us. Women are encouraged to put the knowledge of their life experiences over and above the knowledge of God, giving them the authority to act independently of God. The social goals of improving the condition of women in third world countries, imparting education to women, and uplifting the status of women are all good things to pursue. However, it is the ideology and methodology of feminism with which Southern Baptist beliefs and tenets can never merge. . . . Feminism is not only inconsistent with biblical Christianity but it seeks to exalt personal experiences over scripture, and it seeks to eradicate gender differences and roles that God designed at creation.

Similarly, Debra Hochgraber of the Baptist General Convention of Texas sees feminists "as women with a primary agenda that focuses on rights for women. My primary agenda is for women to walk closer to the Lord, that all people come to know Christ, and then know him better."

Candi Finch explored feminist writings in college after a professor challenged her to think about feminist contributions. Although Candi believes in equal opportunity and equal pay for equal work, she is firmly convinced that many of the basic philosophical tenets of feminism conflict with her understanding of the Bible. "So, no," she responded, "I would not consider myself a feminist by any stretch of the imagination." Although Candi acknowledges feminism's contributions to women's progress, she now sees feminism generally and feminist theology in particular as a threat to the church because it waters down the authority of scripture and relies more on secular thinking than biblical teaching.

For many conservative women, feminism challenges God's authority and design for creation. They perceive feminism as focusing on the self and on human rights rather than on God and one's personal relationship with Christ. They, too, acknowledge the importance of social change and improving the status of women, but they believe that those changes come about as a result of personal conversion and subsequent Christian ministry in the world. Primarily, they see feminism as an assault on the gender characteristics and roles God has given to women and men and an undermining of the scriptures on which those gender understandings are based.

Bra-Burning Militants and Other Mythical Feminist Beasts

For Southern Baptist women, the stereotypes they hold on to are probably the greatest barrier to an identification with feminism. In fact, I was surprised at the extent to which both conservative and progressive Southern Baptist women distanced themselves from what they consider to be feminist extremes. I suppose I shouldn't have been. After all, these are mostly southern women for whom "making a fuss" is a social no-no. Karen Massey answered unequivocally that she is a feminist. Then she elaborated:

> This is probably where my southern upbringing influenced me. Now, am I one of those bra-burning, parade-marching, protest sign–carrying feminists? No, I'm not that. Now do I oppose that? No. No I don't. Because I

think feminism is a big enough camp to encompass all kinds of women. For me, bottom line, a feminist is someone who believes in, supports, and encourages the potential of women in all areas of life: socioeconomically, politically, religiously, all across the gamut. That women have the same rights as men, period. So, do I consider myself a feminist? Yes. I am more of a feminist who works within the system to change it than one on the outside screaming and yelling about it. And do we need those [who are] screaming and yelling? Absolutely. It's the loud voices who help push toward change; so, yes, we need those. But because I am Baptist, that necessarily means that the crowd of people that I find myself going to typically [is] more conservative. So I have to work within the system.

Karen's response is typical of many of the progressive women I interviewed. They fully claim feminism and support the goals of the women's movement. They even support, to a large extent, the actions of those on the more activist end of the feminist spectrum. But they do not consider themselves activist feminists. They work quietly within the system rather than making a public fuss about sexism in Baptist life and in the larger society. The more radical elements of feminism are necessary, they believe, but if Southern Baptist women are to continue to work within the system, they have to conform to culturally expected and accepted norms for women in leadership.

Similarly, many contemporary Southern Baptist feminists appeal to Baptists' sense of justice and fair play in support of issues such as equal employment opportunity and wages, while distinguishing themselves from those feminists who carry signs and march in protests. Sheri Klouda doesn't like the connotations and nuances of the word *feminist*. When I asked her what those connotations are, she replied, "Folks that are loud and boisterous and always trying to prove their point, and this is like their primary agenda. . . . I do have to say, though, that I would be in agreement with basic equalities. To me, it appears that those who have a feminist perspective are outspoken, and oftentimes it's like they're really trying to challenge basic tenets and structures and things. And I don't like confrontation. So I stay out."

Not surprisingly, the most commonly mentioned extreme was bra burning, whether I was talking to progressive Southern Baptists or conservative ones. A former WMU staff member took steps to support women in the late 1960s, but "I wouldn't say I was a bra-burner or anything like that," she added. One seminary student said, "I don't consider myself a feminist. I don't go around burning my bra or anything.

That's still what I think of when I think feminist." When I asked another student at Truett whether she considers herself a feminist, she replied, "Well, I'm not burning my bra, but basically, yeah."

None of the Clique members was very aware of the women's movement, except for the images they caught on television, but almost all of them mentioned bra burnings. One told me that she equates feminism with bra burning, although, she said, "I think they probably had a lot to say that was important too." Two others said that what they remember most from the women's movement is the "bra rebellion" and that "they burned the bra." Yet another pointed out that she "didn't agree with burning bras." A campus minister who is in her early forties doesn't remember a lot about the movement, but she does remember the bra burnings. One laywoman from Georgia said that feminism makes her think of the "bra-burning era" and Billie Jean King. Another participant thinks feminism can be a good thing, but she doesn't like to see it used in an "okay, I'm a feminist; I'm radical; I'm gonna go braless" way. When I offered my definition of feminism to the group of women from one church, someone said, "Oh, well! I thought that was a bra thing."

"Most of us wear our bras these days," I quipped, launching into my explanation of feminist history, the varieties of feminism, and the benefits of feminism, upon which they all agreed that the question of whether they are feminists is foolish. Of course they are.

The myth of bra-burning feminists demonstrates the power of misinformation and stereotypes. They can take hold in our collective consciousness to the extent that women born long after the protests of the 1960s and 1970s still have bra burning as their primary image of feminism. But now I want to settle this issue once and for all: FEMINISTS DID NOT BURN THEIR BRAS! The myth arose in response to the feminist protest at the 1968 Miss America pageant in Atlantic City. A group called New York Radical Women decided to organize a protest against the negative impact of beauty pageants, which told women that their most valuable asset was their appearance. The protesters engaged in a number of acts of street theater, including placing a Freedom Trash Can on the boardwalk and tossing in objects that represented women's oppression—high heels, dishwashing detergent, copies of *Ladies' Home Journal* and *Playboy*, tweezers, false eyelashes, girdles, curlers, and, yes, bras. Someone had suggested setting the contents on fire, but because doing so might endanger the wooden boardwalk, the women were unable to obtain a fire permit. A number of protesters also got tickets to get into the pageant, and during the speech of the outgoing Miss America, they unfurled a banner that read "Women's Liberation" and shouted "Freedom for women" and "No more Miss America!" Two stink bombs were also set off in the hall, and the protesters were removed. This public protest against one of America's preeminent female icons caught the attention of the press, which erroneously reported that the feminists had burned their bras. The image stuck, even though it had no basis in reality, and to this day, it continues to prevent many women from embracing a feminist identity for fear of being perceived as too extreme.

The image of extremism came up in my conversations with Southern Baptist women again and again. Angelyn Turner told me, "I think a lot of times when people say 'feminist,' you think of these radical people, and it's more the people who are very outspoken about issues that we don't all agree with that you consider feminist." Another, very progressive woman refused the label of feminist "because some women want to be feminists just so they can shout about something." Fang-Lan Hsieh, a librarian at Southwestern Seminary, said that some feminists just want to fight about women's issues. "I think that's going to the extreme," she explained. "That's my understanding of feminism." Many participants also associate images of man hating and anger with feminist extremes. Many women believe that feminism is anti-men or strives to place women above men. Another very progressive woman said that she probably agrees with the goals of feminism, but because she has met so many angry women, she doesn't want to be called a feminist. Several women referred to feminists as "mean" and "manly." One participant dismissed second-wave feminists and suggested that there's a new wave of young women who will be "more constructive and not destructive and that don't act like men or so mean and hateful." These women, she said, will interact better with men, because they won't be assuming "he's about to rape and pillage the universe."

In my opinion, underlying many women's apprehension about feminist extremism is their fear of losing male approval and male support. Once, one of my male colleagues was arrested for making anonymous sexually harassing phone calls to a woman. In our staff meeting, the other men repeatedly talked about how important it was to pray for him and how concerned they were for him. After listening to several minutes of this, I said, "Why are we so worried about him? What about her? She's the one who was terrorized by his behavior. She's the one we should pray for." After the meeting, one of the men took me aside and told me that he was concerned I was becoming too feminist. Similarly, when Melissa Browning, who now works for the Cooperative Baptist Fellowship, was a seminary student, a certain man who spoke in chapel "kept saying, 'We need a few good men. We need a few good men.'" He repeated that phrase more than thirty times throughout the sermon. When Melissa found out that this man was going to be a dean, she asked him whether he was really going to support women and encourage churches to support women. He told her that she was "getting too much on the feminist side" and being "too testy" and that she "just needed to calm down."

Often, when women stand up for their rights, they lose male approval —they're told that they're too feminist or too sensitive or too angry. And for many women, those words are frightening, because male approval also brings certain rewards, whether that involves being heralded as an ideal woman, having doors held open, or being supported financially. These are things that women, on the whole, have been socialized to believe that they need, and the threat of losing these things is felt deeply when males disapprove. Ginny Hickman of Broadway Baptist Church in Fort Worth explained that when women challenge cultural constructions of gender, "that's when the negative connotation of feminism comes up, and all of a sudden it becomes ugly, and you're a troublemaker, you're out of your place, and I think it's uncomfortable to raise those issues, even as far as we've come."

Many participants also believe that feminism has devalued the family and their roles within it. One woman who identifies as feminist nevertheless distinguishes herself from radical feminists "because I value the family a lot." Because of their emphasis on women in public life, some feminists have "gone too far," she said. Both Audrey Crabtree and Betty Sue Drury blame feminism for some of contemporary women's suffering. Audrey contends that for women of her generation (she's fifty years old), feminism disrupted the gender roles they had been socialized to perform. She explained:

> We got to be teenagers, and the whole world was in turmoil. We had the Vietnam War; we had people burning their bras and protesting and fighting and people being shot. And then we were told that everything we had been taught was wrong. And that we had no value unless we saw things the way they saw it. And while I will admit that I believe the women's movement probably did do some things that needed to be done, I truly don't like the way

they've done it. And I don't like that to this day. I feel that I am devalued by the women's movement because I am not in agreement with them.

Audrey chose to be a stay-at-home mother because she believes that the Bible teaches that raising children is the most important contribution a woman can make. When the women's movement challenged women's roles in the home, Audrey said, it did women, men, the family, and society a disservice.

Likewise, Betty Sue believes that the feminist movement has actually lowered women's status by challenging the idea that women should be supported and cared for by men. "Now the feminists wouldn't agree with this because they think they've made great strides, and, of course, they've done some things that are good, I suppose. But they've caused an awful lot of problems, and we're still suffering through some of those problems now."

Why do these myths of bra-burning, man-hating, angry, militant feminists persist? Within Southern Baptist subculture, they are rarely challenged; in fact, denominational leaders who demonize feminism as anti-Christian and unbiblical often reinforce these myths.[5] In addition, popular antifeminist writers and radio personalities blame many contemporary social problems on feminism. For example, much of the recent discussion about the so-called boy problem contends that feminism is the cause of boys' violence and failure in school.[6] Seldom do these analyses point to patriarchy as the problem. And recently, a closer analysis of the data has shown that many of the problems are more related to social class and race than to gender.[7]

On the whole, Southern Baptist women agree that women and men are equal in worth. They also agree on a wide variety of feminist issues (although they certainly disagree on others). Generally, they believe that women are capable of doing just about anything a man can do, although many question the propriety of some activities (such as military combat). Others oppose women taking on some roles that they believe are God-ordained for men, such as pastoring a church. They have all been deeply influenced by the women's movement, although many seem largely unaware of how their views have been shaped by the historical moment in which they live. Similarly, very few expressed a sense that gender itself is constructed within a social and historical context. Almost all of them, progressive women included, spoke of gender as an essential characteristic to some degree. Over and over they told me: "Men are men, and women are women."

Untroubling Gender: Southern Baptist Women's Construction of Gender

The participants in my research could easily identify gender roles—doing the dishes or preaching—within their contexts, and they recognized that these roles are culturally assigned. They don't believe that there's any inherent biological reason why men can't do the dishes or women can't preach, although many offer theological reasons for these gender rules—that is, God says women are supposed to take care of the home and men are supposed to preach. Nonetheless, for many participants, recognition of the social construction of gender roles is precisely what allows them to challenge these roles, with men becoming primary caregivers in the home and women becoming pastors. WMU staffer Kristy Carr believes in women's equality. She also believes that men do some things better than women and vice versa, but for her, these differences don't mean that women's leadership roles in the church should be limited. She suggested that "just because of our culture, [women's staff leadership] is still not the norm in our denomination."

What struck me as I talked to these women is that although they recognize the cultural construction of gender roles, most of them see gender itself as an inherent attribute of identity: women are feminine, and men are masculine. Women can do some things better than men because they are women, and vice versa. For these women, gender roles are something one does; gender is something one is.

For them, gender is predicated on difference. Clique member Alicia Bennett is all for equality of the sexes, "but I think they're different, different roles and different ways it plays out." Gwen Dellinger concurred: "Women really are different than men, and we got a bad rap that we wanted to be like men or we wanted to be men. I don't want to be a man; I just want to be respected for being a woman!" Paige Trotter explained, "Men and women are different. God made us different. We think different. Our emotions are not the same. Our needs are not the same. So we're different." Fang-Lan Hsieh agreed that "women and men are really different" and suggested that women should look like women. Clique member Shelby Christie said that she likes to "be feminine. I like to be as feminine-looking as I can to my husband, to my friends, the people I know because I am a woman. If I was a man, I'd like to be manly. But I am a woman, so I like to be feminine." Minerva Escobedo said, "God did make us different than men. . . . Being feminine in God's eyes is what God intended for us to be."

For many Southern Baptist women, feminism's challenge to gender is most frightening. They see feminism as attempting to erase gender distinctions, which they believe are ordained by God. Elaine Richards explained, "One of the worst fallouts from the feminist movement is it just erased the difference between men and women, and it's totally confused our young men on what their roles in life are to be, who they are supposed to be. And it's really made the young women coming up, they're not very feminine anymore. There are some tough girls. . . . There's not many girly girls, and there's a lot of girly boys out there now." For Elaine, feminism's explanation of gender as a social process has undermined the certainty of gendered behavior (being girly or manly) that comes with fixed notions of gender. Paige Trotter suggested, "Feminist groups have demoralized men to the point that they're not as manly as they used to be. I like chivalry, I like for a man to open the door for me. I like for a man to put me up on a pedestal, but you don't see that kind of thing anymore."

Heather King expressed these concerns:

> I am most concerned about how Christian women have allowed secular and political feminism to creep into the church and into their belief system. Christian women are succumbing to the lie that they must be liberated from gender roles assigned by God at creation. Feminism asserts that a woman has the right to determine her own truth. A woman's feelings, emotions, and experiences determine theological concepts and doctrine. When interacting and interpreting scripture, if God's Word does not line up with a woman's personal experiences or feelings on a given subject she is then free to disregard it or even worse redefine God's Word based on her experiences. This type of approach to scripture undermines the authority and validity of God's Word and places her on a slippery slope.

For Heather, feminism's deconstruction of gender challenges God's design for women and men. It is an assault on the authority of scripture and, ultimately, on the sovereignty of God, who assigned gender to women and men.

Of course, by recognizing that men and women can take on behaviors associated with the other sex, these women are implicitly (albeit unknowingly) acknowledging gender as a construct. They recognize, as Sheri Klouda put it, "that it's important to maintain gender distinctions." They also recognize, however, that people can make choices about whether they perform the "appropriate" behavior assigned to them by virtue of their anatomy. Sheri continued, "I don't want to be one of the guys or like the guys; I want to be myself. So I think it's important to not necessarily mold yourself into the pattern of all the guys."

Many participants described the very processes by which they were taught to be feminine. Clique member Nancy Moore explained, "Back when we were coming up, the roles were very clearly defined. The boys played with certain toys, and the girls played with certain toys. You were always mindful to keep your dress down. . . . I don't have any pictures of us in anything other than little dresses. . . . And we were always reminded to be a lady." Nonetheless, Nancy was at times transgressive. "It was kind of a special thing to be a tomboy," she told me, "behind Mother's back. We wanted to be as good as the boys at some things. And since we didn't have any boys in our family, my daddy would always call me his boy. . . . I always enjoyed being a girl, but like I say, behind everybody's back I wanted to be a strong little boy." By the time she was a teenager, Karen Massey "just knew how you were supposed to behave as a female. Polite and proper and, you know, you were to be cooperative. And I don't know if it was ever explicitly said, but you just knew you were to grow up and get married and have children." Karen's church also gently nudged her toward typically female professions—nursing or teaching. "We always had to wear dresses," she continued. "Makeup was okay; makeup was almost encouraged. You knew that you had to have your hair fixed perfectly and your makeup on perfectly, you know? You were supposed to look like a girl. You were to look feminine."

Gender, for Southern Baptist women, seems to be a complicated and contradictory terrain. On the one hand, most of these women believe that gender is somehow essentially related to biology, that women and men are different, and that being female means being a particular way. On the other hand, they can readily describe the ways they learned to be female and acknowledge the possibility that one might not necessarily act out one's "appropriate" gender. They are especially cognizant of culture's influence on gender roles. Although some believe that God has assigned certain roles based on gender, most contend that these roles are flexible and depend more on the context of the individual than on the individual's anatomy. For most participants, *gender* is not a particularly troubled term. Some of them dislike people in authority who deny them equality based on their gender, but most of them are fairly accepting of contemporary American cultural constructions of women and femininity. At this point, the more radical feminist notions of gender are highly threatening and represent the "extreme" that so many participants decried. Truett student Sarah Carbajal, who is actually much more left-leaning in her views than most, made an interesting observation. She fears that as women try to do what men can do, they will lose some of their ability to connect as women. She is trying to value herself as a woman, with womanly attributes.

As a feminist researcher, I was acutely aware of the potential for consciousness-raising among the participants, which is why I offered my general definition of feminism. Southern Baptist women seem pretty comfortable with the broader goals of equality, but most of them have real problems with truly disruptive feminist theories. For me, the question has become how academic and activist feminists can embrace these women and work on shared goals, while acknowledging our very real differences. As I talked with these women, I realized the subversive potential of women who claim their right to equality and soul competency within a highly patriarchal framework. If feminists see them only as part of the Religious Right or naive participants in their own oppression, I fear that we will miss an opportunity to build alliances that may further women's causes. Some of the causes that some of these women support are absolutely antithetical to feminist goals, and some feminist ideas no doubt evoke the ire and righteous wrath of many Southern Baptist women. Yet there is common ground, and it is greater than I expected when I started my research. The problem is how to talk to each other respectfully and authentically. I think that many of these women understand more about feminism after talking to me, and I certainly understand more about their faith having talked to them.

8

Competent before God

Southern Baptist Women and Soul Competency

My faith has found a resting place, not in device nor creed;
I trust the Ever-living One, His wounds for me shall plead.
I need no other argument, I need no other plea,
It is enough that Jesus died, and that he died for me.
—Lidie H. Edmunds, "My Faith Has Found a Resting Place"

I heard this story: A little girl in Sunday school was working intently on her artwork. Her teacher asked the little girl what she was drawing. "I'm drawing a picture of God," the little girl replied. "But," the teacher said, "no one knows what God looks like." "Well," answered the little girl, "they will in a few minutes." Once, a friend of mine who is a lapsed Catholic told me that she'd come hear me preach if I'd preach on "What is God?" I decided to accept her challenge and make that my next sermon. A couple of weeks before I was going to preach it, I was talking to the choir director about the music for the service, and I told her the sermon would be "What is God?" Without missing a beat, she replied, "You know the answer to that?"

The audacious claim of soul competency is that the individual can know and deal directly with God. At best, the answer to the question of my sermon was, to quote T. S. Eliot, "hints and guesses," but the confidence behind the question is that it can be asked at all, that I can presume for myself to come to some conclusions (if only more questions) about who and what God is based on my own experiences and interpretations of scripture. My Baptist forebears didn't leave these matters up to popes or councils or creeds. Rather, they entrusted them to the individual before God. As Pam Tanner put it, "I was taught that being

Baptist meant being independent. Priesthood of the believers, and every church and every person got to decide and view scriptures and have their own opinion, and nobody told them how to believe."

Certainly, that has made things messier. Baptists have fought and split and fought and split for nearly four centuries now. The principles of soul competency, the priesthood of believers, the autonomy of the local church, religious liberty, and the separation of church and state have played a tremendous role in Baptist identity, and those of us brought up believing those things have continued stubbornly to affirm our right to have direct dealings with God. For Southern Baptist women, this message has been particularly powerful in the midst of their participation in a denomination that is highly patriarchal. The idea of soul competency has empowered some women to defy the cultural norms that limit women's roles, from Lottie Moon to the young women now studying for the pastorate at McAfee or Truett. For more Southern Baptist women, soul competency has meant that they have the right to claim and enact their own agency and autonomy, even in terms of how they understand such problematic issues as submission and headship.

Southern Baptist women are surprisingly complex and contradictory. As historical subjects, they are situated in a moment influenced strongly by the civil rights and women's movements, as well as Baptist and southern history. In some ways, they have much in common; in others, they are miles apart. They believe a lot of different things. They're all over the place on social issues. They participate in different worship styles. What they do share, however, is an unwavering sense of their own ability to hear the voice of God and act on what they believe God calls them to do. Like the little girl in Sunday school, they are confidently drawing away.

Being Baptist

Probably because of the influence of Landmarkism, Southern Baptists grew as a denomination relatively isolated from the rest of the Protestant world. Rarely did Southern Baptists cooperate with other denominations, and Southern Baptists generally had a sense that they did church and missions better than other groups anyway. Particularly as the denomination grew in size and assets, Southern Baptists felt no need to work with other groups because they had the resources to do whatever they wanted in the ways they wanted. This relative isolation has meant that, in many ways, Southern Baptists have developed an identity that is separate from those of other conservative and evangelical Christians. Although many Southern Baptists, particularly the more conservative ones, share a number of theological convictions with evangelical Christians, on the whole, Southern Baptists have a separate and unique identity that sets them apart from the rest of the evangelical world. However, with the rise of fundamentalism in the denomination, some of the new leaders may have more in common with fundamentalists in other conservative denominations than with moderates in their own. But on the whole, this unique Southern Baptist identity has been extremely powerful in shaping the identities of Southern Baptist women.

Because the denomination has excelled at providing a shared educational program and common worship resources, Southern Baptists across the nation have had similar experiences that have forged this denominational identity. Again, in recent years this has begun to vary, as some churches have moved toward a "community" church identity and emphasized their conservative and evangelistic identity rather than their Baptist one. Nonetheless, certain ideas about what being Baptist means have remained central. For women, these ideas are especially significant because they provide the means by which women negotiate agency and power within the patriarchal structures of the denomination and Southern Baptist churches. Although most of my participants affirmed that their Christian identity is the more important one, they also recognize that the practical form that identity takes—for them, a Baptist identity—is very important. For many participants, this is because they believe Southern Baptists to be most correct in their theological thinking, particularly in terms of valuing the Bible. For others, Baptist identity is important because of its historical distinctiveness, which many participants see as eroding under the fundamentalist leadership in the Convention.

Perhaps the greatest testament to the power of Southern Baptist identity comes from those women who have left the denomination because of the Controversy. They may no longer identify as Southern Baptists at a denominational level, but almost all of them still hold to those ideals of Baptist identity they learned in GAs and Training Union. In their words, the Convention changed; they didn't. Carolyn Matthews sometimes wonders "if Baptists have forgotten who they are. That goes back to what I said about autonomy of the local church and the priesthood of believers. I find all that kind of thing eroding when I see what is going on in the Convention." Gwen Dellinger of North Broad Baptist

Church in Rome, Georgia, said, "I don't think that the people who call themselves Southern Baptists are what Southern Baptists used to be." Another member of that group added, "I don't feel like we moved; I feel like the Southern Baptists moved." When I asked what had defined Southern Baptists previously, Gwen answered, "The priesthood of all believers. And that includes women in that group, along with men."

As I interviewed Southern Baptist women, I asked them what being Baptist means to them. The responses could have been from a survey for *Family Feud*, they fell so neatly into a limited number of categories. And so, the survey says, the number-one answer is . . .

The Priesthood of Believers

At the root of Baptist identity is the notion that each person can go directly to God without the need for any mediator. Jean Cullen defined the priesthood of believers this way: "The Spirit moves in all of us, and God talks to all of us. . . . God works and is in all of us, and we have the ability to have that relationship with God." LaDonna Burton explained, "It means that you don't have to go to anybody; you just go straight to the source. I mean, you don't depend on somebody else to say prayers for you." Joyce Reed agreed: "[Being Baptist] means freedom of my spirit to be directed by God's spirit in whatever way God wants to direct my life and to have freedom to be who I am in Christ." That idea gives rise to its corollary statements in biblical interpretation, polity, and missions. As Janet Dickerson put it, "I love the freedoms that I have in a Baptist church." Charlean Hayes Hughes pointed out that being Baptist means both being part of a community with a long history and having an individual relationship with God that is nurtured by that community.

Almost every woman I asked listed the priesthood of believers as key to what being Baptist means to her. Many used that phrase specifically. Others talked about it in terms of their ability to deal with God themselves, apart from any other person or church. Some talked about how they had been taught explicitly about the priesthood of believers in various church programs. Others hadn't necessarily heard those words growing up but had witnessed them in practice in every facet of the church's life. April Baker explained, "You don't do Sunday school and Training Union and GAs and Acteens, all of those, and do all of the camps and all of the extra stuff, without some of that being really ingrained in you . . . we didn't have big sessions that I remember about the priesthood of all believers. But I knew what that meant because I grew up in a culture where it really was a prevailing attitude. And an expectation. And that's just in my bones." When I asked Barbara Elder whether the church she grew up in had emphasized the priesthood of believers, local church autonomy, religious liberty, and the separation of church and state, she replied, "I don't think they emphasized it; they just lived it!"

Even among the most conservative Southern Baptists, the ability of both women and men to go directly to God is assumed; in fact, according to Baptists, only the individual person can and must deal with God in relation to her or his own life. Carolyn Blevins explained that Baptists emphasize the individual. "I think Baptist theology places a lot of confidence in the individual," she explained, "which I don't think the Southern Baptist Convention does now." This emphasis, Sheri Adams noted, means that only the individual is "able to interpret God's will for a person's own life." Phyllis Rodgerson Pleasants explained that when she was studying the earliest English Baptist confessions of faith, she realized "what keeps me in this unbelievably convoluted tradition is the freedom, not to believe whatever you want to, but for me it's the freedom to follow. It is the first London Confession that has this wonderful phrase in the preface about being free to follow the Lamb wheresoever he goes." She added that faithfulness to this ideal has sometimes meant that people have had to break off from what they know. "If God was going to reveal Godself to you through scripture and the family of faith—both of which were necessary—you could not go off and have these dreams and interpretations on your own—but if God was going to reveal Godself through scripture and the faith community, then you had to be free to follow." Patty Carter has always been taught that her spiritual development is her own responsibility and "there was not someone, pastor, deacon, whoever, that was going to tell me how I had to believe."

For more progressive women, the priesthood of believers provides empowerment for them to challenge the patriarchal structures of the church and denomination that oppress women. They can claim equally with men to hear the call of God because that call comes directly to them and not through some other person. Professor Carolyn Blevins noted that debates among Baptists are not new; they date back to Baptist beginnings. She explained, "Baptists were dissenters to begin with, and the dissent didn't stop at the door of the church. When they formed the church, it continued in the church as well. And you know that's part of Baptist tradition, that ability for each person to have a voice. And it's a little message to us. But that dissent has been part of this whole women's thing as long as we've been Baptists."

For women called to ministry, the priesthood of believers plays a significant role in their understanding of their calling. It allows them to say in the face of those who oppose women in ministry that God has called them. Because God deals directly with the individual, only the individual can determine what God asks her or him to do. Therefore, for women in ministry, the priesthood of believers provides a strong affirmation of their sense of calling. Many women noted the irony that the same churches that taught them this concept didn't support them when they answered God's call. When Brenda Flowers was growing up and participating in GAs and Acteens and youth group, she never heard anyone say there was something she couldn't do. Instead, she always heard, "You can be what you want to be in Christ. If you are called to be a leader, you be a leader." No one ever told her that she couldn't be a preacher. Instead, they challenged her to learn the scriptures and become a good speaker. "Well," she asked, "what do you do with that?" Martha Gilmore, one of the first Southern Baptist women ordained in Texas, told me, "I often talk about a hymn that stuck in my mind that said, 'Whosoever surely meaneth me.' Somehow I think that sense of the priesthood of the believer and your own possibility to have a relationship with Jesus that was personal, that really was very reinforcing to me."

Joanne Parker fretted about the stained-glass ceiling that Southern Baptist women face. She often thinks, "Okay, you've given me the ability to go directly to God in prayer without thinking I have to go through the saints and through a priest; and you've given me the ability to open my Bible; but you've not given me the ability to lead in my church. . . . That does not make sense." For Linda McKinnish Bridges, the irony of the priesthood of believers that both keeps women in line and empowers them to challenge limited roles is very personal. She said:

> My father was saying to me, "There are prescribed roles." He would say it to me; then he would say, "Get out there and give it to them, Linda." But then he'd say, "Do it like a lady." The irony of that is: "Go do it, but you've got constraints." So you're always living in this paradox. You know: "You can do it; you can do anything—but you gotta do it in this way." So that kind of tension of living in the paradox is kind of like that doctrine of the priest-

hood of believers. I mean that was bedrock to denominational structure, denominational thought forms. And so that may have had some of the doctrinal impetus for being able to create my own space in a place that said I had no space. But yet it did give me place.

Lynda Weaver-Williams had to learn to value her own spiritual authority before God gave her the strength to claim her calling in the face of those who would "beat me over the head" with their interpretations of the Bible's statements about women. "My priesthood of the believer," she explained, meant "I had the right to say, 'This is my calling.' It took me a long time to figure that out, but I do believe the seeds of that were given to me, were planted in my soul, in that little Baptist church."

I Can Read It for Myself

Closely connected to the priesthood of believers for Southern Baptist women is their relationship to scripture. Many participants, both conservative and progressive, value Southern Baptists' emphasis on reading, knowing, and understanding the Bible. Paula Sheridan expressed what many of the women feel—that Southern Baptists do a good job teaching the Bible. She explained:

> I think in many ways I will always be a Southern Baptist, although I intentionally do not affiliate with a Southern Baptist congregation here in Southern California. Many of the ideas of Southern Baptists are very precious to me, such as the priesthood of the believer and the autonomy of the local congregation and this wonderful emphasis on knowing the stories of the Bible. I have wandered as a pilgrim from denomination to denomination, and I realize that those things are something I always took for granted as a Baptist, and now, in other denominations, I sit in adult classes with people who've been in a congregation all their lives, and they know none of the stories that are so dear to us as Baptists.

Angela Cofer said, "Being Baptist means to me that my belief system is based on the Bible, the holy scriptures; that there is also a history of Baptists being those who seek religious freedom. The priesthood of the believer; all those things that come to mind being Baptist." Barbara Elder noted, "Being Baptist is more than a denomination; it's more about a particular group of people who look at the scriptures and try to apply the scriptures as accurately as possible." Dot Walsh said, "The Bible is open; you are welcome to read it; the interpretation is there for you."

The priesthood of believers means that the responsibility for interpreting the Bible belongs to the individual. Of course, this also means that Southern Baptists will always have disagreements about what the Bible says, but as Pat Brown told me, "Being Baptist has traditionally meant being free to think. That is part of being Baptist that I have treasured and continue to treasure." Carolyn Weatherford Crumpler added, "Being Baptist means to me, first of all, the priesthood of the believer. I don't have to follow a set of rules. I don't have to follow *The Baptist Faith and Message;* I don't have to sign any kind of statement. . . . I do believe that the Bible is God's Word and that I should read it and I have the power through the Spirit to interpret it and apply it to my life." Similarly, to Sue Turner, being Baptist "means I am free; I am an autonomous person belonging to an autonomous group of people. I can read the Bible for myself, and I can depend on the Holy Spirit for interpretation without any outside interference from any other hierarchy." Becky Kennedy explained, "Being Baptist means . . . priesthood of the believer . . . that we interpret the scriptures as we are led by the Holy Spirit. Being Baptist means to me being open-minded; it means taking care of, paying attention to, and being aware of Christian responsibility. Taking care of the hungry, being aware of what needs need to be met. I think those are values that Baptists hold dear." Likewise, Carolyn Matthews noted, "I do embrace the idea of the priesthood of the believer, autonomy of the local church, and that people are able to interpret the Bible for themselves. And in that way, I would say being a Baptist has been influential. No priests, no higher church fathers interpreting the Bible for me."

As a convert from Catholicism, Joanne Parker finds the priesthood of believers to be an essential aspect of Baptist identity. "To me," she explained, "being Baptist means I have the freedom to go directly to God in prayer; I have the freedom to open my Bible and study it without someone else telling me, 'This is what you need to learn.'"

The priesthood of believers means that individuals have the freedom to come to their own understandings of scripture. During the Controversy, the limits of this freedom became a central line of division between fundamentalists and moderates, with fundamentalists suggesting a very narrowly defined range of interpretations and moderates emphasizing the broader parameters of the priesthood of believers.

Autonomy of the Local Church

One of the most common errors I see when journalists write about Southern Baptists is that they refer to the Southern Baptist Church. No such thing exists; there are only Southern Baptist churches that choose to affiliate with the Southern Baptist Convention. All governing authority for the local church resides in that church. The Southern Baptist Convention, state conventions, and local Southern Baptist associations exist to support the local church; they don't have any power over it. Each church is autonomous; it makes its own decisions about leadership, membership, and participation in other Baptist bodies. No matter what the Southern Baptist Convention proclaims or does, the local church is still completely free to chart its own course.

Beth Crawford, who recently became a Presbyterian campus minister, still struggles when she has to go to a meeting of the presbytery. She loves Baptists' idea of independence: "I love the idea that each individual community was able to discern for themselves what made sense for them." Jean Cullen noted that being Baptist means "that we are self-governing and that we as local groups of believers determine what's best in particular situations for that particular church." Tisa Lewis pointed out, "People who are Baptists shouldn't have to answer to a higher authority as far as hierarchy in the church is concerned, and the church does its decision making based on what the church wants to do; we don't have to go along with what the denominational leadership says. We basically decide for ourselves in the church what we want to do on certain issues, and we don't have to conform to the whole denomination . . . that's the way it used to be anyway." Leah McCullough pointed out, "I think autonomy of the local church allowed each church to live out its call to be and do in the world what God has called it to be and do, . . . without being told how to do that and in ways that constrain that. Use the resources and gifts you have to most faithfully live into the Gospel."

Of course, the Controversy redefined the limits of local church autonomy, as some local churches were tossed out of their associations because they ordained women or called women as pastors. Eventually, the Southern Baptist Convention itself amended its constitution to remove local churches that in any way affirmed gay and lesbian people.

Democratic Church Governance

The implication of the priesthood of believers for the polity of the local church is that its system of governance is democratic. Because each person can deal directly with God, each person's voice is equally valued (at least in theory) and therefore has a right to be heard in issues of church governance. Carolyn Hale Cubbedge acknowledged that churches can certainly function in all kinds of congregational patterns but added, "I do like the congregational, democratic form of government that goes on in Baptist churches."

The priesthood of believers also means that the pastor has no institutional or theological authority over members of the congregation. The pastor is usually given a great deal of authority based on the position and the congregation's respect for the position, but that authority is persuasive, not coercive. The pastor leads but does not command. In Baptist polity, the pastor is the servant-leader of the church, the one who leads by serving. For Katrina Brooks, who was raised Catholic, this distinction is especially important in how she defines her pastoral ministry: "The pastor is a servant. The pope doesn't call all the shots." Likewise, Joyce Reed stated emphatically, "The pastor is the shepherd; the pastor is someone I have always loved and respected, but the pastor has never been my authority; as far as my Christian authority, God is my authority."

When I asked some of the women of First Baptist Church in Batesburg, South Carolina, whether there's room for disagreement in the church, Bettie Akins said, "I hope there is because we want to disagree about a lot." Annie Cockrell added, "I'm like Bettie. I hope it is. We still love one another." Then I asked whether disagreeing with the pastor would be okay. "Absolutely," Paige Trotter responded. "And I speak up when I disagree; I don't talk behind his back, but I'd go to him and tell him. And I have done that before."

"And I've heard her do it, too," Grace Geddes affirmed.

"There should be room for disagreement," Paige added.

"This is the house of the Lord," Grace concurred, "and if you don't disagree once in a while, you'll never get it right."

During the Controversy, moderates reemphasized the doctrine of the priesthood of believers as a direct challenge to fundamentalists' critique of biblical interpretations that differed from their own. Many of the fundamentalist leaders were pastors who relied on the authority of their personal charisma and people's respect for their positions to sway Southern Baptists to believe as they did. Moderates responded by encouraging individual congregants to think and interpret the Bible for themselves, relying on the historic notions of soul competency and the priesthood of believers. In 1988 the Convention passed a startling resolution that actually de-emphasized the importance of the doctrine of the priesthood of believers and asserted pastoral authority:

> WHEREAS, None of the five major writing systematic theologians in Southern Baptist history have given more than passing reference to the doctrine of the priesthood of the believer in their systematic theologies; and

> WHEREAS, *The Baptist Faith and Message* preamble refers to the priesthood of the believer, but provides no definition or content to the term; and

> WHEREAS, The high profile emphasis on the doctrine of the priesthood of the believer in Southern Baptist life is a recent historical development; and

> WHEREAS, The priesthood of the believer is a term which is subject to both misunderstanding and abuse; and

> WHEREAS, The doctrine of the priesthood of the believer has been used to justify wrongly the attitude that a Christian may believe whatever he so chooses and still be considered a loyal Southern Baptist; and

> WHEREAS, The doctrine of the priesthood of the believer can be used to justify the undermining of pastoral authority in the local church.

> Be it therefore RESOLVED, That the Southern Baptist Convention, meeting in San Antonio, Texas, June 14–16, 1988, affirm its belief in the biblical doctrine of the priesthood of the believer (1 Peter 2:9 and Revelation 1:6); and

> Be it further RESOLVED, That we affirm that this doctrine in no way gives license to misinterpret, explain away, demythologize, or extrapolate out elements of the supernatural from the Bible; and

> Be it further RESOLVED, That the doctrine of the priesthood of the believer in no way contradicts the biblical understanding of the role, responsibility, and authority of the pastor which is seen in the command to the local church in Hebrews 13:17, "Obey your leaders, and submit to them; for they keep watch over your souls, as those who will give an account"; and

> Be it finally RESOLVED, That we affirm the truth that elders, or pastors, are called of God to lead the local church (Acts 20:28).[1]

For most of us, the resolution was shocking because, until the Controversy, even those of us in fundamentalist congregations had been raised to question pastoral authority. I clearly remember my pastor telling us, "Don't take what I say for truth. Examine the Bible for yourselves to make sure." Joyce Reed described a similar experience: "We were really always encouraged to listen to the sermon through the filter of the Holy Spirit and to make sure what was coming out from the pulpit jibed with what we knew about God and the Holy Spirit, and to never take everything that was said from the pulpit as gospel unless it did mesh with what God was speaking to us."

My sister's experience was different. I had already finished my first year in college when fundamentalists elected their first president of the Convention in 1979. At that point, our pastor became actively involved with the fundamentalist leadership, and Karen, who was still an adolescent, felt that the pastor's views dominated the church. He was a very charismatic man, an eloquent preacher, and a good pastor, and many church members followed him unquestioningly. Karen said, "I never dreamed of questioning one word in the Bible or one word out of the teachers' or preachers' mouths at West Rome." Nonetheless, she saw the disconnects between what people espoused and how they lived, and she began to ask questions and eventually found another Southern Baptist church that encouraged her to think for herself.

Despite the 1988 resolution, the women I interviewed still feel free to disagree with a pastor on matters of both theology and church business. Most of the laywomen aren't even aware of the resolution. The participants clearly believe that pastors should be respected as leaders, but these women don't give up their own authority simply because a pastor says something is true or something should be done a certain way. Nan Cook doesn't think the Controversy affected local churches too much, except in one way: "through the younger ministers that trained in those seminaries."

"What changes do you see them bringing?" I asked.

"I see them as being more dictat[orial], you know, saying, 'This is the way it will be done.' And they want to bring ideas of the change of the Southern Baptist Convention into the churches; that's one of the changes we don't want."

Members of the First Baptist Church in Hendersonville, Tennessee, also believe that there's room for disagreement in Southern Baptist churches. Melissa Ashley said, "I think it's okay to disagree. Because you want the truth to be spoken there, and if you don't feel like it's the truth, I feel like, yes, I should disagree. I feel that I could easily say that I disagreed. I don't think I feel inhibited or ashamed to speak up." Shannon Daniell also affirmed that it's okay to disagree, but she noted that people shouldn't necessarily undermine the authority of the pastor. In her case, she was part of a church that often unthinkingly accepted whatever the pastor said. So rather than challenging him publicly, she chose to leave that congregation. Mitzi Sayler said, "You still have to check out the truth for yourself. Read the Word for yourself, and [God] will show you right from wrong."

When I asked members of the Mount Alto Baptist Church whether it's okay to disagree with the pastor, LaDonna Burton responded immediately, "Yes."

"Well," another member pointed out, "he's your brother."

It's true that LaDonna's brother Gary Graves is their pastor, but she explained, "He's not better than we are. In the eyes of God, we're just equal. He may be held a little bit more responsible than we are, but we're equal."

The Clique certainly feels free to disagree with the pastor. Doris Bailey spoke with disapproval of people who say the pastor is always right or is the one who should make all the decisions. "I don't think that's true," she explained, "because I think God leads us, not men. And if we feel that God is leading us, then I think we have the right or responsibility to say so." Similarly, Kayne Carter added, "I feel the Lord has given us to know what scripture says too. And if you read the Bible, I think you know if [pastors] are on the right track or not." Nancy Moore certainly thinks it's okay to disagree with a pastor. "I disagree with mine!" she said, laughing, and added, "I think that I just feel like that we are equal in the sight of God, and I don't think that, even though your pastor is responsible for you as far as being the shepherd of the flock, I don't think that he should control your mind and your thoughts and your heart; and if there's something that comes up that bothers me, I go right to him and talk about it and try to disagree agreeably." We reminisced about the time our pastor had suggested in a business meeting that to vote against his wishes (I think it had to do with paving the parking lot) was to vote against God's will because he (the pastor) had prayed about it and God had told him what he (God) wanted to do. We shook our heads. Then Nancy told me this story: "I was in the nursery at the time, and [the pastor's] little boy was in the nursery, and somebody corrected him or something, and he said, 'You can't do that. My daddy is the boss here.'" We laughed appreciatively. "'My daddy is the boss here,'" she continued, "and I thought, 'Something's wrong with this picture, that he has this conception, this early, that his daddy is the boss of the church.'"

Separation of Church and State

Historically, religious liberty and separation of church and state are significant Baptist contributions.[2] Moderate Baptist women absolutely continue to embrace these ideals, and many take pride in them. Judy Baker, who is now a state representative in Missouri, said that being Baptist is one of the things that led her into politics. "I believe very strongly in the separation of church and state, and I believe the Baptist contribution to religious liberty and separation of church and state is profound," she explained. "There were a few people at the very beginning of the foundation of this country that stood up for religious freedom and separation of church and state; among those were the Baptists as leaders. I feel that that's been eroded to some degree in the recent past, and so I have felt that it's very important that strong Baptists come to the public square and reiterate those principles and hold them high and reformulate their importance in the public square."

Nancy Ammerman sees the priesthood of all believers as a "collective trusting in the ability of laypeople pooling their wisdom and figuring out what God wants them to do. It means a real commitment to a voluntary church that is able to stand, when it needs to, in opposition to government and the state." Nancy's comment indicates the close relationship among these Baptist distinctions—priesthood of believers, local church autonomy, democratic church governance, and separation of church and state. They all grow from the idea of soul competency and the freedom and responsibility of the individual before God, and they are interrelated as soul competency gets worked out in relationships within and without the local church, denomination, and larger society.

Many of the more conservative women I spoke with are surprisingly uncomfortable with these notions. They support religious liberty, but they fear that separation of church and state has gone too far. Their rhetoric echoes that of the political Religious Right and demonstrates a lack of knowledge about Baptist and U.S. history. They are more swayed by the revisionist history of the Religious Right, which claims that the United States was founded as a Christian nation, than by the actual historical facts, which reveal that Baptists in particular were the catalysts for religious liberty and separation of church and state in this country. As Southern Baptists have amassed political power, many of them seem to have forgotten the time when Baptists themselves were persecuted as a religious minority—a time when other religious groups held political power and determined law and policy based on their beliefs.[3]

The conversation I had with the women from First Baptist Church in Batesburg, South Carolina, typifies this discomfort with the separation of church and state. They began by affirming other Baptist distinctions, but then some of them expressed reservations about church-state separation. I began by asking, "How does being Southern Baptist affect who you are?"

> BETTIE AKINS: I think that being a Southern Baptist has given me a lot of opportunities to serve God. I don't know a lot about other denominations, but we certainly have a wonderful missions program, teaching, so many programs that you can really learn from, and opportunities to serve God through it.

> NAN COOK: I think that being a Southern Baptist, people know what you stand for.

> EARLINE DURST: I think we're more mission-minded, Baptists are. I just have that feeling, and what is church without missions?

> SUSAN SHAW: Are there any Baptist distinctives that are especially important to you?

> BETTIE: I've already mentioned the missions program, and I think we have a wonderful missions program in the Southern Baptist Convention.

> NAN: I think the Cooperative Program of Southern Baptists is one of the great assets of any denomination.

> BETTIE: I like the fact that we're autonomous too. [Someone asked her to explain.] Well, that means we don't have any higher-ups to dictate to us— that might be a little strong, but that's the way I feel. Each church is individual, and we like to honor and respect what the Convention suggests, but we do not have to follow their instructions.

> SUSAN: What does the priesthood of believers mean to you?

NAN: I think it means that we all can go to God direct. That we do not have to go through anybody else; that we've been saved by Jesus Christ, and we can talk to him directly.

SUSAN: What do you think about the notions of the separation of church and state?

JEAN GASTON: That's a hard one.

SUSAN: Why is that?

JEAN: Well, I taught school for, I guess, thirty-four years. And the first, I don't know, probably twenty years that I taught, there was religion in school. You were free to have a prayer, a little devotion at the beginning of the school day; and I think when they took that out of the schools, that's when we started seeing a lot of violence in the schools, and I just really think that hurt.

PAIGE TROTTER: Personally, I think what is happening in the schools, what is happening in the public arena, is a tragedy. . . . The devil wants God out of the schools, out of government; the devil wants him out of every area that he possibly can. Our battle is not with flesh and blood but with spiritual power. And I believe that every organization that opposes prayer in school, prayer in public places, is in line with the devil. To me, things are simple: I see things in black and white, and that's the way I see it.

The conversation I had with the Clique was similar in many ways. They strongly affirmed the priesthood of believers and the autonomy of the local church, but they had a difference of opinion when I brought up separation of church and state. It began with my own mother disputing the notion that the founders intended church and state to be separate. "[The founders] believed that they came here for religious freedom, that the state should not set a religion that you had to follow. That everybody was free to have their own religion," but, she continued, "[this nation] was founded on God. Every document we have still says, 'In God We Trust.' In Washington, just about every building has the mention of God, on every monument. And no matter what they say, we still trust in God."

When some members voiced their agreement, Nancy Moore challenged them. She is disturbed by religious groups having lobbyists in Washington, "because I don't think that's church business. Church business is winning the lost, one by one." She believes that electing Christians to office is important, but, she said, "I do not want a church state, because religion ultimately gets raped in that. All through history. It doesn't work that well. You don't want to say, 'This is Christian,' because America is composed of a lot of different religions. That is our strength, because it's 'One for All,' and we can't ignore the citizens who are of other faiths."

Mom agreed that all people should have the right to practice their faith. Lidia Abrams noted that people have brought various religious faiths from all over the world, but, she added, "They should respect what they found when they got here."

Nancy again offered a challenge: "Jesus was not organizing groups to go into teaching the government. Jesus was about another kingdom completely separate from these kingdoms on earth. The Christian's business is to work for that other kingdom, which is a heavenly kingdom; it's not of this world." She continued, "Of course, our individual welfare depends upon our government, and we want to elect good men, and the best men are Christian men. So we want to do that, but we have to be careful when we say we want it to be one way, because we are a diverse nation. People have their own things they want to do; they have their own ways, and we should be trying to win them to Christ."

Mom didn't agree: "Christians also have got to speak up and quit being silent." She gave the example of gay marriage. "Our government has to have regulations and has to have morals enforced, evidently, because we're going down, further down, all the time."

Nancy responded: "I think about what Paul said—'I'm determined to know one thing: Jesus Christ crucified.' That's the message of the church."

The Cooperative Program

Many participants pointed to the Cooperative Program as a unique part of Baptist identity.[4] The Cooperative Program is a mechanism by which individual churches are able to fund Southern Baptist agencies, institutions, and missions. When an individual gives an offering to a local church, the church keeps a portion of that offering for its own work and then sends a portion to the local association, state convention, and Southern Baptist Convention (each local congregation determines what portion—if any—to give to these organizations). The association, state convention, and SBC then distribute the money to support various enterprises, from associational soup kitchens to the six Southern Baptist seminaries. A large percentage of the money given through the Cooperative Program goes to support domestic and international missions. The Cooperative Program thus allows these fiercely independent local churches to work together to do more than they would be able to do individually. Brenda Faulkner explained, "We are a cooperating group of people. I think that we're able to carry out the Great Commission more effectively because we cooperate financially. Monies go into the Cooperative Program and are distributed to all our agencies. It just enables us to accomplish a lot more than if we were doing it independently of each other."

Growing up as the child of missionaries, Debra Owens-Hughes saw firsthand the need for cooperation. She explained, "The Cooperative Program of the Southern Baptist Convention makes things possible that one church alone could seldom if ever accomplish. We never went without food; yet some [missionaries from other churches] did when a church that supported them split or the pastor changed and the money wasn't sent. I learned from this that even in my own life, that I can do very little alone, on my own, even though this is my natural personality tendency, that if I work alongside others, much more could be accomplished."

Kathy Sylvest said, "I've always been very proud of Southern Baptists for having the Cooperative Program and knowing I could give what little bit I had in my church and make a difference all over the world." She learned the value of giving from her parents. They were dairy farmers and didn't have a lot, but each year her parents matched the money the children saved for the Lottie Moon Christmas Offering for Foreign Missions. "So," she continued, "we could double our gift to Lottie Moon, and that was always a big deal in my family." Her parents also emphasized tithing. Once, when she was very young, her grandmother gave her a dollar, and she knew she needed to tithe. That Sunday, she faithfully placed ten cents in the offering envelope. The next Sunday, she started to put in another ten cents, and her grandmother asked her what she was doing.

"I'm tithing," Kathy explained.

"Where did you get some more money?" her grandmother asked.

"I didn't," Kathy responded. "This is what I had left from last week."

Her grandmother explained that she only had to tithe once when she got money, not every week. "So," Kathy concluded, "they missed out on me being a *really* good giver." We laughed, and she added, "But we were taught that was part of what being Baptist was all about—cooperative missions giving."

Carolyn Weatherford Crumpler explained, "We study the Bible, we study missions, and then we pray, and then we give money, and then we go." Not surprisingly, Sara Wisdom, who spent thirty-three years in WMU work in state Baptist conventions, chose to align herself with Southern Baptists "first, because of their mission program" and then "because of doctrines."

"Which ones?" I asked.

"Priesthood of the believer is really the most important to me," she answered. For Southern Baptists, the imperative of missions, of evangelism, is deeply connected to soul competency. Because salvation is an individual decision, each individual must make a decision about the Gospel. Therefore, for Southern Baptists, carrying the Gospel to all the world is essential. Kate Campbell learned from her father, pastor Jim Henry, that for Baptists, "the main thing was sharing the love of Christ. And the second emphasis was on the individual priesthood of the believer." Lisa Vang said, "Being Baptist means that we can work together with others who have the same beliefs to reach out to the lost and make more disciples." Similarly, Libo Krieg explained that when she sees the work that Southern Baptists do around the world, "I feel proud about it; we're not fake; we're real. We're doing the work. And I feel so honored to be part of Baptists."

Minerva Escobedo explained that, to her, part of the appeal of Southern Baptists is that she feels connected to something larger than herself. "I'm involved in my church," she said, "but my church is involved in the association and the Cooperative Program." She offered the example of the relief work done by Southern Baptists in the aftermath of Hurricane Katrina. "It has just helped me to become very missions-minded because of being involved with Southern Baptist work," she asserted. Jennifer Adamson also emphasized the importance of working together for missions. She said, "One of the things I love about being Baptist is that we not only focus inwardly and help each other grow, but we look to the world really. It goes to the missions and to the help that we seek to give others outside our denomination. To really let Christ be known. It makes me proud that we could do those kinds of things and have those food kitchens and just that support when we have disasters because I do think that we are reaching [out] to the world as we demonstrate Christ in our lives."

Although the participants see themselves first as Christians, their Christian faith is profoundly shaped by their experiences as Southern Baptists, and their identities as Christian and Southern Baptist women have been and continue to be deeply influenced by Baptist distinctions. They see the Baptist way of doing things as most closely aligned with their own convictions (though this may be a bit of a chicken and egg situation, in that their convictions may be the result of their experiences of being Baptist). At the core of their understanding of being Baptist is a belief in the authority of scripture, the priesthood of believers, the autonomy of the local church, democratic church governance, and religious liberty (with separation of church and state as a corollary for most, but not all). Central to these understandings of being Baptist are issues of agency and autonomy. For Baptists, the Christian life begins in free choice and is lived with free choice. Faith is not coerced; neither is cooperation. Associations are voluntary, whether an individual's decision to be part of a local congregation or a local congregation's decision to be part of a local association, state convention, or the Southern Baptist Convention itself.

For women, the implications of this Baptist emphasis on the individual and freedom are profound, for inherent in Baptist thinking is the underpinning for women's agency, autonomy, and equality. Although the denominational structures themselves are patriarchal (as is a great deal of the theology), these historical Baptist beliefs provide the possibility of an alternative discourse for women. Despite any pronouncements by the Convention or its leaders, these women know that ultimately they are their own free agents, competent before God. So even though the Convention may blame women for the Fall, and various churches, associations, and the SBC itself may denounce the ordination of women, Baptist women continue to do exactly what they believe God has called them to do. For some women, their resistance is overt; they pursue ordination and the pastorate. For others, resistance is more subtle; they remain in their very conservative churches and each year quietly nominate women to be deacons. Some may not even feel that they are resisting; they simply find ways to do what they think is right, and they are comfortable within the framework of male leadership and headship as they understand it. Even for these women, however, their positions are choices made as free agents, fully aware of their ability to choose otherwise. Certainly, some women are less thoughtful; some go along with whatever the male leadership says; some completely buy into the idea of women's subordination. But from my conversations with Southern Baptist women, I have found that most do not. They may espouse submission, but they are able to frame the notion in ways that give them great latitude, and they know how to work the system to get what they want.

These women are not feminists in the same sense that I am, but they believe in the equality of women and men, and they support women's rights in relation to such things as equal employment opportunity and safety from domestic violence and sexual assault. Because they believe that God has created them as men's equals and that God deals directly with them, across the board, their faith is empowering to them as women. The belief that God speaks to them gives them a profound sense of agency and autonomy; they are able to do whatever they believe God calls them to do. And this deeply held conviction provides an ongoing counterdiscourse to the dominant patriarchal discourse of the Southern Baptist Convention. At their core, these women believe in their own soul competency, and this belief finds expression in myriad ways as they seek to live and be faithful to their calling.

In one of the focus groups with the Clique, Mom said, "I believe in the Bible Phoebe was a deacon, because the Bible says she was."

"So that means it's okay for women to be deacons then?" I asked.

Nancy replied, "I'm a deacon. It's a necessity in our church because there's not enough leaders in the church. I think ideally if the men were more spiritual, the women would be glad for them to be the deacons, if they are willing to serve when they are needed."

Alicia added, "I don't have anything against women serving like that, but I think it's better if the men have the leadership role. And I really think women have enough responsibilities."

"Amen," several replied.

Lidia spoke up. "This is what I'm saying, that I cannot be against anything, as long as it's something that is from the Lord and is good." She then told us that one of her friends became a church usher, and some church members complained because they disapproved of a woman being an usher. "But I know what good qualities she has," Lidia continued, "and I know who she is. So therefore I can't be against something that's pure and good, and so [Lidia's friend and her husband] usher together a lot of times, and I'm not against it for it is something from the Lord that is good."

Mom jumped back in. "I believe Lydia in the Bible was a deacon too."

"More likely a pastor," I suggested.

"You think she was a pastor?" Mom asked.

"The church was in her house," I pointed out.

Mom told us that her pastor had recently called her to ask what she thought about women as deacons. He was thinking that maybe female deacons could minister better to single and widowed women than men could. Mom pointed out that when Kayne's husband, Bill, was ordained a deacon in their church, Kayne made a commitment to the ministry of deacons too. Mom added, "We find, in most of the deacon ministries, the women are the ones that are doing the visiting and doing the contacting because the men are working. And so, they're really doing it. So I consider Kayne my deacon."

I decided to up the ante. "What do you all think of women as pastors?"

"That's a whole new ball game," Mom replied.

"What's the difference?" I asked.

Mom's ambivalence on the issue came out in her response: "A pastor, there are qualifications for pastors. And I believe that Annie Armstrong and Lottie Moon were pastors to their flock because they preached. And when you expound the Word, that's what a pastor is. Preacher, pastor, same word in the Bible. But women are emotional, and we're just a different makeup than men. And I just believe the pastor of a church should be a man. That's just my opinion. But the Bible probably does teach that women could be. Because when it says 'prophetess'—I was telling Susan this morning, we're studying in 2 Kings, and I got my lesson out to read it and there was one verse in there that said it was a prophetess after Hezekiah, and it says 'the prophetess gave the Word of the Lord to the new king.' No different: preacher, pastor, prophetess."

Lidia spoke again: "I love to see a man [as] the head of a church, but I have heard some women preaching, and I don't have nothing against it."

Judy chimed in at this point: "I really don't have anything against a woman pastor; I just prefer to have a man. But I think that women can minister in so many other ways. And I see nothing wrong with it. When I think of Lottie Moon and a lot of missionaries; I hear people like Shirley Randall [a missionary who used to speak at West Rome Baptist Church when she was home on furlough], oh, I can sit and listen to Shirley Randall all day! And I would have no problem listening to [a woman]. But as head of the church, pastor, so to speak, I always think of those in terms of being a male. But I have no objection to a woman who has the same beliefs and can expound the Word as well. I have no problem with that."

"Aren't you surprised at us, Susan?" Mom asked.

My response: yes and no. On the one hand, they surprised me with their openness to women as deacons, preachers, and pastors. On the other hand, I'm not so sure that I was surprised at all. For my entire life, these women have made their own way, made up their own minds, and claimed their own voices in the church. Certainly, Southern Baptist women are often full of contradictions; they disagree with one another on a regular basis, and sometimes, they don't even agree with themselves. Nonetheless, they have a strong sense of their own ability to think through issues and come to their own conclusions. They are faithful women whose religious experiences and convictions play a profound role in how they understand themselves and act in the world. As Baptists, they end up in different places; they disagree on many significant theological and social issues, sometimes to such an extent that they can no longer work together because of these profound differences. Still, they share a central aspect of self that grows from their formative experiences as Baptists—singing hymns, walking the aisle, being a GA, living the priesthood of believers. They are competent before God, capable individuals, agents of their own lives.

Cast of Characters

The Clique

Details about the Clique are provided in the introduction. They are Lidia Abrams, Doris Bailey, Alicia Bennett, Kayne Carter, Shelby Christie, Judy Masters, Nancy Moore, and JoAnn Shaw.

Other Participants

Sheri Adams, professor of theology and church history at the M. Christopher White School of Divinity at Gardner-Webb University, Boiling Springs, North Carolina

Jennifer Adamson, director of women's ministries, First Baptist Church, Orlando, Florida

Bettie Akins, homemaker, member of First Baptist Church, Batesburg, South Carolina

Nancy Ammerman, professor of sociology, Boston University

Sarah Frances Anders, emeritus professor of social work, Louisiana Baptist College

Melissa Ashley, pharmacist, member of First Baptist Church, Hendersonville, Tennessee

April Baker, co-pastor of Glendale Baptist Church, Nashville, Tennessee

Judy Baker, Missouri state representative

Rosalie Beck, professor of church history at Baylor University, Waco, Texas

Meghan Becker, student at Truett Theological Seminary, Waco, Texas

Amy Bigbee, student at Truett Theological Seminary, Waco, Texas

Carolyn Blevins, professor of religion at Carson-Newman College, Jefferson City, Tennessee

Doris Borchert, retired professor of Christian education

Pamela Boucher, minister of childhood development, Magnolia Avenue Baptist Church, Riverside, California

Linda McKinnish Bridges, associate dean for arts and sciences at Wake Forest University, Winston-Salem, North Carolina

Katrina Stipe Brooks, co-pastor of North Broad Baptist Church, Rome, Georgia

Pat Brown, librarian at Lifeway Christian Resources, Nashville, Tennessee

Melissa Browning, Cooperative Baptist Fellowship fieldworker, Birmingham, Alabama

Eva Buford, student at Truett Theological Seminary, Waco, Texas

LaDonna Burton, paralegal, member of Mount Alto Baptist Church, Rome, Georgia

Mary Beth Byram, student at McAfee School of Theology, Atlanta, Georgia

Kate Campbell, folk singer, Nashville, Tennessee

Sarah Chism Carbajal, student at Truett Theological Seminary, Waco, Texas

Kristy Carr, volunteer missions coordinator, Woman's Missionary Union, Auxiliary to the Southern Baptist Convention

Patty Carter, teacher, member of North Broad Baptist Church, Rome, Georgia

Candice Christian, children's ministry, First Baptist Church, Orlando, Florida

Sheryl Churchill, consultant, Woman's Missionary Union, Auxiliary to the Southern Baptist Convention

Sandra J. Cisneros, minister of education, Templo Jerusalem Baptist Church, Victoria, Texas

Jamie Cline, teacher, member of First Baptist Church, Hendersonville, Tennessee

Annie M. Cockrell, homemaker, member of First Baptist Church, Batesburg, South Carolina

Angela Faith Cofer, professor of voice at Southwestern Baptist Theological Seminary, Fort Worth, Texas

Nan Cook, homemaker, member of First Baptist Church, Batesburg, South Carolina

Amy Corbin, kindergarten teacher, member of First Baptist Church, Hendersonville, Tennessee

Beth Cox, speech pathologist, member of North Broad Baptist Church, Rome, Georgia

Audrey Crabtree, secretary, member of First Baptist Church, Orlando, Florida

Beth Crawford, law student at the University of Oregon

Carolyn Weatherford Crumpler, former executive director of Woman's Missionary Union, Auxiliary to the Southern Baptist Convention

Carolyn Hale Cubbedge, regional coordinator for Morning Star Treatment Services, Savannah, Georgia

Jean Cullen, mission involvement specialist, Woman's Missionary Union, Auxiliary to the Southern Baptist Convention

Millie Culp, teacher, member of Mount Alto Baptist Church, Rome, Georgia

Shannon Daniell, pharmacist, member of First Baptist Church, Hendersonville, Tennessee

Gwen Dellinger, workforce development director, member of North Broad Baptist Church, Rome, Georgia

Priscilla L. Denham, minister, spiritual director, clinical pastoral education supervisor, New Hampshire; one of the early group of Southern Baptist women to be ordained in the mid-1970s

Janet Dickerson, homemaker, member of Second Ponce de Leon Baptist Church, Atlanta, Georgia

Betty Sue Drury, homemaker, member of Travis Avenue Baptist Church, Fort Worth, Texas

Beth Duke, registered nurse, Tennessee

Joye Ardyn Durham, photographer, Black Mountain, North Carolina

Earline K. Durst, homemaker, member of First Baptist Church, Batesburg, South Carolina

Nancy Echols, retired teacher, member of North Broad Baptist Church, Rome, Georgia

Barbara Elder, program development consultant, Woman's Missionary Union, Auxiliary to the Southern Baptist Convention

Lucy Elizalde (pseudonym), missions worker, Texas

Raquel Ellis, research assistant, Illinois

Minerva Escobedo, retired administrator, California State University, Fresno

Brenda Faulkner, administrative assistant, First Baptist Church, Orlando, Florida

Candi Finch, PhD student at Southwestern Baptist Theological Seminary, Fort Worth, Texas

Kathy Manis Findley, trauma counselor, Arkansas

Brenda Flowers, assistant to the mayor, Riverside, California

Sara H. Fox, homemaker, member of First Baptist Church, Batesburg, South Carolina

Kryn Freehling-Burton, graduate student in women studies at Oregon State University

Jennifer Fuller, Cooperative Baptist Fellowship student missions staff, Birmingham, Alabama

Jimmie Nell Galbraith, homemaker, member of Broadway Baptist Church, Fort Worth, Texas

LeAnn Gardner, student at Truett Theological Seminary, Waco, Texas

Diana Garland, dean of the School of Social Work at Baylor University, Waco, Texas

Cari Garrett, women's ministry assistant, First Baptist Church, Hendersonville, Tennessee

Jean Gaston, homemaker, member of First Baptist Church, Batesburg, South Carolina

Grace Geddes, homemaker, member of First Baptist Church, Batesburg, South Carolina

Martha Gilmore, retired United Methodist pastor, Dallas, Texas; one of the early group of Southern Baptist women ordained during the mid-1970s

Leigh Ann Grubbs, administrative assistant, First Baptist Church, Orlando, Florida

Leah Grundset, student at Truett Theological Seminary and intern at Baylor Baptist Student Ministries, Waco, Texas

Becca Gurney, hospital chaplain, Austin, Texas

Nikki Hardeman, student at McAfee School of Theology, Atlanta, Georgia

Tammy Hayes, homemaker, member of First Baptist Church, Hendersonville, Tennessee

Kim Heath, student at McAfee School of Theology, Atlanta, Georgia

Melissa Hellem, homemaker, member of Second Ponce de Leon Baptist Church, Atlanta, Georgia

Ginny Hickman, child advocate, member of Broadway Baptist Church, Fort Worth, Texas

Debra Hochgraber, women's ministries specialist, Baptist General Convention of Texas

Nancy Hollomon-Peede, minister for community involvement, Westwood Baptist Church, Springfield, Virginia

Beverly Howard, professor of music at California Baptist University, Riverside

Fang-Lan Hsieh, music librarian at Southwestern Baptist Theological Seminary, Fort Worth, Texas

Charlean Hayes Hughes, homemaker, former collegiate missions consultant, Vancouver, Washington

Leigh Jackson, director of community ministries at First Baptist Church, Waco, Texas

Phyllis Jenkins, pastor's wife, Plano, Texas

Cynthia Johnson, retreat leader, member of Broadway Baptist Church, Fort Worth, Texas

Rebecca A. Kennedy, campus minister at Baylor University, Waco, Texas

Mary Key, homemaker, adjunct psychology instructor at California Baptist University, Riverside

Heather King, former director of women's ministries at Southern Baptist Theological Seminary, Louisville, Kentucky

Zana Juanita Kizzee, director of human resources for an engineering firm in Virginia

Sheri Klouda, former professor of Hebrew at Southwestern Baptist Theological Seminary, now a professor at Taylor University in Indiana

Libo Krieg, physical therapist, Houston, Texas

Amanda Lake, hospitality sales, Gaylord Opryland Hotel, Nashville, Tennessee

Patty Lamb, retired from the banking and finance profession, member of Second Ponce de Leon Baptist Church, Atlanta, Georgia

Wanda S. Lee, executive director of Woman's Missionary Union, Auxiliary to the Southern Baptist Convention

Joan Lewis, homemaker, member of First Baptist Church, Batesburg, South Carolina

Tisa Lewis, director of accreditation and institutional evaluation, Association of Theological Schools, Pittsburgh, Pennsylvania

Missy Loper, occupational therapist, member of First Baptist Church, Hendersonville, Tennessee

Karen G. Massey, professor of Christian education at McAfee School of Theology, Atlanta, Georgia

Carolyn Matthews, computer programmer, California

Leah McCullough, campus minister at Westminster House, Oregon State University

Katie McKown, student at Truett Theological Seminary, Waco, Texas

Amy L. Mears, co-pastor of Glendale Baptist Church, Nashville, Tennessee

Dee Miller, piano teacher, former Southern Baptist missionary in central Africa

Charla Milligan, student at Truett Theological Seminary, Waco, Texas

Carla Moldavan, math professor at Berry College, Mount Berry, Georgia; member of North Broad Baptist Church, Rome, Georgia

Danielle Mongin, art teacher, member of Second Ponce de Leon Baptist Church, Atlanta, Georgia

Karrie A. Oertli, director of pastoral care at a Baptist medical center in Oklahoma

Debra Owens-Hughes, Southern Baptist missionary in Colombia

Joanne Parker, editor of *Missions Mosaic,* Woman's Missionary Union, Auxiliary to the Southern Baptist Convention

Dorothy Kelley Patterson, first lady and professor of theology and women's studies at Southwestern Baptist Theological Seminary, Fort Worth, Texas

Julie Pennington-Russell, pastor of Calvary Baptist Church, Waco, Texas

Dorcas Pérez, church worker, First Baptist Church, Orlando, Florida

Gladys M. Peterson, former American Baptist missionary to Japan

Dixie Lea Petrey, director of pastoral care in a Tennessee retirement community

Carolyn Goodman Plampin, former Southern Baptist missionary to Brazil

Phyllis Rodgerson Pleasants, professor of church history at the Baptist Theological Seminary, Richmond, Virginia

Peggy Sanderford Ponder, hospice chaplain and pastoral counselor, Birmingham, Alabama

Shirley Powell, homemaker, member of Travis Avenue Baptist Church, Fort Worth, Texas

Kandy Queen-Sutherland, professor of religion at Stetson University, DeLand, Florida

Joyce Reed, youth services librarian, Arizona

Rhonda Reeves, preschool resources editor at Woman's Missionary Union, Southern Baptist Convention

Elaine Richards, homemaker, member of Travis Avenue Baptist Church, Fort Worth, Texas

Chris Ritter, library research department staff, member of Travis Avenue Baptist Church, Fort Worth, Texas

Mitzi Sayler, respiratory therapist, Tennessee

Lilla Schmeltekopf, interior designer, member of Broadway Baptist Church, Fort Worth, Texas

Kathryn Seay, student at Truett Theological Seminary, Waco, Texas

Karen J. Shaw, development director, Oregon State University

Sarah J. Shelton, pastor of Baptist Church of the Covenant, Birmingham, Alabama

Paula M. Sheridan, professor of social work at Whittier College, Whittier, California

Joye Smith, preschool consultant for Woman's Missionary Union, Auxiliary to the Southern Baptist Convention

Louisa Smith (pseudonym), PhD student in Texas

Pat Smith, church worker, member of Broadway Baptist Church, Fort Worth, Texas

Jorene Taylor Swift, minister of congregational care at Broadway Baptist Church, Fort Worth, Texas

Kathy Sylvest, librarian, Southern Baptist Historical Library and Archives, Nashville, Tennessee

Pamela K. Tanner, high school choir director and fine arts chair, Sugar Land, Texas

Paige Trotter, homemaker, member of First Baptist Church, Batesburg, South Carolina

Angelyn Turner, home office worker, member of Second Ponce de Leon Baptist Church, Atlanta, Georgia

Sue E. Turner, retired educational consultant, Fort Worth, Texas

Lisa Vang, tax manager, Allen, Texas

Jennifer Wagley, student at Truett Theological Seminary, Waco, Texas

Dorothy Walsh, retired courtroom deputy, member of Second Ponce de Leon Baptist Church, Atlanta, Georgia

Lynda Weaver-Williams, professor of religious studies at Virginia Commonwealth University, Richmond

Suzanne Lenae Whisler, intern at Baylor Baptist Student Ministries, Waco, Texas

Debbie Williams, attorney, Atlanta, Georgia

Lisa A. Williams, student at Truett Theological Seminary, Waco, Texas

Helen Winstead, clerical worker, member of First Baptist Church, Batesburg, South Carolina

Sara Wisdom, former executive director of Northwest Woman's Missionary Union

Jennifer Wofford, teacher, member of Mount Alto Baptist Church, Rome, Georgia

Carol Woodfin, history professor at Palm Beach Atlantic University, West Palm Beach, Florida

Faith Wu (pseudonym), Southern Baptist seminary professor

Melodie Yocum (now deceased), professor of theater at California Baptist University, Riverside

Laura Gene York, homemaker, member of Travis Avenue Baptist Church, Fort Worth, Texas

Mary Zimmer, director of social services for long-term health care, Louisville, Kentucky

Notes

All the chapter epigraphs are from the *Baptist Hymnal* (Nashville: Convention Press, 1975).

Introduction

1. Ted Ownby, "Evangelical but Differentiated: Religion by the Numbers," in *Religion and Public Life in the South in the Evangelical Mode,* ed. Charles Reagan Wilson and Mark Silk (Walnut Creek, Calif.: Alta Mira Press, 2005), 31–61.

2. For more on Baptist history, see Bill J. Leonard, *Baptist Ways: A History* (Valley Forge, Pa.: Judson Press, 2003), and Leon McBeth, *The Baptist Heritage: Four Centuries of Baptist Witness* (Nashville: Broadman Press, 1987).

3. Walter B. Shurden, *Not a Silent People: Controversies that Have Shaped Southern Baptists* (Nashville: Broadman Press, 1972), 13.

4. For more on the emergence of Republican identity in the Southern Baptist Convention, see Oran P. Smith, *The Rise of Baptist Republicanism* (New York: New York University Press, 1997).

5. "Agency and Communion as Conceptual Coordinates for the Understanding and Measurement of Interpersonal Behavior," in *Thinking Clearly about Psychology: Essays in Honor of Paul E. Meehl,* vol. 2, *Personality and Psychopathology,* ed. D. Cicchetti (Minneapolis: University of Minnesota Press, 1991); M. Friedman, "Autonomy and Social Relationships: Rethinking the Feminist Critique," in *Feminists Rethink the Self,* ed. D. Tietjens Meyers (Oxford: Westview Press, 1997).

6. Julie Nelson-Kuna and Stephanie Riger, "Women's Agency in Psychological Contexts," in *Provoking Agents: Gender and Agency in Theory and Practice,* ed. Judith Kegan Gardiner (Urbana: University of Illinois Press, 1995), 176.

7. Numerous excellent histories of Baptists in the United States have been published in recent years. For example, see Pamela R. Durso and Keith E. Dur-

so, *The Story of Baptists in the United States* (Brentwood, Tenn.: Baptist History and Heritage Society, 2006); William H. Brackney, *Baptists in North America* (Malden, Mass.: Blackwell, 2006); Bill J. Leonard, *Baptists in America* (New York: Columbia University Press, 2005).

8. Cited in Robert A. Baker, ed., *A Baptist Source Book* (Nashville: Broadman Press, 1966), 106.

9. McBeth, *Baptist Heritage*, 391.

10. Findley Edge, *A Quest for Vitality in Religion: A Theological Approach to Religious Education* (Nashville: Broadman Press, 1963), 201. See also Glenn Hinson's critique of the corporatization of the Southern Baptist Convention in "Oh, Baptists, How Your Corporation Has Grown!" in *Distinctively Baptist: Essays on Baptist History,* ed. Marc A. Jolley (Macon, Ga.: Mercer University Press, 2005), 17–33.

11. James Fowler, *Stages of Faith: The Psychology of Human Development and the Quest for Meaning* (San Francisco: HarperSanFrancisco, 1995).

12. Carl L. Hunt, ed., *Exiled: Voices of the Southern Baptist Convention Holy War* (Knoxville: University of Tennessee Press, 2006).

13. Leonard claims that the system of denominational connectionalism in the South "is experiencing significant transition, restructuring, and reevaluation by persons and churches spread across a wide geographical and theological spectrum. While the SBC remains the largest Protestant denomination in the U.S., claiming over 15 million members in nearly 40,000 churches, elements of fragmentation, redefinition, and schism in denominational connectionalism and identity are currently impacting all segments of the old denominational system." Bill Leonard, "Baptists in the South: A New Connectionalism," *American Baptist Quarterly* 19 (2000): 208–9.

14. E. Y. Mullins, *The Axioms of Religion* (Philadelphia: American Baptist Publication Society, 1908); James Leo Garrett, Glenn Hinson, and James E. Tull, *Are Southern Baptists "Evangelicals"?* (Macon, Ga.: Mercer University Press, 1983); Walter B. Shurden, *The Baptist Identity: Four Fragile Freedoms* (Macon, Ga.: Smyth & Helwys, 1993). I also want to thank the professors at Southern Baptist Theological Seminary from 1982 to 1987 who so profoundly shaped my understandings of Baptist history, theology, polity, and education: John Hendrix, Bill Rogers, Dan Aleshire, James Blevins, Paige Kelly, and Henlee Barnette. And I thank the women from the fourth floor of Mullins Hall, with whom I endlessly discussed, analyzed, synthesized, and occasionally lamented. Much of what I learned came from those late-night conversations around the kitchen table. In particular, I thank Tisa Lewis, my best friend and theological sparring partner for the last twenty-six years.

15. Torbet identifies five principles that define Baptist identity. Although different Baptists interpret these in different ways and may add other principles, agreement in some form generally exists among Baptist groups on these key principles: the Bible as the norm for faith and practice, baptized believers as the

constituents of the church, the priesthood of believers, the autonomy of the local church, and religious liberty and the separation of church and state. Robert G. Torbet, *A History of the Baptists* (Philadelphia: Judson Press, 1950).

16. Ferrol Sams, *The Whisper of the River* (New York: Penguin, 1984), 3.

17. Givens suggests that, influenced by twentieth-century business models, the SBC became so efficient at creating programs that defined the nature, function, and organizational structure of local churches that it lost sight of empowering the churches to do these things for themselves. She argues that by 1960, religious education had become highly standardized and tied to denominational and church programs and showed an affinity for church growth, efficient organization, and how-to guides. Linda Mays Givens, "A Programmed Piety: Education for Spirituality in Southern Baptist Study Course Literature, 1908–1986" (dissertation, Southern Baptist Theological Seminary, 1988), 134.

18. Kay Shurden, "An Analysis of the Images of Women in Selected Southern Baptist Literature," in *Findings of the Consultation on Women in Church-Related Vocations* (Inter-agency Council of the Southern Baptist Convention, 1978).

19. Roger Williams, "The Bloudy Tennent of Persecution," in *A Sourcebook for Baptist Heritage*, ed. Leon McBeth (Nashville: Broadman Press, 1990), 83–84.

20. Letter from Thomas Jefferson to Danbury Baptist Association, January 1, 1802, Library of Congress, http://www.loc.gov/loc/lcib/9806/danpre.html (accessed November 10, 2005).

21. Letter from James Madison to Edward Livingston, July 10, 1822, in *The Writings of James Madison*, ed. Gaillard Hunt (Chicago: University of Chicago Press, 1900), http://press-pubs.uchicago.edu/founders/documents/amendI_religions66.html (accessed November 10, 2005).

22. For more on Baptist successionism, see Shurden, *Not a Silent People*, 21–33; McBeth, *Baptist Heritage*, 447–61; James R. Graves, *Old Landmarkism: What Is It?* (Memphis: Baptist Book House, 1880); James M. Pendelton, *Distinctive Principles of Baptists* (Philadelphia: American Baptist Publication Society, 1882).

23. Leonard, *Baptist Ways*, 183.

24. Mullins, *Axioms of Religion*.

25. Shurden, *Baptist Identity*, 24.

26. Ibid., 31.

1. Just as I Am

1. Linda Mays Givens, "A Programmed Piety: Education for Spirituality in Southern Baptist Study Course Literature, 1908–1986" (dissertation, Southern Baptist Theological Seminary, 1988).

2. Marcus Borg, *The God We Never Knew: Beyond Dogmatic Religion to a More Authentic Contemporary Faith* (New York: HarperSanFrancisco, 1997), 17.

3. Ibid., 71.

4. SBC Web site: http://www.sbc.net/knowjesus/theplan.asp (accessed November 23, 2005).

5. Horace Bushnell, *Christian Nurture* (Eugene, Ore.: Wipf & Stock, 2001); Daniel O. Aleshire, *Faithcare: Ministering to All God's People through the Ages of Life* (Louisville, Ky.: Westminster John Knox Press, 1988).

6. Findley Edge, *A Quest for Vitality in Religion: A Theological Approach to Religious Education* (Nashville: Broadman Press, 1963).

7. Ibid.

8. Will L. Thompson, "Softy and Tenderly" [1880], in *Baptist Hymnal* (Nashville: Convention Press, 1975), 190.

9. William J. Kirkpatrick, "Lord, I'm Coming Home" [1892], in ibid., 174.

10. Jean Heriot, *Blessed Assurance: Beliefs, Actions, and the Experience of Salvation in a Carolina Baptist Church* (Knoxville: University of Tennessee Press, 1994).

11. Bill J. Leonard, *Baptist Ways: A History* (Valley Forge, Pa.: Judson Press, 2003), 25.

12. Edward Barber, *A Small Treatise of Baptisme, or, Dipping* (London, 1641).

13. William L. Lumpkin, ed., *Baptist Confessions of Faith* (Valley Forge, Pa.: Judson Press, 1959), 167.

14. "Short Confession of Faith in XX Articles by John Smyth," in ibid., 100.

15. Lumpkin, *Baptist Confessions,* 167.

16. Leonard, *Baptist Ways,* 48.

17. Lumpkin, *Baptist Confessions,* 330–31.

18. Second London Confession, in ibid., 265.

19. For example, see www.founders.org.

20. E. Y. Mullins, *The Christian Religion in Its Doctrinal Expression* (Nashville: Baptist Sunday School Board, 1917), 347.

21. *The Baptist Faith and Message* (1963; reprint, Nashville: Convention Press, 1971), 64.

22. Bill Leonard, "When the Denominational Center Doesn't Hold: The Southern Baptist Experience," *Christian Century,* September 22, 1993, 909.

23. Timothy George, *Theology of the Reformers* (Nashville: Broadman & Holman, 1988), 318.

24. Leonard, "When the Denominational Center Doesn't Hold," 909.

25. Tisa Lewis, *Faith Influences: Gospel Responsibilities in a Changing World* (Birmingham, Ala.: Woman's Missionary Union, 2000), 55.

26. Ibid., 56.

27. Ibid.

28. For more on the Landmark controversy, see Walter Shurden's chapter, "The 'What about Other Denominations?' Controversy, or Baptists Argue about the Church," in his *Not a Silent People: Controversies that Have Shaped Southern Baptists* (Nashville: Broadman Press, 1972), 65–81.

2. The B-I-B-L-E

1. Cynthia Lynn Lyerly, "In Service, Silence, and Strength: Women in Southern Churches," in *Religion and Public Life in the South in the Evangelical Mode*, ed. Charles Reagan Wilson and Mark Silk (Walnut Creek, Calif.: Alta Mira Press, 2005), 104.

2. Martha Sconyers, *The Sword Drill* (Montgomery, Ala.: Baptist Training Union Department, n.d.).

3. E. Y. Mullins, *The Axioms of Religion* (Philadelphia: American Baptist Publication Society, 1908).

4. See, for example, W. A. Criswell's influential *Why I Preach that the Bible Is Literally True* (Nashville: Broadman Press, 1969) and Paul Pressler, *A Hill on which to Die: One Southern Baptist's Journey* (Nashville: Broadman & Holman, 2002). Criswell was the theological force behind the fundamentalists who conceived the takeover of the SBC. Pressler, a federal appellate court judge, was one of the architects of the takeover, along with Paige Patterson, who is now president of Southwestern Baptist Theological Seminary.

5. Criswell, *Why I Preach*, 33.

6. See, for example, James Carl Hefley, *The Truth in Crisis*, vols. 1–5 (Dallas: Clarion Publications; Hannibal, Mo.: Hannibal Books, 1986–1990); Joe Edward Barnhart, *The Southern Baptist Holy War* (Austin: Texas Monthly Press, 1986); Ellen M. Rosenberg, *The Southern Baptists: A Subculture in Transition* (Knoxville: University of Tennessee Press, 1989); Nancy Ammerman, *Baptist Battles: Social Change and Religious Conflict in the Southern Baptist Convention* (New Brunswick, N.J.: Rutgers University Press, 1990); Bill J. Leonard, *God's Last and Only Hope: The Fragmentation of the Southern Baptist Convention* (Grand Rapids, Mich.: Eerdmans, 1990); Grady C. Cothen, *What Happened to the Southern Baptist Convention? A Memoir of the Controversy* (Macon, Ga.: Smyth & Helwys, 1993); Walter B. Shurden, *The Struggle for the Soul of the SBC: Moderate Responses to Fundamentalist Movement* (Macon, Ga.: Mercer University Press, 1993); Fisher Humphreys, *The Way We Were: How Southern Baptist Theology Has Changed and What It Means to Us All* (New York: McCracken Press, 1994); Grady C. Cothen, *The New SBC: Fundamentalism's Impact on the Southern Baptist Convention* (Macon, Ga.: Mercer University Press, 1995); David T. Morgan, *The New Crusades, the New Holy Land: Conflict in the Southern Baptist Convention* (Tuscaloosa: University of Alabama Press, 1996); John W. Merritt, *The Betrayal: The Hostile Takeover of the Southern Baptist Convention and a Missionary's Fight for Freedom in Christ* (Asheville, N.C.: R. Brent, 2005). For an excellent sourcebook of documents produced during the Controversy, see Walter B. Shurden and Randy Shepley, eds., *Going for the Jugular: A Documentary History of the SBC Holy War* (Macon, Ga.: Mercer University Press, 1996).

7. Fisher Humphreys, *The Way We Were: How Southern Baptist Theology Has*

Changed and What It Means to Us All, rev. ed. (Macon, Ga.: Smyth & Helwys, 2002); Jerry Sutton, *The Baptist Reformation: The Conservative Resurgence in the Southern Baptist Convention* (Nashville: Broadman, 2000); Jeff B. Pool, *Against Returning to Egypt: Exposing and Resisting Credalism in the Southern Baptist Convention* (Macon, Ga.: Mercer University, 1998); Cothen, *What Happened to the Southern Baptist Convention;* Timothy George, "Toward an Evangelical Future," in *Southern Baptists Observed: Multiple Perspectives on a Changing Denomination,* ed. Nancy Ammerman (Knoxville: University of Tennessee, 1993), 276–300.

8. Sutton, *Baptist Reformation;* Samuel S. Hill, "The Story before the Story: Southern Baptists since World War II," in Ammerman, *Southern Baptists Observed,* 30–46; Arthur E. Farnsley, "'Judicious Concentration': Decision Making in the Southern Baptist Convention," in ibid., 47–70; David Ray Norsworthy, "Rationalization and Reaction among Southern Baptists," in ibid., 71–97; Ammerman, *Baptist Battles.*

9. Ellen M. Rosenberg, "The Southern Baptist Response to the Newest South," in Ammerman, *Southern Baptists Observed,* 144–64; Rosenberg, *Southern Baptists: A Subculture in Transition.*

10. E. Luther Copeland, *The Southern Baptist Convention and the Judgment of History: The Taint of an Original Sin,* rev. ed. (Lanham, Md.: University Press of America, 2002).

11. Ammerman, *Baptist Battles.*

12. Walter B. Shurden, "Major Issues in the SBC Controversy," in *Amidst Babel, Speak the Truth: Reflections on the Southern Baptist Convention Struggle,* ed. Robert U. Ferguson Jr. (Macon, Ga.: Smyth & Helwys, 1993), 1–10.

13. Walter B. Shurden, *Not an Easy Journey: Some Transitions in Baptist Life* (Macon, Ga.: Mercer University Press, 2005).

14. Arthur E. Farnsley II, *Southern Baptist Politics: Authority and Power in the Restructuring of an American Denomination* (University Park: University of Pennsylvania Press, 1994).

15. Morgan, *New Crusades;* Barry Hankins, *Uneasy in Babylon: Southern Baptist Conservatives and American Culture* (Tuscaloosa: University of Alabama Press, 2002).

16. David T. Morgan, *Southern Baptist Sisters: In Search of Status, 1845–2000* (Macon, Ga.: Mercer University Press, 2003); Leonard, *God's Last and Only Hope.*

17. Rosenberg, "Southern Baptist Response to the Newest South."

18. See, for example, Audra Trull, "Women Leaders in the Bible: Disobedient Daughters or Models of Ministry?" in *Putting Women in Their Place: Moving beyond Gender Stereotypes in Church and Home,* ed. Audra Trull and Joe Trull (Macon, Ga.: Smyth & Helwys, 2003), 63–79.

19. Bruce Ware, "The Beauty of Biblical Womanhood," *Tie* 71 (winter 2003): 4, 5.

20. Daniel Akin, "The Role of Men and Women in the Church," *Tie* 71 (winter 2003): 8.

21. Evelyn Stagg and Frank Stagg, *Women in the World of Jesus* (Philadelphia: Westminster Press, 1978); Virginia Ramey Mollenkott, *Women, Men, & the Bible* (Nashville: Abingdon Press, 1977); Jann Aldredge Clanton, *In Whose Image? God and Gender* (New York: Crossroad Press, 1991); Paul K. Jewett, *Man as Male and Female* (Grand Rapids, Mich.: Eerdmans, 1975). The Web site of Christians for Biblical Equality (www.cbeinternational.org), an organization of conservative evangelical Christians, states, "Christians for Biblical Equality is a non-profit organization comprised of individual and church members from over 80 denominations who believe that the Bible, properly interpreted, teaches the fundamental equality of men and women of all ethnicities and all economic classes, based on the teachings of scripture as reflected in Galatians 3:28: There is neither Jew nor Greek, there is neither slave nor free, there is neither male nor female; for you are all one in Christ Jesus." The Web site also offers a number of publications exploring the biblical and theological bases for equality.

22. Ferrol Sams, *The Whisper of the River* (New York: Penguin, 1984), 260.

23. Brenda Brasher, *Godly Women: Fundamentalism and Female Power* (New Brunswick, N.J.: Rutgers University Press, 1998), 67.

3. Casseroles and Covered Dishes

1. www.cathye.com/jkrelig.htm (accessed November 30, 2005).

2. *The American Women's Cook Book,* ed. and rev. Ruth Berolzheimer (Chicago: Consolidated Book Publishers, 1940), 701–2.

3. Anne R. Kaplan, Marjorie A. Hoover, and Willard B. Moore, "Introduction: On Ethnic Foodways," in *The Taste of American Place: A Reader on Regional and Ethnic Foods* (Lanham, Md.: Rowman & Littlefield, 1998), 121.

4. Sidney W. Mintz, *Tasting Food and Tasting Freedom: Excursions into Eating, Culture, and the Past* (Boston: Beacon Press, 1996), 7.

5. Daniel Sack, *Whitebread Protestants: Food and Religion in American Culture* (New York: St. Martin's Press, 2000), 61–62.

6. Kate Campbell, Ira Campbell, Johnny Pierce. © 1997 Large River Music (BMI)/Cedarsong Publishing (BMI). Used by permission.

7. Deborah Lupton, *Food, the Body, and the Self* (London: Sage, 1996), 1.

8. Cynthia A. Kierner, "Hospitality, Sociability, and Gender in the Southern Colonies," *Journal of Southern History* 62 (1996): 451.

9. Ibid., 455.

10. Ibid., 460.

11. J. D. Salinger, *Franny and Zooey* (New York: Bantam Books, 1961), 196.

12. Pat O'Connor, *Friendships between Women: A Critical Review* (New York: Guilford Press, 1992).

13. John Westerhoff, *Will Our Children Have Faith?* (New York: Seabury Press, 1976).

14. Barbara Brown Zikmund, Adair T. Lummis, and Patricia Mei Yin Chang, *Clergy Women: An Uphill Calling* (Louisville, Ky.: Westminster John Knox Press, 1998), 103.

15. K. A. Roberto and P. Kimboko, "Friendships in Later Life: Definitions and Maintenance Patterns," *International Journal of Aging and Human Development* 28 (1989): 9–19.

16. Karen A. Roberto, "Qualities of Older Women's Friendships: Stable or Volatile?" *International Journal of Aging and Human Development* 44 (1997): 1–14.

17. Joseph Scriven, "What a Friend We Have in Jesus" [1855], in *Baptist Hymnal* (Nashville: Convention Press, 1975), 403.

18. Charles W. Fry, "The Lily of the Valley" [1881], in ibid., 459.

19. See, for example, Ruth Ann Foster, "Jesus and Women," in *Putting Women in Their Place: Moving beyond Gender Stereotypes in Church and Home,* ed. Audra Trull and Joe Trull (Macon, Ga.: Smyth & Helwys, 2003), 81–90.

4. Red and Yellow, Black and White

1. Gloria Yamato, "Something about the Subject Makes It Hard to Name," in *Women's Voices, Feminist Visions: Classic and Contemporary Readings,* ed. Susan M. Shaw and Janet Lee (New York: McGraw-Hill, 2007), 100.

2. Mark Newman, "The Georgia Baptist Convention and Desegregation, 1945–1980," *Georgia Historical Quarterly* 83 (winter 1999): 683–711. See also Norman Alexander Yance, "Southern Baptist Race Relations, 1947–1977: Changing Attitudes from Harry Truman to Jimmy Carter," *Journal of Religious Thought* 35 (spring/summer 1978): 45–54.

3. Quoted in Catherine Allen, *A Century to Celebrate: History of Woman's Missionary Union* (Birmingham, Ala.: Woman's Missionary Union, 1987), 254.

4. Ibid.

5. Alan Scot Willis, *All According to God's Plan: Southern Baptist Missions and Race, 1945–1970* (Lexington: University Press of Kentucky, 2005).

6. For more details on the role of the Christian Life Commission in racial reconciliation, see Holly Reed Harrison, "'Our Relation to Persons of African Descent Has Been Less than Ideal . . .': The Southern Baptist Convention, the Christian Life Commission, and Race Relations," *West Tennessee Historical Society Papers* 53 (1999): 118–34.

7. Andy Manis, "'Dying from the Neck Up': Southern Baptist Resistance to the Civil Rights Movement," *Baptist History and Heritage* 34 (winter 1999): 33–48.

8. For an early assessment of Southern Baptists' progress on race issues, see Leon McBeth, "Southern Baptists and Race since 1947," *Baptist History and Heritage* 7 (1972): 155–68.

9. Tandy McConnell, "Religion, Segregation, and the Ideology of Cooperation: A Southern Baptist Church Responds to the Brown Decision," *Southern Studies* 4 (1993): 19–38.

10. SBC, "Resolution on Racial Reconciliation on the 150th Anniversary of the Southern Baptist Convention," June 1995, http://www.sbc.net/resolutions/amResolution.asp?ID=899 (accessed August 10, 2006).

11. Douglas A. Blackmon, "For Heaven's Sake: Racial Reconciliation Becomes a Priority for the Religious Right," *Wall Street Journal,* June 23, 1997, A1.

12. Timothy C. Morgan, "Racist No More? Black Leaders Ask," *Christianity Today* 39 (August 1995): 53.

13. "Southern Baptists Seek More Blacks," *New York Times,* June 20, 1999, 29.

14. Amy Green, "Southern Baptist Surprise," *Christianity Today* 48 (September 2004): 54–56.

15. Joe Maxwell, "Black Southern Baptists," *Christianity Today* 39 (May 1995): 26–31.

16. For a history of Southern Baptist work among persons of Latin or Spanish descent in the United States, see Joshua Grijalva, "The Story of Hispanic Southern Baptists," *Baptist History and Heritage* 18 (1983): 40–47.

5. We've a Story to Tell

1. Transcript of oral history interview with Nancy Sehested by Bill Sumners, July 1, 1994, Southern Baptist Historical Library and Archives.

2. For an excellent biography of Lottie Moon, see Catherine Allen, *The New Lottie Moon Story,* 2nd ed. (Birmingham, Ala.: Woman's Missionary Union, 1980).

3. *Woman's Work in China,* November 1883.

4. *Foreign Mission Journal,* May 1885.

5. Quoted in Allen, *The New Lottie Moon Story,* 177.

6. Quoted in Catherine Allen, *A Century to Celebrate: History of Woman's Missionary Union* (Birmingham, Ala.: Woman's Missionary Union, 1987), 263.

7. For a comprehensive history of the WMU Training School, see T. Laine Scales, *All that Fits a Woman: Training Southern Baptist Women for Charity and Mission, 1907–1926* (Macon, Ga.: Mercer University Press, 2000).

8. Vickers argues that early female participants in missions and WMU challenged traditional constructions of womanhood. Their involvement in mission work emphasized women's role as worker over the traditional construction of women as wives and mothers. Gregory Vickers, "Models of Womanhood and the Early Woman's Missionary Union," *Baptist History and Heritage* 24 (1989): 41–53.

9. Sehested oral history interview.

10. Nicola Hoggard Creegan and Christine D. Pohl, *Living on the Boundaries: Evangelical Women, Feminism, and the Theological Academy* (Downers Grove, Ill.: InterVarsity Press, 2005), 79.

11. SBC, "Resolution on Ordination and the Role of Women in Ministry," 1984, http://www.sbc.net/resolutions (accessed February 2, 2004).

12. Ferrol Sams, *The Whisper of the River* (New York: Penguin Books, 1984), 3.

13. Susan M. Shaw and Tisa Lewis, "'Once There Was a Camelot': Women Doctoral Graduates of the Southern Baptist Theological Seminary, 1982–1992, Talk about the Seminary, the Fundamentalist Takeover, and Their Lives since SBTS," *Review & Expositor* 95 (1998): 397–423.

14. For more on the changes at Southern under Al Mohler's leadership, see Julie Ingersoll, *Evangelical Christian Women: War Stories in the Gender Battles* (New York: New York University Press, 2003), 47–59.

15. Addie Davis, taped interview by Eljee Bentley, June 9, 1985, WMU archives, Woman's Missionary Union Alma Hunt Library, Birmingham, Ala.

16. Ibid.

17. Keith E. Durso and Pamela R. Durso, "'Cherish the Dream God Has Given You': The Story of Addie Davis," in *Courage and Hope: The Stories of Ten Baptist Women Ministers,* ed. Pamela R. Durso and Keith E. Durso (Macon, Ga.: Mercer University Press, 2005), 23.

18. Ancient Irish hymn text, trans. Mary Byrne, 1905, versified by Eleanor Hull, 1912, in *Baptist Hymnal* (Nashville: Convention Press, 1975), 212.

19. Bruce A. Ware, "The Beauty of Biblical Womanhood," *Tie* 71 (winter 2003): 4–5.

20. John Hall, "NAMB Stops Endorsing Female Military Chaplains," http://www.bpnews.net (accessed February 14, 2004).

21. Morris H. Chapman et al., "Report of the Southern Baptist Convention/Baptist World Alliance Study Committee," *Biblical Recorder,* December 26, 2003, http://www.biblicalrecorder.org (accessed February 3, 2004).

22. Molly Marshall, "God Does Indeed Call to Ministry Whom God Will, Gender Notwithstanding," in Durso and Durso, *Courage and Hope,* 122.

23. Molly tells this story in the documentary film *Battle for the Minds* (Lipscomb, 1996).

24. Creegan and Pohl, *Living on the Boundaries,* 102.

25. Barbara Brown Zikmund, Adair T. Lummis, and Patricia Mei Yin Chang, *Clergy Women: An Uphill Calling* (Louisville, Ky.: Westminster John Knox Press, 1998), 130.

26. Howell Williams, "'That's the Way We've Always Done It': The Myth of Progress and the Identity of Women in Baptist Life" (master's thesis, Florida State University, 2003).

27. David T. Morgan, *Southern Baptist Sisters: In Search of Status, 1845–2000* (Macon, Ga.: Mercer University Press, 2003).

28. Ingersoll, *Evangelical Christian Women,* 136–38.

29. "First Person: Virginia WMU & Women in Ministry," *Baptist Press,* November 18, 2004, www.bpnews.net/printerfirendly.asp?ID=19575 (accessed November 19, 2004).

30. Dorothy Patterson, "Why I Believe Southern Baptist Churches Should Not Ordain Women" (unpublished ms., Southern Baptist Historical Library and Archives, 1988), 16.

31. For more on Sheri Klouda's dismissal, see Thomas Bartlett, "'I Suffer Not a Woman to Teach,'" *Chronicle of Higher Education,* April 13, 2007, A10; Sam Hodges, "Gender Suit Hits Seminary," *Dallas Morning News,* March 9, 2007, http://www.dallasnews.com/sharedcontent/dws/dn/latestnews/stories/031007dnmetklouda.34547c9c.html (accessed April 11, 2007); and Hannah Elliott, "Dismissed Professor Files Lawsuit against Southwestern Seminary," *Baptist Standard,* March 30, 2007, http://www.baptiststandard.com/postnuke/index.php?module=htmlpages&func=display&pid=6135 (accessed April 11, 2007).

32. Frederick Buechner, *Wishful Thinking: A Seeker's ABC* (San Francisco: HarperSanFrancisco, 1993), 118–19.

6. Gracious Submission

1. For more on 1970s Southern Baptist publications and women, see Susan M. Shaw, "Of Words and Women: Southern Baptist Publications and the Progress of Women in the 1970s," *Baptist History and Heritage* 42 (spring 2007).

2. http://www.sbc.net/bfm/bfm2000.asp#xviii (accessed April 21, 2006). For an examination of fundamentalist statements on women, see Susan M. Shaw, "Gracious Submission: Southern Baptist Fundamentalists and Women," *National Women's Studies Association Journal* (forthcoming).

3. Oral memoirs of Dorothy Patterson, interviewed by Barry Hankins, June 8, 1999, Religion and Culture Project, Baylor Institute for Oral History, 2003, 21.

4. Ibid., 24.

5. Ibid.

6. http://www.sbc.net/resolutions/amResolution.asp?ID=530 (accessed May 18, 2006).

7. http://www.sbc.net/resolutions/amResolution.asp?ID=534 (accessed May 18, 2006).

8. http://www.sbc.net/resolutions/amResolutionasp?ID=1125 (accessed May 18, 2006).

9. Bruce Ware, "The Beauty of Biblical Womanhood," *Tie* 71 (winter 2003): 2–5.

10. Daniel L. Akin, "The Role of Men and Women in the Church," *Tie* 71 (winter 2003): 6–9.

11. Randy L. Stinson, "Show Yourself a Man," *Tie* 73 (winter 2005): 7.

12. Al Mohler, "The Boy Problem, Then and Now," *Tie* 73 (winter 2005): inside cover.

13. Stinson, "Show Yourself a Man," 4.

14. Jaye Martin, "The Marks of a Godly Husband," *Tie* 73 (winter 2005): 17.

15. Sally Gallagher, *Evangelical Identity and Gendered Family Life* (New Brunswick, N.J.: Rutgers University Press, 1999), 92.

16. Kathy Manis Findley is now a therapist who treats survivors of trauma. She herself was a victim of abuse as a child and adolescent and has written about surviving violence and abuse in *The Survivor's Voice: Healing the Invisible Wounds of Violence and Abuse* (Macon, Ga.: Smyth & Helwys, 1999).

17. Thaeda Franz, "Power, Patriarchy and Sexual Abuse in the Christian Church," *Traumatology* 8 (March 2002): 3–4.

18. Louisa L. Foss and Melanie A. Warnke, "Fundamentalist Protestant Christian Women: Recognizing Cultural and Gender Influences on Domestic Violence," *Counseling and Values* 48 (October 2003): 14–23.

19. Nancy Nason-Clark, "When Terror Strikes at Home: The Interface between Religion and Domestic Violence," *Journal for the Scientific Study of Religion* 43 (2004): 304.

20. Karolyn Elizabeth Senter and Karen Caldwell, "Spirituality and the Maintenance of Change: A Phenomenological Study of Women Who Leave Abusive Relationships," *Contemporary Family Therapy* 24 (December 2002): 543–64; Norman Giesbrecht and Irene Sevcik, "The Process of Recovery and Rebuilding among Abused Women in the Conservative Evangelical Subculture," *Journal of Family Violence* 13 (September 2000): 229–48.

21. Sue Wong Gengler and Jerry W. Lee, "Ministers' Understandings of Battered Women: Differences among Catholic Male Priests, Protestant Female Ministers and Protestant Male Ministers," *Journal of Religion & Abuse* 3 (2001): 55.

22. Margaret Kennedy, "Sexual Abuse of Women by Priests and Ministers to Whom They Go for Pastoral Care and Support," *Feminist Theology* 11 (2003): 226–35; Patricia L. Liberty, "'It's Difficult to Explain'—The Compromise of Moral Agency for Victims of Abuse by Religious Leaders," *Journal of Religion & Abuse* 3 (2001): 81–90.

23. Dee Ann Miller, *How Little We Knew: Collusion and Confusion with Sexual Misconduct* (Lafayette, La.: Prescott Press, 1993).

24. See, for example, Gallagher, *Evangelical Identity and Gendered Family Life,* 165.

25. Ellison and Bartkowski found that in conservative Protestant families (including Southern Baptists), wives do more housework than husbands and spend more time doing traditionally female forms of labor in the home. Christopher G. Ellison and John P. Bartkowski, "Conservative Protestantism and the Division of Household Labor among Married Couples," *Journal of Family Issues* 23 (November 2002): 950–85.

26. Carolyn W. Crumpler, "'Yes, Lord, I'll Go,'" in *Courage and Hope: The Stories of Ten Baptist Women Ministers,* ed. Pamela R. Durso and Keith E. Durso (Macon, Ga.: Mercer University Press, 2005), 55.

27. Ibid., 56.

28. Lydia Huffman Hoyle, "Nineteenth-Century Single Women and Motivation for Mission," *International Bulletin of Missionary Research* 20 (April 1996): 58.

29. Ruth A. Tucker, *Guardians of the Great Commission: The Story of Women in Modern Missions* (Grand Rapids, Mich.: Academic Books, 1988), 227.

30. For more on single women missionaries in other denominations, see Janet Lee, "Between Subordination and the She-Tiger: Social Constructions of White Femininity in the Lives of Single, Protestant Missionaries in China, 1905–1930," *Women's Studies International Forum* 19 (1996): 621–32, and Nancy Rose Hunt, "'Single Ladies on the Congo': Protestant Missionary Tensions and Voices," *Women's Studies International Forum* 13 (1990): 395–403.

31. Annie Jenkins Sallee Papers, Texas Collection, Baylor University, Waco, Tex.

32. Ibid.

33. Ibid.

34. Catherine Allen, *The New Lottie Moon Story*, 2nd ed. (Birmingham, Ala.: Woman's Missionary Union, 1980), 139.

35. Una Roberts Lawrence, *Lottie Moon* (Nashville: Sunday School Board of the Southern Baptist Convention, 1927), cited in ibid.

36. Daniel McGinn, "Marriage by the Numbers," *Newsweek*, June 5, 2006, 43.

37. Constitution of the Southern Baptist Convention, http://www.sbc.net/aboutus/legal/constitution.asp (accessed June 7, 2006).

38. SBC, "On the Marriage Protection Amendment," http://www.sbc.net/resolutions/amResolution.asp?ID=1152 (accessed July 6, 2006).

39. For more on this organization, see http://www.wabaptists.org/index.htm.

40. Alliance of Baptists, "Statement on Same Sex Marriage," April 17, 2004, http://www.allianceofbaptists.org/sssm-2004.htm (accessed July 6, 2006).

41. Kimberly A. Mahaffy, "Cognitive Dissonance and Its Resolution: A Study of Lesbian Christians," *Journal for the Scientific Study of Religion* 35 (1996): 392–402.

7. I Am Woman

1. Ada Maria Isasi-Diaz, *Mujerista Theology: A Theology for the Twenty-first Century* (Maryknoll, N.Y.: Orbis, 1996): 1. See also Ada Maria Isasi-Diaz and Yolanda Tarango, *Hispanic Women: Prophetic Voice in the Church* (San Francisco: Harper & Row, 1988). Similarly, black female theologians have developed "womanist" theology that draws on the experiences of black women. See Stephanie Y. Mitchem, *Introducing Womanist Theology* (Maryknoll, N.Y.: Orbis, 2002).

2. Molly Marshall, "God Does Indeed Call to Ministry Whom God Will,

Gender Notwithstanding," in *Courage and Hope: The Stories of Ten Baptist Women Ministers*, ed. Pamela R. Durso and Keith E. Durso (Macon, Ga.: Mercer University Press, 2005), 129.

3. "The *Ms.* Poll: Support High for Being a Feminist," *Ms.* 16 (summer 2006): 44.

4. See, for example, Lori G. Beaman, *Shared Beliefs, Different Lives: Women's Identities in Evangelical Context* (St. Louis: Chalice Press, 1999), 87–109; Christel Manning, *God Gave Us the Right: Conservative Catholic, Evangelical Protestant, and Orthodox Jewish Women Grapple with Feminism* (New Brunswick, N.J.: Rutgers University Press, 1999), 85–103.

5. For example, see Al Mohler's blog approving Harvey Mansfeld's denouncement of feminism, at http://almohler.com/blog.php (accessed July 18, 2006), or Southern Seminary professor Mary Kassian's *The Feminist Mistake: The Radical Impact of Feminism on Church and Culture* (Wheaton, Ill.: Crossways, 2005).

6. See, for example, Christina Hoff Sommers, *The War against Boys: How Misguided Feminism Is Harming Our Young Men* (New York: Simon & Schuster, 2001).

7. See, for example, the American Association of University Women's Report, "Beyond the Gender Wars: A Conversation about Girls, Boys, and Education" (Washington, D.C., 2001).

8. Soul Competency

1. SBC, "Resolution on the Priesthood of the Believer," http://www.sbc.net/resolutions/amResolution.asp?ID=872 (accessed July 31, 2006).

2. See G. Hugh Wamble, "Baptist Contributions to Separation of Church and State," *Baptist History and Heritage* 20 (1985): 3–13, 34.

3. Prevost, drawing evidence from resolutions passed by the Southern Baptist Convention, likewise argues that Southern Baptists have shifted in their stance on church-state separation. Ronnie Prevost, "SBC Resolutions Regarding Religious Liberty and the Separation of Church and State (1940–1997): A Fundamental Shift," *Baptist History and Heritage* 34 (1999): 73–94. See also Barry Hankins, "The Evangelical Accommodationism of Southern Baptist Convention Conservatives," *Baptist History and Heritage* 33 (1998): 54–65.

4. For more detailed information on the Cooperative Program, see Chad Owen and David E. Hankins, *One Sacred Effort: The Cooperative Program of Southern Baptists* (Nashville: Broadman & Holman, 2005).

Index